Indexed in

EGLI 1994

INCRIMINATIONS

INCRIMINATIONS

GUILTY WOMEN / TELLING STORIES

Karen S. McPherson

PRINCETON UNIVERSITY PRESS   PRINCETON, NEW JERSEY

Copyright © 1994 by Princeton University Press
Published by Princeton University Press, 41 William Street,
Princeton, New Jersey 08540
In the United Kingdom: Princeton University Press,
Chichester, West Sussex

Library of Congress Cataloging-in-Publication Data

McPherson, Karen S., 1950–
Incriminations : guilty women/telling stories /
Karen S. McPherson
p.   cm.
Includes bibliographical references and index.
ISBN 0-691-03252-1 (cl)
1. Fiction—Women authors—History and criticism.
2. Fiction—20th century—History and criticism.
3. Guilt in literature. 4. Women in literature.
5. Feminism and literature. I. Title
PN3401.M27   1994
843'.9109352042—dc20   93-39520

This book has been composed in Galliard

Princeton University Press books are printed
on acid-free paper and meet the guidelines
for permanence and durability of the Committee
on Production Guidelines for Book Longevity
of the Council on Library Resources

Printed in the United States of America

10 9 8 7 6 5 4 3 2 1

For Eden, for Leslie, and for my parents

Contents

Acknowledgments

MANY FRIENDS, colleagues, and students nourished me intellectually and emotionally throughout the long gestation of this book. My warmest thanks go to the students in my Canadian Women Writers course and in my 1992 graduate seminar, for their intellectual energy and their concern for things that matter, and to Nicole Brossard for her vision, her language, and her resonant voice. I also owe a special debt of gratitude to Hélène V. Wenzel who inspired and guided me when I was just beginning and to Suzanne Nash whose penetrating critical insights, wisdom, and caring helped me find my way as I was nearing the end. I am deeply appreciative of the criticisms and suggestions offered by Maria DiBattista. Sincere thanks also to Randi Brox with whom I first read Woolf and Beauvoir, to Alison Bernstein for her support, to Mary Jean Green, Karen Gould, Jane Moss, Janet Paterson, and Robbie Schwartzwald for their spirit of community and their example, and to Anne Garréta, André Aciman, Yolanda Paterson, Tom Trezise, Susan Brison, Brigitte Mahuzier, Elise Hansen, Alain Toumayan, and Deborah Hockstein for friendship, encouragement, and inspiration. I am grateful to my research assistants, Carolyn Josenhans Simmons, Pamela DeRuiter Prach, Miléna Andrews, and Neil Blackadder, as well as to Robert Brown and Lauren Lepow at Princeton University Press, for their editorial expertise and intelligent counsel. A Mellon preceptorship and grants from Princeton University's Committee on Research in the Humanities and Social Sciences greatly facilitated the completion of this project.

INCRIMINATIONS

Prologue _____

incriminate: 1. to accuse of or present proof of
a crime or fault; 2. to involve in an accusation;
cause to be or appear to be guilty; implicate;
3. to charge with responsibility for all or part
of an undesirable situation, harmful effect, etc.[1]

Guilty as Charged

Incrimination and guilt *involve* one another, but incrimination is not necessarily *proof* of guilt. It is because of their shared participation in the semantic field of "crime" that the two concepts are naturally but loosely
associated. The association comes to appear motivated, however, even in
the absence of proof or compelling evidence, as the incriminating force of
the charges makes them stick—as incrimination articulates guilt. Incrimination may, after all, by definition "*cause to be or [cause to] appear to be*
guilty."[2] It is easy to miss the tautological sleight of hand here (incrimination incriminates *because it is incriminating*) and to conclude that incrimination and guilt prove and justify one another. Like the police and the law
that back them up, incriminations *make* (and make out to be) criminal(s);
and, again like the police and the law, they concentrate their power (the
power of *meaning* what they say) in order to assert their primacy and their
right. A person is guilty *as* charged because "guilty" *is* charged.[3]

We cannot deny or ignore the story of "guilty women telling." Inscribed at the center of my title, bracketed and held in place by the
matched pair "incriminations" and "stories," this three-word phrase con-
jures up a familiar script in which incriminations are cunningly predeter-
mined and women can only plead guilty. The seventeenth-century practice of witchducking might be cited as a paradigmatic version of this
scenario. The water test was one of many folk trials used to determine the
guilt or innocence of accused witches. A woman charged with sorcery was
thrown into the water to sink or swim. The diabolical twist to the process
was that if the woman floated, she was guilty. Only by sinking could she
prove her innocence. In other words, the woman could plead "not guilty"
only through her silence, her drowning. Any ability to survive the ordeal,
to speak in her own defense, condemned her.[4]

Neither can we, however, accuse the "guilty women" who occupy a
central place in my title of having passively submitted to such condemna-

tion. The title may indict, but it does not convict. Its "guilty women" may either prove or challenge the story that incriminates them. If "guilty women/telling" tells the same old story, "women/telling stories" makes room for other tales, other voices, previously unarticulated or unheeded. Furthermore, just as the polysemy of "incriminations" made guilty women paradoxically both object and subject of incrimination (that is, both incriminated and self-incriminating),[5] so the semantic breadth of "telling stories," in concert with the title's indeterminate and nonrestrictive syntax, leaves open the question of whether the *women* or the *stories* are telling, and in what sense.

If the stories of or about women are *telling* (revealing), what do they tell? On whom do they tell? Do telling stories explain incrimination or invite it? Are women guilty of lying (telling stories) or just of speaking for themselves (telling their own stories)? Does storytelling *constitute* self-incrimination? Or does incrimination of women come about through others telling stories (blaming, tattling)? The title *Incriminations: Guilty Women/Telling Stories* means to leave room for all of these questions.

Hearing Voices

> It remains a humanist truism that literature
> speaks to us. The work of deconstruction might
> be understood to have resurrected the dead
> metaphor of such a notion in order to lay its
> ghost for good. Literature has no voice. It is
> text, not talk.
> —Garrett Stewart, *Reading Voices*[6]

> Learning to sing one's own songs, to trust the
> particular cadences of one's own voice, is also
> the goal of any writer.
> —Henry Louis Gates, Jr., *Figures in Black*[7]

Listen. *Is there a voice in this text?*[8] Or is it folly to suggest, in this age of texts, that words on a page might "speak" to us? Have we not learned to mistrust the Siren's silky voice that would lure us back into secure and complacent faith in some original safe harbor from which we may have ventured and to which we may always return? Certainly since Derrida it is no longer possible naively to believe in the temporal or moral precedence of the spoken over the written?[9] The primacy of voice has been contested. The text commands our attention.[10] Guilty by association with humanistic myths of self-presence and origin, the deposed voice is not to be trusted in the text. And readers and critics, out of fear of being (or being seen as) naively subscribing to these myths, hasten to repudiate voice. *Of course* there was not a voice in this text. Whose voice were we expecting?

Suggesting that one might describe the "work of deconstruction" as "hav[ing] resurrected" the "dead metaphor" of a textual voice "in order to lay its ghost for good," Garrett Stewart relays deconstruction's broad cautionary message: "Literature has no voice. It is text, not talk."[11]

Is it any wonder, then, that readers and critics should take pains not to be caught hearing voices? *And yet . . . listen . . .*

MUCH of the work of contemporary literary critics gives ample evidence of just how hard it is to "lay this ghost for good." A preoccupation with voices (saying, speaking, telling) is reflected in the titles of many recently published articles and books.[12] Stewart, even as he takes pains to demonstrate his consideration for and adherence to deconstruction's lessons, is nevertheless undeniably reluctant to relinquish voice—and in fact it is precisely this reluctance that seems to motivate him. Despite his insistence upon "the definitive divorce of textuality from oral presence,"[13] his attention to the ways in which "reading voices" (that is to say, the act of reading gives voice to the text) does have us readers and critics hearing voices again.[14]

Neither is Geoffrey Hartman, another of the resurrecting ghost-layers, ready to give up voice entirely. Alert to "the reality of words that conduct voice-feeling," he remarks on the "self-involve[ment]" of the deconstructionist approach.[15] What interests him is something that this self-involved process may fail to recognize: "At some point *the affective power of voice*, as well as the relation of particular words to that resonating field we call the psyche, *must be considered.*"[16]

Unlike "deconstructors" who are sensitive about "dead metaphors" and therefore understandably wary about voice, "narratological" critics base their analyses largely on the fiction of voice and the voices of fiction. Storytelling after all assumes both a tale and a teller. In a sense, then, texts, as narratives, reintroduce, *reinscribe* voice(s). But is this the same "voice" that we have been so busy banishing? It is. And it isn't. It is not some original and originating *presence* encoded in and reconstituted as text. But it *is* an evocative fiction that echoes through our reading.[17]

My approach in this book is narratological inasmuch as the organizing principle of my investigation is a general focus on the act of telling (witnessing, incriminating, testifying) and on the telling voices in and of the text. I embrace the convention of talking about voice; it serves me well both practically and ideologically. Like the narratologically oriented critics to whose work I am indebted, I conceive of narrative voices in more than merely formalistic terms. I agree with Susan Sniader Lanser that "narration entails social relationships and thus involves far more than the technical imperatives for getting a story told."[18] Lanser's discussion highlights the frequent tension between orthodox versions of narratology and of feminism and suggests that, instead of finding each other lacking (the one "naively empiricist" and the other "naively subjectivist"), they might fruitfully engage one another. Lanser's analysis suggests that what is happening in *textual practice* reflects and has a bearing upon what is happening in the world.[19] As narratology brushes up against feminism, it seems inevitable that real women and real voices should haunt the grammatical "person" and "voice."

Rising Voices

> Could it possibly be that the new philosophically valorized "neuter anonymity" of the text or world—a valorization of singularities beyond sexual difference—is but *a new attempt to escape the rising voices of women?*
> —Alice Jardine, *Gynesis*[20]

The rising voices of women. Could they be narrating themselves into meaning, into existence as subjects of their own stories and lives? Identifying themselves, *personalizing*, speaking up, speaking out?

Joanne S. Frye boldly evokes what she sees as a vital connection for women (writers and protagonists) between their narrating and their "lived" experience:

> In giving their protagonists the right to speak in their own voices, women writers thus give them not only the capacity to tell their own stories; they also give them the interpretive power over their own reality and self-definition.

> In claiming the right to narrate their own lives, female protagonists thereby claim the authority to name and construct their own experience.[21]

By emphasizing the *interpretation* of reality, the *definition* of self, and the *construction* of experience within fiction, Frye sidesteps some of the problems that "experience" inevitably poses—especially when it is made to serve as ballast for "essence." Frye is *not* simplistically appealing to an essential, shared experience of "being a woman" from which women writers would then be said to draw. The experience that she evokes, inseparable from the language that names and tells it, is dynamic and complex. It is also fictional: Frye is talking about protagonists' reality and protagonists' experience.[22]

The danger for women telling their stories, relating their *particular* experiences as indicative of some *common* experience, is precisely that they may, or may appear to, be reinvesting in the very structures of identity, referentiality, and authority that their voices would be rising up against. Why, then, take this risk?[23]

Why insist upon hearing the rising voices?

The answer is simple. It is one thing always to have had a voice to take for granted; it is another to find one, after centuries of silence. Those who are just now trying their voices can hardly be expected to relinquish or repudiate them; they know too well what they have to lose in the process. Lanser puts it succinctly: "For the collectively and personally silenced the term ["voice"] is a trope of identity and power."[24] When critics and readers hear the voices coming from the margins, they are recognizing and validating that identity and that power.[25]

It might seem inconsistent to associate women's voices with power when women's speech is so frequently dismissed as essentially irrelevant. The nag and the gossip, possibly the most prevalent stereotypes of speaking women in Western culture, are hardly looked upon as empowered or empowering figures.[26]

The easy dismissal of women's speech (and the concomitant emphasis on its irrepressible nature) may, however, be the expression of some deeper anxiety on the listener's part. There is, after all, a long literary and mythic tradition associating women's voices with fatal seduction. Singing a song that no man can resist, the Sirens lure the hapless sailor to his death. A spider(woman) sweetly and melodiously asks a fly, "Won't you come into my chamber?"[27]

A different perspective on the seductive power of a woman's voice is suggested in the framing narrative of *The Thousand and One Nights*, in which the sultana Scheherezade repeatedly forestalls her own death at her husband's hand by telling him stories, involving him again and again in her provocative narrative foreplay.[28] In this scenario, seduction is the key to the woman's survival, a survival both secured and represented by her capacity to keep narrating, by her unstoppable voice. What is common to both seduction scenarios, however, is that the woman, whether predator or intended victim, is the one in control—and this by virtue of the power of her voice.

Perhaps the most graphic illustration of the silencing of a woman's voice is the story of Tereus and Philomela. After Tereus took his wife's young sister Philomela into the forest and raped her, Philomela vowed to proclaim his crime to the world. To prevent this, Tereus imprisoned Philomela and cut out her tongue. But the violated and mutilated young woman, robbed of her voice, sat at her loom and wove the story of her violation into a cloth that she then sent to her sister Procne. After "reading" Philomela's story, Procne rushed to free her sister and shortly thereafter exacted her revenge: she killed her son Itys and fed him to his unwitting father. When Tereus learned the truth about the meal he had just eaten, he drew his sword to kill the sisters. At that moment, however, Procne was transformed into a swallow, Philomela into a nightingale, and Tereus himself into a hoopoe. It is hardly surprising that this tale should be a favorite of feminist readers, as it so clearly makes a connection between the initial rape and the ensuing "rape" of Philomela's voice. That Philomela has been violated and cannot tell her story *is* her story. The silencing repeats and continues the violation.[29] Yet when Philomela finds a voice ("the voice of the shuttle") with which to tell her tale, her act of witnessing provokes Procne's monstrous act of revenge. As the horror of the crime committed by the woman then tends, in some readings, to overshadow the earlier crime of which the woman was the victim, we see once again the extent to which the breaking of silence by a woman may come to be identified with transgression.[30] Silence is indeed a gendered question, and Philomela (the virgin, the weaver, and the nightingale) is emblematic of what may be at stake for a woman in the complexly configured constellation of narration, transgression, and voice. Philomela reminds us that the silence of women may be the site of the violence against them. The raised voices of women will be voices of outrage. The rising voices of women will be voices of uprising.[31]

Interdictions

Any study of transgression probably ought to take into account Georges Bataille's notion of an essential complicity between prohibition and transgression. Proceeding from the idea that "there is no interdiction that cannot be transgressed," Bataille even goes so far as to advance "the proposition" that "the interdiction is there to be violated."[32] He further articulates how the collaborative coupling of law and violation is a function of *social* organization: "Transgression of the interdiction is not animal violence. . . . Organized transgression and interdiction together form a whole that defines social life [la vie sociale]."[33] Violence only becomes *transgression* in relation to societal prohibition, which makes society in a sense an accomplice to the crime.

In "A Preface to Transgression," Michel Foucault elaborates upon Bataille's concept of transgression in relation to borders or limits:

> Transgression is an action which involves the limit, that narrow zone of a line where it displays the flash of its passage, but perhaps also its entire trajectory, even its origin; it is likely that transgression has its entire space in the line it crosses. The play of limits and transgression seems to be regulated by a simple

obstinacy: transgression incessantly crosses and recrosses a line which closes up behind it in a wave of extremely short duration, and thus it is made to return once more right to the horizon of the uncrossable.[34]

Foucault's border is interminably described by its transgression. This difficult *spatialization* of the Bataillian concept nevertheless allows us to focus upon two important aspects of transgression: its relation to language and its relation to gender. Bataille explicitly connects transgression both to erotic excess and to death. He himself then introduces the question of gender when he makes the woman the privileged *objet érotique*, which is to say not only the erotic object but also the object of the crime:

> Eroticism—which is fusion—which shifts interest in the direction of exceeding one's personal being and every limit, is nevertheless expressed by an object. Thus we are faced with this paradox: we are faced with an object indicative of the negation of the limits of all objects; we are faced with *an erotic object.*[35]

In Susan Suleiman's incisive reading of what she calls "Bataille's blind spot," she asks the obvious question: "Why is it a woman who embodies most fully the paradoxical combination of pleasure and anguish that characterizes transgression—in whose body the contradictory impulses toward excess on the one hand and respect of the limit on the other are played out?"[36] Noting that the female body, "in its duplicity as asexual maternal and sexual feminine, is the very emblem of the contradictory coexistence of transgression and prohibition," Suleiman wonders if there is any other model of sexuality and textuality possible besides

> the eternal Oedipal drama of transgression and the Law—a drama which always, ultimately, ends up maintaining the latter [and which is envisaged as] a confrontation between an all-powerful father and a traumatized son, a confrontation staged across and over the body of the mother.[37]

With the mother (the woman) thus representing a space, a stage, the *place* of the transgression, I cannot at this point help hearing Luce Irigaray's question: "But what if the 'object' started to speak?"[38] That is, what if the "interdite qui est là pour être violée" (to borrow and adapt Bataille's formulation) were somehow paradoxically at the same time *not interdite* (in the sense of speechless)?[39] What happens, in other words, if the object becomes at the same time subject? Obviously this would entail a radical subversion of Bataille's *erotic* and of the *definition of the border* as well.

Alice Jardine seems to me to give one of the best descriptions and analyses of this kind of subversion:

> One is tempted to see the exploration of boundaries and spaces as the very essence of philosophy. . . . What was disrupted, decentered, put into question . . .

was the "Big Dichotomies," those that had allowed Western philosophers to think about boundaries and spaces, about structures—most especially about Culture and Nature—up until the nineteenth century.[40]

Noting that "the dichotomies necessary to those structures have never been sexually neuter," she then goes on to declare, "What is henceforth necessary for any human subject who desires to describe the modern world will be to walk through the mirror, dismantle the frame held together by the Big Dichotomies and operate a *trans-position of the boundaries* and spaces now tangled in a figurative confusion."[41] This figurative tangle incessantly repeats the semantic slippage at the heart of the *interdit* where the prohibited is also the unspeakable. When she looks at herself in the mirror that the world holds up to her, a woman sees that she has indeed been *framed*: she has been made to embody the interdiction and its transgression. Unspeaking, unspoken, unspeakable, she must, in the language of the law, be there to be violated. And if she were herself to violate that law and speak her violation? If she were to dismantle the frame?

Conviction Pieces

> How much it takes to become a writer. . . . how
> much conviction as to the importance of what
> one has to say, one's right to say it.
>   —Tillie Olsen, *Silences*[42]

As I earlier suggested, I believe that it is possible, without making blanket generalizations about women writers, female protagonists, or women's stories, to argue prudently and justifiably for the existence of a script in which narration, transgression, and gender are interrelated.[43] I would further contend that while we find pieces of this story of "guilty women telling" throughout Western cultural and literary history, there is increasingly explicit evidence of this script's being *recognized and inscribed as a kind of intertext* in many novels by twentieth-century women writers.

   Modern women writers' attention to this scenario might in part be attributed to the fact that over the course of the last two hundred years there has been a growing consciousness of (and tendency to theorize about) the relationship between social authority and sexual politics.[44] The 1792 publication of Mary Wollstonecraft's *Vindication of the Rights of Woman* heralded the rising women's voices of the nineteenth century, a century that was to see dramatic changes in women's social and economic status in both Europe and America. By the 1850s, the "woman question" was being, and would continue to be, widely debated, and feminist activists were calling more and more loudly for legal, economic, and social reforms.[45] At the same time, "women's unprecedented invasion of the public sphere"[46] was finding literary expression in the emergence of a women's literature of social action produced by such writers as Harriet Beecher Stowe and George Sand.[47]

By the turn of the century, women had made significant advances in gaining access to higher education in both England and the United States, and the struggles for women's suffrage were intensifying. There was also—not surprisingly—a growing awareness of the inevitable intersections and interimplications of sexual politics and women's literary production. Looking back across a nineteenth century indelibly marked by the industrial revolution, the writings of Marx and Engels, the abolition of slavery, the decline of colonial empires, and the revolutionary theories of Darwin and Freud, twentieth-century writers and theorists began to apprehend and articulate newly configured economic, social, political, and psychological paradigms in the contexts of which to reconsider the role and place of women in literary history.

If a seminal text has the virtue of voicing for the first time ideas that can never after that be unimagined, *A Room of One's Own* must be considered such a text. It seems fair to say that people were able—perhaps even compelled—to think about women and writing differently after this book's appearance in 1929. Virginia Woolf's incisive and eloquent analysis of the influence of material conditions upon women's literary production put into circulation a feminist discourse about the historical and social determinants of women's silence and about women's *right* to write. Woolf's text anticipated by several decades many of the issues that feminist critics today are still exploring and debating: the nature and significance of a female literary tradition; women's different relationships to public and private spheres; the self-authorizing structures that predetermine access to and reception of women's writing; the tensions between sociopolitical and artistic values and their implications for writers; the challenges and paradoxes of writing *as a woman*; the theoretical and practical dilemmas posed (both politically and aesthetically) by taking the category of gender into account.

A Room of One's Own in many ways initiated the conversation about language and sexual politics upon which the modern story of "guilty women telling" depends. Twenty years later, with the publication of Simone de Beauvoir's *Le deuxième sexe*, another voice was raised that was also to have a profound and lasting influence upon the way people thought about gender. In its sweeping analysis of the historical and social construction of "woman" as "inessential Other," Beauvoir's landmark work exposed the gender bias at the very root of those philosophies and ideologies being used to authorize such constructions. Of course, as has been widely recognized, Beauvoir's critique of women's subordinate situation is not without its own androcentric bias. Nevertheless, *The Second Sex* is deservedly considered a classic of modern feminism, and Beauvoir herself "one of the founding mothers of contemporary feminist theory."[48] Beauvoir unquestionably "changed the terms of the discourse" and in the process left fissures in the foundations of those political and philosophical systems that had previously made certain feminist questions unaskable.[49] Indeed, both Woolf and Beauvoir were instrumental in opening spaces where one could begin at last to identify the "guilty women telling" story and to read it *differently*.

Although eloquent on the subject of women's rights, Woolf and Beauvoir were both on occasion somewhat defensive on the subject of "women's writing." They both clearly recognized the hazards of writing "*as a woman*,"[50] and each was to some extent constrained by her sense that in en-gendering herself she risked subjecting herself to the trap of essentialism. In asserting her convictions she might find herself convicted. It took the feminisms of the second half of the twentieth century to bring this double bind clearly into focus.

Where the work of early feminist theorists like Woolf and Beauvoir focused on the consequences of the conceptual "gendering" of social and literary history, later generations of feminist thinkers not only continued that work but also began asking *other* questions. Could one just simply take gender into account without calling the account itself radically into question? Alice Jardine expresses the problem succinctly: "Our ways of understanding in the West have been and continue to be complicitous with our ways of oppressing."[51] Recognition and articulation of this complicity has led to radical critiques and conceptual reorientations within linguistics, philosophy, science, history, politics, psychoanalysis, and literary theory—and the changes in all of these disciplines have had an enormous impact on the language and theories of feminism. On both sides of the Atlantic, important work was begun in the 1970s on the relationships between language and power and on the implications of such relationships for women's writing and for feminist discourse.[52] Feminist inquiries and discourses of the last twenty-five years have furthermore been variously shaped and challenged by the epistemological and ontological crises that have come to represent the modern/postmodern age. Often figuring themselves both within and against a legacy of Derridean poststructuralism and/or Lacanian psychoanalysis, many post-1960s feminist theorists turned their attention to language and law as interrelated sites of patriarchal oppression. The connections between law and language had of course been there—and even been addressed—all along, but contemporary feminisms began looking at them specifically in relation to sexual politics.

Indelicate Indictments

> To write: I am a woman is heavy with consequences.
> —Nicole Brossard[53]

To write I am a woman, one must first be able to conceive of the idea. Twentieth-century feminist thought is marked by its growing self-awareness. In conceiving (of) itself, it generates a self-concept that radically challenges earlier definitions and conceptualizations. There can be nothing dainty about such a challenge. *I am a woman* is an indelicate proposition. Presumptuous. Immodest. Unfeminine. Transgressive. *I am a woman* names "guilty women telling" in all of their self-conscious splendor. The women whose novels I explore in this book are familiar with this story and aware of its incriminating implications. Each of them, writing, takes the risk of that indelicate proposition.

I have chosen to focus the main body of my study on Simone de Beauvoir's *L'Invitée*, Virginia Woolf's *Mrs. Dalloway*, Marguerite Duras's *Le ravissement de Lol V. Stein*, and Anne Hébert's *Kamouraska* for reasons both studied and capricious. Proceeding from four distinct moments and contexts in twentieth-century writing by women, these novels offer four very different perspectives on the "guilty women telling" script. They present different authorial stances and different narrative voices in relation to different imputed "crimes." All four novels contain (more or less literal and readable) inscriptions of police and law, and in all of them one finds female protagonists who are somehow "incriminated." But there are wide and significant variations in the degree to which finding guilty women implies finding women guilty.

The investigative procedure in each of my four chapters is basically to look first for inscriptions of the police—that is, formal or substantive structures of authority—in the novel. I then proceed to identify "criminal circumstances," the pattern and logic of incrimination, and finally the articulation of a woman's voice that is telling. (What could she be telling?) Since none of the four novels can be said to be completely or unambiguously subversive of its own unavoidable incrimination of women, any triumphant, recuperative reading of the "guilty women telling" script would be forced, quickly revealing its own agenda. Even so, by seeking out and exposing the policing of meaning and interpretation in the novels, I do find it possible to begin to imagine other *places* from which that script might be read—differently.

The Postscript, reading Nicole Brossard's *Le désert mauve*, is then neither summary nor conclusion, but rather an attempt to suggest what the "guilty women telling" script might be when not only read but *written*

from a new place—and by a new generation of women. Even as it rein-
scribes the familiar script, Brossard's feminist, "postmodern" novel seemingly *gives voice to* a radically different story.

Breaking the Law/Narrating the Unspeakable

In all five of the novels that I consider, incrimination is associated with the
liberation of a different (woman's) voice. In every case as well the story is
in part a story of survival. The voice of the witness, the voice of she who
has lived to tell, tells the unspeakable story of that survival. It is around
these voices that I have organized my study.

I begin with Beauvoir's *L'Invitée*, in some ways the most (deceptively)
accessible and the most frustrating of the four texts. Written before *The
Second Sex*, Beauvoir's first novel tells a great deal more than it intends to
tell or is aware of telling about the author's compromised position, as a
woman, within her own philosophical system of incrimination and vindication. Beauvoir's is the "Voice of Reason" that cannot make sense of
itself.

I turn in chapter 2 to the "Cries and Lies" that are so telling in Duras's
Le ravissement de Lol V. Stein. Published some twenty years after
L'Invitée, Duras's novel in many ways reads like a subversive response to
Beauvoir's controlled argument. The elusive female subject of *Lol V. Stein*
bears a certain resemblance to the "other woman" in *L'Invitée*, and one
might even say that Lol puts into free circulation all of the anxieties that
Beauvoir's narrator was so determinedly denying. The psychological landscape evoked by Duras might easily be the messy underside of Beauvoir's
reasonable world.

Kamouraska, the subject of my third chapter, appears to be a more
conventional novel than *Lol V. Stein*, more obviously rooted in the historical and narrative traditions that produced it.[54] Yet Hébert's *Kamouraska*,
in examining the implications and complications of "Bearing Witness,"
grapples with the complex problematics of women's guilt and the letter of
the law in ways that clearly signal its modernity.

I have kept Virginia Woolf's novel for the last chapter because although
she was a generation older than the others, growing up in the England of
Queen Victoria,[55] her voice seems in many ways to carry the farthest. Virginia Woolf began work on *Mrs. Dalloway* in 1922, the year in which she
wrote in her diary that she had "found out how to begin (at 40) to say
something in [her] own voice."[56] Woolf knew the risk and the promise of
"Speaking Madness," of venturing beyond the confines of conventional
discourse. Her voice (like Mrs. Dalloway's) was ever so polite, but in its
own soft-spoken way it pushed against the boundaries of sense and cus-

tom. In placing the chapter on *Mrs. Dalloway* after the others, I want to insist upon that voice's ability to speak beyond itself into a future it may not even imagine. And to be speaking about what matters.

In a sense it is the possibility of such speaking that motivates the "Post(modern)script" that follows chapter 4. Reading Nicole Brossard's *Le désert mauve* as a postscript to the story of incriminations is one way of calling into question—by speaking beyond—the end of the story. A postscript, after all, is by definition *writing after writing*. A postscript may pretend to be a tacked-on afterthought of no real significance, but in fact it always undoes closure, challenges conclusions, and opens up a text to untold possibilities.[57] It cannot help but decenter our reading. Where there is one postscript there could always be another.[58]

Le désert mauve, published in 1987, itself poses the question of writing *beyond* the ending.[59] Constructed around and through the problematics of translation, it is (all about) its own "postscript." And the *matter* of this postscript is precisely the question of survival, for the novel inscribes the fragility of a civilization on a collision course with its own future. In Brossard's novel, a horizon is both the promise of dawn and the end of the world. The narrator Mélanie voices this awareness when she says: "Very young, I was already crying over humanity. With every new year I could see it dissolving in hope and in violence."[60] There are no illusions in Brossard's novel about the political and social realities that women face: traces of the incriminating script of "guilty women telling" are clearly there. But the radical gestures in and of Brossard's narration—her post(modern)scripts and her feminist plots—may indeed challenge or subvert incrimination and rewrite the woman's guilty sentence. As a radically decentering departure from the patterns of incrimination in the other four novels, *Le désert mauve* may finally permit us to *realize* and to allow to speak what was unspoken in the earlier texts.

One

The Voice of Reason: *L'Invitée*

Arousing Suspicion

In marked contrast with the other novels that we shall be considering, Simone de Beauvoir's *L'Invitée* includes no obvious inscription of the police: society's watchdogs are conspicuously absent.[1] While the police presence in the other novels to some extent authorizes our investigations, pointing us in the direction of transgressions and enabling us to "read for the crime," in *L'Invitée* there is no police trail to follow. Yet we read suspiciously.

Even without police present to trigger or reinforce the reader's investigative curiosity, suspicions are aroused by a lexicon of guilt, blame, and complicity. Indeed, one need only cursorily scan the novel's pages to be struck by the pervasive use of crime-related vocabulary that seems to suggest some "criminal circumstance." Françoise refers time and again (though without referring to any single, common transgression) to her "error [erreur]," her "wrong [tort]," her "fault [faute]." Xavière becomes "a living blame [un blâme vivant]." Pierre admits that his desire to make Xavière love him is a "culpable mania [coupable manie]." Pierre and Xavière stand before Françoise looking at each other like "two guilty people [deux coupables]." A while later they smile at each other "in tender complicity [avec une complicité tendre]."[2] The vocabulary of guilt and complicity arises in many different contexts, and the words are given many different weights. In fact, the individual interpretation of each of these instances is far less important or useful to our investigation than a recognition of the general atmosphere that they evoke; what the reader retains above all from the relentless and broadly applied use of such vocabulary is the fact that fault, blame, and complicity are in constant circulation.

Language employed earlier in the novel also foreshadows the ending and helps to establish, prepare, and, through contrast, emphasize the seriously criminal nature of the final drama played out between Françoise and Xavière. Responding to Pierre's hurt and jealousy over Xavière's sleeping with Gerbert, Françoise remarks that "in any case, an evening out with Gerbert isn't criminal" (304), a judgment that she later repeats in almost the same terms: "After all, it wasn't such a crime to sleep with Gerbert"

(347). Ironically, it is precisely Françoise's own intimate relationship with Gerbert that precipitates the final crisis between the two women and triggers the naming of the *crime* in the final chapter. In other words, terms like "crime," whose potential force in the novel is originally controlled through relatively benign or even empty reference, reemerge at the end with frightening significance.

In similar fashion, both Françoise and Xavière may be said to foretell their story's criminal climax, but in contexts which at the time undercut the significance of the language that they use. Long before the novel's end, Françoise muses that however much Xavière idolized someone, that person would still never be anything but an object to her. Françoise's startling conclusion, "One would have to kill Xavière" (302), is not an actual threat, not even a serious consideration, but merely part of Françoise's theoretical meditation on an existential problem. We must read in the same way the note that Xavière leaves on her door after her night with Gerbert: "Don't forgive me. Tomorrow morning you ought to kill me yourself if I've been too cowardly. . . . No forgiveness" (310). Neither Xavière's histrionic proclamation nor Françoise's shocking pronouncement is to be taken seriously. Yet, innocently and inexorably through the language of Beauvoir's narrative, the atmosphere is charged; the stage has been set.

At the novel's climax, when all of these scattered and free-floating "criminal" references gather and focus upon Françoise, she comes face to face with her "crime" and finds herself guilty, for "she had fallen into the trap, she was at the mercy of this voracious conscience [cette conscience vorace] that had been waiting in the shadow for the moment to swallow her up" (402). At this point, however, we must ask by what means this culpability has come to attach itself to her. Who or what has laid the trap? What and where exactly is the "conscience" that accuses her? Clearly we must now read *backwards* for the law; if we are to read the ending and thereby to understand the "crime" of *L'Invitée*, our customary direction of inquiry must be reversed.

In Beauvoir's novel it is the final articulation of crime and guilt that has suggested some shadowing police presence, some "conscience vorace" that had been waiting all along, unperceived, "in the shadow." But neither the crime nor the "conscience" lends itself to an easy and linear reading for, as our analysis of the novel's ending later in this chapter will demonstrate, neither can be read without reference to the other. A criminal investigation of *L'Invitée* depends upon looking for and locating the crime and the law *together*, using each to hold the other in place. So we find ourselves returning to look for the law and its enforcers, reading, that is, for the police. How and where did we miss them in the shadows?

An Unpoliced World

While both *Kamouraska* and *Mrs. Dalloway* open with scenes of proper bourgeois order, and while Lol V. Stein is treated from the beginning of Duras's novel as a "case" that stymies such an order, the early pages of *L'Invitée* evoke a different context and seem to put into place a different order. The world in which Françoise, Pierre, Xavière, Elisabeth, and Gerbert live and work is definitely on the margins of mainstream, bourgeois French society. These are the artists and actors, the intellectuals and writers who frequent cafés and bars, who sleep half the day and stay out all night, whose unconventional lives and life-styles unabashedly proclaim their *freedom from* societal constraints. But what is perhaps most significant about this freedom, as it is inscribed in the first chapter of Beauvoir's novel, is precisely that it is a *freedom from* rather than a *challenge to* those constraints. The alternative reality here portrayed puts the emphasis not on "alternative," which would imply contrasting it with a more conventional and socially sanctioned existence, but on "reality": the marginal world is treated quite naturally as having or being its own center.

At the beginning of *L'Invitée*, Françoise and Gerbert are in Françoise's study in the theater, working together on finishing the script of a play. It is past two in the morning. Since, as we learn, Françoise is somehow associated with the absent Pierre, and is to some extent defined and self-defined by her role in that couple, this innocent yet intimate middle-of-the-night collaboration with Gerbert would seem to defy societal conventions. In the first chapter it is not, however, merely the situation that inscribes freedom. Pierre's absence has also awakened in Françoise a mood of self-reflection that prompts her to contemplate elements of what one might call her personal philosophy, a philosophy concerned with individual freedom and self-definition. The unaccustomed solitude gives Françoise a heightened awareness of her power to order the world around her: "When she was not there, this smell of dust, this half-light, this forlorn solitude did not exist for anyone; all of this did not exist at all. . . . *She had that power: her presence snatched things from their unconsciousness*, gave them their colour, their smell" (12, emphasis added). Françoise's refusal to define her place in the world as contingent upon external factors is a forceful gesture of self-determination: "She alone evoked the significance [elle était seule à dégager le sens] of these abandoned places, of these slumbering things. She was there and they belonged to her. The world belonged to her" (12). Françoise makes her individual consciousness the point of reference for her experience, the seat of both judgment and privilege, affirming: "'I don't need to try to cut out a special place for myself in the world. I feel that I am already in it'" (17).

Her point of view is, unsurprisingly, neither entirely clear nor entirely consistent. After all, an existential awareness of the autonomy of one's experience and of the absence of any separate or higher authority to define or validate that experience is hardly simple or reassuring. Yet, although Françoise's reflections and her conversations with Gerbert hint at her uneasy relationship with her own self-assertion, she at first seems determined above all to avoid looking at the implications. Indeed, she is disturbingly adamant in her denial of any regret. For instance, as she turns to leave the empty square where she has for a moment experienced "the joys of solitude" she has a brief pang of misgiving: "She put her hand on the doorknob, then turned back with a qualm of conscience. This was desertion, an act of treason [un abandon, une trahison]" (13). But she will not entertain this troubling nostalgia: "She had long since given up this kind of regret. Only her own life was real" (13). Françoise explains to Gerbert: "'I feel calmer now, because I've persuaded myself that wherever I may go, the rest of the world will move with me. That's what keeps me from having any regrets'" (15). Firmly planted in the here and now and allowing herself no reason or right to regret the loss of the *there* and *then*, Françoise would seem to be unaware that her words reveal the extent to which the past still haunts most of her declarations of tranquillity. She tells Gerbert: "'*It used to break my heart* to think that I'd never know anything but one small section of the world. . . . I feel calmer now. . . . I came to understand that I must be resigned to making a choice. . . . *At first it was hard for me*; but now I have no more regrets'" (15 and 16, emphasis added). Nor will her present be allowed to fuel any future nostalgia, for "her own life" will displace itself with her. For instance, on the point of acknowledging that something precious with Gerbert is about to be lost—"Now all that was all over. She would often be seeing him again, but only with Pierre or with all the others. . . . 'It's almost a pity that we've finished,' she said" (13 and 14)—she immediately defends herself against both her reaction and her interpretation: "He was apparently not at all sorry to see the end of their ten days together; that was only natural. *She was not sorry either*" (14, emphasis added). Indeed, her conclusion, "*I am here, at the heart of my life*" (14), operates as a kind of credo to secure her identity. Yet this identity, boldly brandished, does not in fact secure Françoise, for although she repeatedly asserts, "I am here," she cannot present a coherent, unproblematic self. One might even go so far as to claim that she fails to present an incoherent, problematic one. The irony of the solitude that she rediscovers with joy in the empty square is that her experience of it is characterized by her own erasure: "There was this passing sound, the sky, the quivering foliage of the trees, and the one rose-coloured window in a black façade. There was no Françoise any longer; no one existed any longer, anywhere" (12). Then when she returns to consciousness of her-

self, she apparently perceives her self-assertion not only as a kind of betrayal of the enabling power of her absence, but also paradoxically as a
reduction or weakening of the very individuality she would seem to be
asserting: "It was strange to become someone once more, a woman to be
exact . . . and this present moment but one moment in her life like all the
others" (12–13).

It is unclear whether she is regretting her presence or her absence when
she notes that now, upon her departure, "the rose-coloured window
would gleam in vain; it would no longer shine for anyone" (13). Françoise
seems unwilling—or unable—to read the ambiguities of the passage from
"*no one* existed any longer, anywhere [*personne* n'existait plus nulle part]"
to "[the window] would *no longer* shine for *anyone* [il ne luirait plus pour
personne]" as in any way signaling her own problematic status or her ambivalence about having been, for an instant, "no one" and about now becoming "someone, a woman to be exact." There finally seems to be no
way to locate the *individual* at either extreme ("no one" or "someone")
of Françoise's experience. Granted, Françoise has not yet explicitly acknowledged or articulated either of these extremes as particularly problematic for her. Nevertheless, a probing reading of the first chapter of
L'Invitée shows her individual consciousness, asserted or absent, to be one
of the central and developing issues in the novel.

Existentialism provides the philosophical basis for Françoise's story.[3]
References to "an unpoliced world" can be explained and justified in part
by the fact that according to the existentialist view there is no moral code,
no human nature, no God-judge to answer to. It is important to keep in
mind, however, that in this "unpoliced" existentialist world the individual's freedom entails and is inseparable from an absolute responsibility:
"when we say that man is responsible for himself, we do not mean that he
is responsible only for his own individuality, but that he is responsible for
all men."[4]

Françoise's untroubled proclamations of self are attempts to assert her
individual liberty without accounting for the responsibility that it entails.
Indeed, one might interpret the regret and melancholy that she seems determined to deny as corresponding to the "anguish" that Sartre locates
alongside existential responsibility:

> The existentialist frankly states that man is in anguish. His meaning is as fol-
> lows—When a man commits himself to anything, fully realising that he is not
> only choosing what he will be, but is at the same time a legislator deciding for
> the whole of mankind—in such a moment a man cannot escape from the sense
> of complete and profound responsibility.[5]

This responsibility and anguish are a very powerful subtext in Françoise's
story, and they add an important dimension, another kind of policing, to
the "unpoliced" world. In the very first chapter, when Françoise is at-

tracted to but does not sleep with Gerbert, her decision has nothing to do with a reluctance to transgress society's laws and morals. She "sacrifices" the possibility of intimacy with Gerbert not because it would be *wrong*, but because she freely chooses to refrain. Nevertheless, the juxtaposition of fantasy and renunciation implies that while Françoise's choices are *externally* unpoliced, there is a strong current of self-policing underlying her free choice.

That Françoise is indeed policing her actions comes through dramatically in her language, which is full of interdictions: "Françoise looked at his fine green eyes beneath their curling lashes, at his expectant mouth—'If I had wanted to. . . .' Perhaps it was still not too late. But *what could she want?*" (16, ellipsis in original, emphasis added). The suspension points that interrupt the articulation of Françoise's fantasy and the question "what could she want?" with which she effectively buries it clearly illustrate the self-censorship at work here. What follows is almost a series of commandments: she will not let herself *say, think, wish*. She does not even have the right to regret:

> She shut her eyes. *She could not say:* "I love you." *She could not think it.* She loved Pierre. There was no room in her life for another love. . . . Gerbert did not love her; *she could not wish that he might love her.* . . . And yet she had no regrets; *she had not even a right* to that melancholy which was beginning to numb her drowsy body. (18, emphasis added)

Although Françoise seems totally preoccupied with being answerable to her own demanding censor, a vital aspect of existential responsibility, as Sartre pointed out, is that it must also respond to the existence of "others." In other words, while refusing the possibility of a separate, absolute referent beyond the individual, existentialism nevertheless makes clear that liberty is not the same thing as *license*. Responsibility is a way of acknowledging that each person's freedom is constantly informed and challenged by the freedom of the other. The anguish of this (which is to become the central problematic of the novel) is expressed by Françoise when she says to Gerbert: "'It's almost impossible to believe that other people are conscious beings [des consciences], aware of their own inward feelings, as we ourselves are aware of our own. . . . To me, it's terrifying when we grasp that.'" (16) Of course Françoise is quick to dismiss the scandalous implications of this terrifying revelation: "'But that hardly ever happens, and never completely'" (16). Indeed, the only "other" that Françoise allows to inform her own freedom is Pierre, and *his* existence is never perceived as a challenge. Pierre and Françoise have a relationship unique and unprecedented in its absolute commitment and absolute freedom. Describing their unassailable union to Françoise, Pierre waxes eloquent: "'It's impossible to talk about faithfulness and unfaithfulness where we are concerned. . . . You and I are simply one [Toi et moi, on ne

fait qu'un]. Neither of us can be described/defined without the other'"
(25). Françoise is equally eloquent as she reflects later that "there was but
one life and at its core but one entity, which could be termed neither he
nor I, but we" (51). Harmony is, by definition, guaranteed. And yet this
indivisible "we" is at the same time composed of two individuals engaged
in living according to a shared philosophy of openness, trust, mutual respect. These two individuals form an outlaw couple that then follows its
own "rules," rules consisting precisely in the *absence* of rules, and
Françoise's *autonomy* and *liberty* as woman and writer are theoretically
part of this arrangement. When she makes her choice not to become involved with Gerbert, it is in reference not to fidelity or to duty but to this
liberty: "She looked at Gerbert. She was free in her words, in her acts.
Pierre left her free" (18).

We see here, however, just how well the outlaw couple polices itself, or
at least polices Françoise, for the declared freedom once again inscribes
constraints: Pierre may leave her free, but Françoise cannot wholly embrace that liberty. Having already reflected that "she loved Pierre. There
was no room in her life for another love," she now defines even the idea
of loving Gerbert as an untruth: "but acts and words would be only lies,
as the weight of that head on her shoulder was already a lie. Gerbert did
not love her" (18). We sense here an essential discrepancy in the ways
Françoise and Pierre understand their arrangement; they clearly perceive
space differently. While subscribing to a philosophy of free choice,
Françoise does not move easily from the intention to the realization, for
she sees her choices limiting one another. Her love for Pierre and her desire for Gerbert cannot be reconciled: one or the other must cede its place
in her world. She therefore hastens to relinquish the fantasy, declaring it
"a lie." We see that Françoise's limits are self-imposed and that Pierre
clearly fills up Françoise's "space" as she obviously does *not* pervade his (as
evidenced by his ability to act on his freedom and to have other lovers).
Even more striking is the paradoxical dynamic of "allowed" freedom
within the "unpoliced" world of the outlaw couple. "*Pierre* left her free":
it is not the couple, but *Pierre* who gives her license.

Policing the Text

L'Invitée may purport to tell the story of an unpoliced world, but if we
consider not the *énoncé* but the *énonciation*, we find what appears to be a
remarkably well-behaved narration.[6] The narrative logic here employed is
so familiar and expected that we easily forget that this law must be en-
forced and may be questioned; indeed, the policing is so natural as to
seem innocuous. The straightforward style of Beauvoir's novel contrasts

with a certain unruliness in the other novels that we will be considering. In the novels by Duras, Hébert, and Woolf, we will see that beneath and around the implied context of bourgeois order is a narration so problematized that the law there inscribed is shaken. *L'Invitée* would seem, by contrast, to be supremely readable, with far less indulgence in stream of consciousness, dream sequences, self-reflective, reflexive, and deconstructive techniques. Françoise's penchant for rationalization and justification sets the tone, and the narration is ordered along traditional, predictable, logical lines.[7] Beauvoir herself admits that this is not a particularly experimental work: "I accepted, as did the Americans, a certain number of traditional conventions."[8] She further explains that she also adopted a method and standard later codified by Sartre:

> I was working by one rule which both Sartre and I regarded as fundamental, and which he expounded shortly afterward in an article on Mauriac and the French novel. In each successive chapter I identified myself with one of my characters [je coïncidais avec un de mes héros], and did not allow myself to possess any knowledge or notion beyond what he or she would have had. (*Prime*, 269)

This "rule" that Beauvoir and Sartre considered fundamental precluded any possibility of authorial or narratorial omniscience. Point of view was strictly limited to what one character (at a time) might be expected to see or know. In a third-person narrative, this technique meant that the narrator's point of view was determined by and confined to that of the privileged character. Such delimitations, however, worked in two directions: the character's point of view limited the narrator, but the character was in turn controlled. Through the use of a third-person rather than a first-person narrative voice and as a result of shifting from one character's perspective to another, Beauvoir imposed certain limitations on her characters:

> Because of each character's limited knowledge [Grâce à l'ignorance où je tiens mes héros], the plot development is often . . . enigmatic. . . . [N]o definitive interpretation . . . can ever be made, since no character is the repository of absolute truth. . . . Since I refused to examine my characters' various outlooks [multiples consciences] with an all-seeing author's eye, I refrained likewise from intervening in the natural time sequence they followed. (*Prime*, 273–274)

Vigorously rejecting authorial intrusion or totalizing gestures, Beauvoir seems to be suggesting a system of author-character checks and balances. She keeps her characters from knowing too much; they keep her from knowing too much. Each holds the other in partial ignorance, through a kind of reciprocal policing of what can be known and told.

The narrator of *L'Invitée* is basically unobtrusive, primarily responsible for straight descriptions of locale and situation and for the explanatory, contextualizing "she said"s and "he said"s. Indeed, the "connecting tissue" of the story seems generally to be narrated without any particular bias. All of the rhetorical force and immediacy of the narration derives from the abundant and pervasive direct discourse and free indirect discourse or *style indirect libre*.[9] Yet when Beauvoir declares, "Je coïncidais avec un de mes héros," she is actually claiming a closer identification than the English translation ("I identified myself with one of my characters") conveys. In the French she literally *coincided* with a character; this claim effectively fudges the distinction between author and narrator. It is clear from Beauvoir's statements in the memoirs that she takes for granted an author-overseer who manipulates the terms of knowledge and interpretation. Declaring, "I did not allow myself to possess any knowledge or notion beyond what he or she would have had," she is describing a relationship between the Beauvoir who directs the text ("I") and the Beauvoir-surrogate who narrates it ("myself"). She is describing Simone de Beauvoir's control over her narrator.

Beauvoir the author does *not* coincide with her characters. Rather, although she will not impose her own authoritative voice on her story, she clearly manipulates and controls "her" characters in the interest of producing a text whose ambiguity "corresponds to the ambiguity one encounters in real life" (*Prime*, 273). Her strategy thus reflects a traditional belief in the power of writing, when properly exploited by the writer, to reproduce or convey something "real," some objective truth. Furthermore, while the point of view shifts from one character to another (although Françoise is generally privileged, there are chapters devoted to Gerbert's and Elisabeth's perspectives as well), there is nothing random or capricious in this maneuver; it is methodical, tightly controlled and backed up by an implied but determined authorial stance. It is the author who chooses to have her narrator "coincide" with Elisabeth in one chapter and with Gerbert in another. Seemingly supremely self-assured about the process of authoring, Simone de Beauvoir conceives of, observes, and executes the rules.

Beauvoir may seem self-assured and her approach traditional, but the potential for radical disruption is nevertheless inherent in numerous aspects of her narrative technique, particularly the pervasive narrative strategy of *style indirect libre*, but also the fact that the dominant third-person discourse is occasionally interrupted by unmediated statements in the first person, that is, by "I" statements not contained within quotation marks. These unexpected shifts occur primarily in the early pages of the novel and then again at the very end, and they apply only to Françoise.

The effect of juxtaposing third- and first-person discourses to speak for a single character is that *both* voices are problematized. The (third-person) *style indirect libre* is revealed as one step removed from the person whose thoughts and feelings it pretends to express.[10] And the direct and unquoted first-person statements, by virtue of their infrequency and the way in which they break with the prevailing narrative voice, appear somewhat self-conscious and (ironically) inauthentic. The "I" that they assert is hard to locate in the text. Where is this voice coming from, suddenly, without mediation? And where does it disappear to? Martha Noel Evans considers in some detail this "imperious 'I,'" noting: "Beauvoir coincides ambiguously with Françoise as the 'I' of the text. Author and character share a personal pronoun, blend into each other, so that a statement of the character is potentially a statement of the author."[11] She then goes on to remark that "just as the eruption of the 'I' posits the possibility of that fusion [bonding author, character, and reader], so its constant disappearance puts it into question. . . . Each time the switch is made from first to third person, the distance and difference that separate the character, the author, and the reader are emphasized."[12]

Consider the different levels on which Françoise is narratively presented in the following excerpt:

> *She turned over* a page. Two o'clock had struck a short time ago. Usually, at this hour, there was not a living soul left in the theater; tonight it was alive. The typewriter was clicking, the lamp cast a pink glow over the papers. And *I am here*, my heart is beating. Tonight the theatre has a heart and it is beating.
>
> "I like working at night," *she said*. . . .
>
> *She went out* of the office. *She didn't have any particular desire for whiskey*, it was the dark corridors that drew her. *When she was not there*, the smell of dust, the half-light, and their forlorn solitude did not exist for anyone. . . . A moment ago [the red plush seats] weren't waiting for anything. *But now she was there* and their arms were outstretched. (11–12, emphasis added)[13]

Is Françoise object or subject of this narration? Indeed, it is precisely the intrusive first person (*and I am here, my heart is beating*) that calls subjectivity into question.

The way in which this unmediated first person disappears from the text after the first chapters (and only reemerges in the crisis at the end) makes it impossible for the reader to gain any continuous access to Françoise through that voice. It primarily serves, therefore, not to locate and express Françoise but to make the reader more conscious of what the third person and the *style indirect libre* necessarily withhold, reminding us that a narrator (and beyond the narrator an author) is controlling and limiting the point of view in the novel.[14]

In the passage quoted above we note that Françoise appears, in the space of two pages, on four distinct narrative levels that can be represented by the four statements: *she turned over a page*; *I am here*; *"I like working"*; and *she was there* (third person "objective"; unmediated first person; quoted first person; and *style indirect libre*.)[15] This shifting perspective on the protagonist is both broadening and narrowing, for while Françoise admittedly penetrates every level of the narration, the limits of each point of view are at the same time highlighted by the way the narrative levels meet and contrast formally with one another.

In similar fashion, the strategy of shifting the point of view from one character to another in *L'Invitée* also succeeds both in broadening and in limiting the perspective. There is a promise of subjectivity in the way in which the narrative voice "coincides" with a character's point of view, but the shift from one character to another in turn inscribes the failure of subjectivity, that is, its inability to survive the challenge of other subjects. In a variation on Pierre's crucial admission to Françoise that "when I look at her I don't look at you" (166), the author of the novel could address any one of her protagonists saying, "When I am looking out of his/her eyes I am not looking out of yours."

It would be difficult to claim that what may be true for Flaubert, that "free indirect discourse . . . thoroughly confounds the attribution of judgment and tone,"[16] is true in the same way for Beauvoir. We are not confronted with a multiplicity and undecidability of possible owners for the statements. Yet even if we feel *certain* that the point of view is Françoise's, the narrative voice remains, as Michal Peled Ginsburg points out, "functionally independent" of both direct and indirect discourse.[17] The use of *style indirect libre* is Beauvoir's way of having Françoise think or speak without giving her an autonomous voice and unconditional authority.

Furthermore, as Peter Brooks has pointed out, *style indirect libre*, in "pseudo-objectifying" the sentiments expressed, contributes to what he calls "studied irresponsibility."[18] In Beauvoir, we may *know* in a given passage that either Françoise or the author-narrator *must* be responsible, but within the pseudo-objectified artifact of the text we cannot conclusively pin that responsibility on either. *Style indirect libre* offers Beauvoir above all the cover and alibi of *authorial* irresponsibility.

It is significant that our discussion of points of view has focused upon Françoise. Françoise *is* the main character, and the *shifting* point of view to some extent merely encourages us to notice the degree to which her point of view is privileged, making us formally aware of an imbalance in authorial investment. Even if Beauvoir had not admitted in her memoirs that Françoise's story was drawn in part from her own experience, we would sense from the text that the author identifies most closely with Françoise. It is not surprising then to find in certain aspects of Françoise's relationship to Xavière reflections of Beauvoir's own narrative project. In the second chapter of the novel Françoise and Xavière are in an Arab café, and Françoise contemplates her young protégée:

> Françoise had certainly had an inspiration [avait été bien inspirée] in bringing her here; never before had Xavière spoken at such length about herself; *and she had a charming way of telling a story.* Françoise sank back into the cushions; . . .

what especially delighted her was to have annexed this insignificant, pathetic little being into her own life: . . . Xavière now belonged to her. . . . Xavière's gestures, her face, *her very life depended on Françoise for their existence.* Xavière, here and now at this moment, the essence of Xavière, was no more than the flavour of the coffee, than the piercing music or the dance, no more than inde-terminate well-being; but to Françoise, her childhood, her days of stagnation, her distastes, made up a romantic story [composaient une histoire romanesque] as real as the delicate contour of her cheeks. *And that story ended here in this café*, among the vari-coloured hangings, and at this very instant in Françoise's life, as she sat looking at Xavière and studying her. (20, emphasis added)

Xavière, with her "charming way of telling stories," might be called self-narrating as she makes up (composes) a "romantic/novelistic story [une histoire romanesque]" but she only exists, to narrate, because Françoise has annexed her, directing an all-encompassing attention upon her and thereby giving her that existence (in a sense narrating her narrating). In this passage Françoise is the invisible possessor, the ("inspired") motivat-ing force behind the story that is (but is not) Xavière('s). Can we not read in this picture of desire and manipulation some of the motivations and desires of the author of the "histoire romanesque" that is *L'Invitée*? Like Xavière within Françoise's world and story, Françoise herself is self-narrat-ing in a limited way and at the same time possessed and controlled by an unobtrusive storyteller whose desires she both expresses and masks.

Clearly even the potentially radical strategies that we find in this gener-ally conformist and "realist" novel are also instrumental in policing the text. Culler observed that "limited points of view" have not in general lived up to their radical potential:

the concept . . . now has so long and distinguished a critical history that it can no longer be viewed as a revolt against order. In fact, the function of the con-cept, especially when applied to the more radical works of the past hundred years, is to enable us to order them. Anything, however fragmented or incoher-ent . . . can be recuperated, justified.[19]

The predominant critical tendency seems always to be toward recupera-tion, justification, sense making, order. D. A. Miller made a similar obser-vation about the role of *style indirect libre* in policing the novel:

The master voice of monologism never simply soliloquizes. It continually needs to confirm its authority by qualifying, canceling, endorsing, subsuming all the other voices it lets speak. No doubt the need stands behind the great promi-nence the nineteenth-century novel gives to *style indirect libre*, in which, re-speaking a character's thoughts or speeches, *the narration simultaneously sub-verts their authority and secures its own.*[20]

Professing to produce a text ambiguous and open to varied interpretations, a text in which no "truth" may be located, Simone de Beauvoir would seem to reject the seductions of such a "master voice." As we have seen, however, her narrative strategies sometimes fail to conceal the intensity of authorial desires and ambitions. Vestiges of the impossible dream of final and absolute authority haunt both the substance and the execution of the text.

The Role of Gender

The juxtaposition of an "unpoliced" world and a well-policed text in *L'Invitée* sets the scene for an investigation of the law. The complexities and nuances within each of these domains, however, keep decentering and calling that law into question. I would submit that many of these nuances are attributable to the gender of protagonist and author and that they effectively illustrate the uneasy rapport of women and the law. Beauvoir often insisted that gender played no significant role in limiting her own individual experience.[21] But in fact gender is not at all irrelevant to either the philosophical content or the narrative technique of her novel.

I have already suggested some of the complexities in the unpoliced world of *L'Invitée*, for instance, Françoise's malaise regarding her individual liberty and self-definition, as evidenced in her overanxious denial of desires and regrets. Her mental preoccupation with the absent Pierre also seems to contradict her claim to place herself and her consciousness unequivocally at the center of her own life. (She is, in her thoughts, constantly "aware" of his approach, visualizing him in the train, fantasizing about their imminent reunion.) Early hints of Pierre's unique and determining role in Françoise's liberty furthermore suggest that the *self* might be the price Françoise pays for her declarations of independence. I would argue that the complex tensions in Françoise's situation reflect Simone de Beauvoir's not always successful attempts to integrate (or at the very least to keep from clashing) existentialist philosophy and her own ideas, developed in *The Second Sex*, about the situation of women. Beauvoir proclaims that the theories expounded in her landmark treatise do not conflict with existentialist doctrines but are rather an application and extension of those principles: "Our perspective is that of existentialist ethics."[22] Yet she nonetheless clearly recognizes the singularity of the woman's dilemma:

> The drama of woman lies in this conflict between the fundamental aspirations of every subject (ego)—who always regards the self as essential—and the compulsions of a situation in which she is the inessential. How can a human being in woman's situation attain fulfillment? [Comment dans la condition féminine peut s'accomplir un être humain?] (*SS*, xxxv)

Indeed, the whole point of *The Second Sex* is to elucidate the difference between the universal case and the specifically female variation: "Surely woman is, like man, a human being; but such a declaration is abstract. The fact is that every concrete human being is always in a particular situation [singulièrement situé]" (*SS*, xx). As she undertakes to explore the history and consequences of women's exceptional situation within the broad human enterprise (that of individuals attempting to constitute themselves as subjects), Beauvoir makes a critical observation, pointing out that women have traditionally been differently defined: "Thus humanity is male and man defines woman not in herself but as relative to him. . . . He is the Subject, he is the Absolute—she is the Other" (*SS*, xxii). Given this formulation, it would seem reasonable to ask how a woman, defined by society as the Other, is to fit into the existentialist paradigm (already de-centered for her by her "alterity"). But the question is not really asked. Beauvoir acknowledges the singularity of women's situation, yet she is not inclined to question the possibility of masculine bias in the formulation of existentialist theory, that is, to consider that this may be another instance in which the male point of view is taken as the universal.

Clearly there are discrepancies between Beauvoir's focus in *The Second Sex* and the "philosophy" underlying *L'Invitée*. What is conscious in the first was an unintegrated subtext in the other. Although Beauvoir would probably justify this difference in emphasis by repeating her contention that "one is not *born* a woman," that there is no significant *essential* differ-ence between men and women, the more than one thousand pages of *The Second Sex* attest to her belief that the situation which *creates* differences and *produces* women nevertheless merits investigation.[23] In *L'Invitée*, however, the role of gender and the importance of the protagonist's go virtually unacknowledged and unexplored. Gender is, as in Beauvoir's per-sonal story, a relatively insignificant "given condition." The eclipsing of the gender question may be due in part to Beauvoir's desire for universal relevance and appeal and a belief that philosophy and art can and should transcend the particular in order to speak a universal language.

In a 1966 lecture delivered in Japan in which she outlined some of her experiences as a writer, Beauvoir stressed that the novel, "having begun with the singularity that is necessarily at the root of creation, must always strive to discover the universality of a situation."[24] This lecture is itself a brilliant illustration of Beauvoir's need to tell her story under the auspices of a more universal "human" project. Her first words are "Jean-Paul Sar-tre has spoken to you about literature in general," and as she proceeds to offer her own "particular example" to illustrate his generalities, she re-turns again and again to the question of universality. When speaking of the writing of *L'Invitée*, for instance, she uses "universal" or "universal-ity" (and even once the verb "to universalize") eight times in the space of ten sentences. She insists that the essential creative process in the conception of that novel involved a translation of her experience of hostility and antagonism between her and a woman friend into "the problem of *others* [le problème d'*autrui*]": "I found a way to pass from that singular experience to a universality."[25]

The quotation from Sartre that Beauvoir uses as one of the epigraphs for the second book of *The Second Sex* speaks eloquently of her need to ally her project with his, and with the general (and non-gender-specific) concerns of "existentialism": "[We are], *like everybody*, half victim and half accomplice" (emphasis added).[26] But the situation described in *The Second Sex* is *not* that of "everybody." In fact, Beauvoir makes some very astute observations about the particular "paradox" of women's situation. Not only is the woman radically displaced in the male world, she constitutes a challenge to the truths by which men attempt to order that world:

> Woman does not entertain the positive belief that the truth is something *other* than men claim; she recognizes rather, that there *is not* any fixed truth. . . . It is at the heart of the masculine world itself, it is in herself as belonging to this world that she comes upon the ambiguity of all principle, of all value, of everything that exists. (*SS*, 612)

And Beauvoir concludes with a statement that has far-reaching implications for our consideration of women and the law: "She knows that *masculine morality, as it concerns her, is a vast hoax*" (*SS*, 612, emphasis added). Beauvoir points out that this "masculine morality" is founded upon a double standard:

> With other men he has relations in which values are involved; he is a free agent confronting other free agents [une liberté affrontant d'autres libertés] *according to universally recognized laws*. (*SS*, 613, emphasis added)

By contrast

> his relations with woman . . . lie in a contingent region, where morality no longer applies, where conduct is a matter of indifference. (*SS*, 613)

In the terms of the societal laws that Beauvoir is describing, women traditionally mark the place of, or indeed embody, transgression. Using the examples of abortion and prostitution, while at the same time insisting that "not the prostitute only, but all women serve as sewer to the shining, wholesome edifice where respectable people have their abode" (*SS*, 614), Beauvoir declares that men "count openly on the woman's willingness to make herself guilty of a crime" (*SS*, 613). Women are the necessary outlaws and, if need be, the natural scapegoats: "Woman plays the part of those secret agents who are left to the firing squad if they get caught, and are loaded with rewards if they succeed: *it is for her to shoulder all man's immorality*" (*SS*, 614, emphasis added).

The situation in *L'Invitée* does not, however, conform to this stereotype of women in relation to masculine "law." As we have already noted, the "world" of the novel is not that society described in *The Second Sex* but a marginal "unpoliced" world. In addition, the question of the relation of morality to gender is decentered in *L'Invitée* because the two women, Françoise and Xavière, are portrayed as diametrically opposed when it comes to moral values. And not only does Françoise recognize that Xavière has "a complete set of values that [run] counter to hers" (101), but Xavière is aligned (or aligns herself) with *Pierre*, telling him at one point that they, unlike Françoise, are not "moral beings" (356). Françoise feels that Xavière and Pierre relegate her to an austere and superior moral position while they indulge in egotism, selfishness, and passion. In a strange variant on Beauvoir's image of woman shouldering "all man's immorality," Françoise becomes the repository of *morality* for Pierre and Xavière; through a kind of inverted scapegoating, they look to her to transform their potentially "guilty" love into "virtue" (206). Françoise's difficulty in imposing herself on the world is furthermore tied to this morality and to the sacrifice (selflessness) it implies. Unlike Xavière, who, "with calm audacity . . . chose to assert herself [and thus] had a definite place in the world [pesait lourd sur la terre]," Françoise, by denying her jealousy, hatred, anger, and vengefulness, had "under the futile pretext of keeping herself pure . . . created a void within herself" (288 and 287).

These departures from the pattern described in *The Second Sex* do not, however, make the fact of gender any less significant in Françoise's story. The ways in which Pierre is likened to Xavière only render more striking the differences in their relations to Françoise. Both Pierre and Xavière are portrayed as self-centered and both are conspicuous in the novel for their inviolate status—that is, neither is given the point of view; they are equally *objectified* in the text. But it is Xavière, and not Pierre, whom Françoise perceives as a scandalous challenge to her very existence, and this is due primarily to the fact that Xavière is the "other *woman*." Françoise's relationship with Pierre relies upon a fantasized communion that is inconceivable with Xavière. Martha Evans points out that "[Françoise's] consciousness . . . resides altogether in Pierre. . . . [W]ithout realizing it, [she] is living as a kind of parasite . . . [and the] payoff is Françoise's unacknowledged enjoyment of an imperious power for which she does not have to take responsibility."[27] On the other hand, what Françoise finds reflected in Xavière is not empowering. Xavière will not share: she guards her sanctum (her room) jealously; she walls herself up in sulks and caprice; and Françoise ultimately concludes that she is, and can only be, an "enemy presence" (389).

The estrangement of the two women comes about as a direct result of the triangle. In the beginning, Françoise was involved in two *separate* relationships, each marked by its singularity, its exclusivity, and in each of which she felt herself integral, indispensable. When a relationship begins to develop between Pierre and Xavière, the three players are suddenly faced with all of the complicated angles of a triangle. Calling it "a beautiful trio" (210), "a perfectly harmonious trio" (232), Pierre and Françoise would like to believe that the new configuration, like any equilateral triangle, can be "well-balanced." But, in truth, the triangle, as a picture of a relationship, is a far from stable structure, and the Pierre-Xavière relationship, by completing the triangle, introduces those vicious angles of triangular desire: exclusion and jealousy.

The triangle introduces gender-specific conflicts, as Xavière confronts Françoise with the double threat of indifference (in the sense both of not caring and not differing) and displacement. Xavière's indifference is typified for Françoise by what she perceives as the younger woman's "too monstrous selfishness": "it isn't only that she considers herself superior to other people, she is utterly unaware of their existence" (134). Furthermore, as Martha Evans points out, Xavière, as a woman, confronts Françoise with the "difference of no difference," and, as a sexual being, she mirrors Françoise's own troubling, unspeakable, unthinkable "desire of and as a woman."[28] But, Evans notes, Françoise "cannot conceive the possibility of giving shape or expression to a desire for another woman as an autonomous being, to her own desire as an autonomous woman."[29] Pierre is the essential focal point of the triangle, as he had already been for Françoise in their dyadic relationship, for, as the power of desire is acknowledged, the possibility of desire between the two women is inhibited and denied. The symbiotic mother-daughter nature of the two women's relationship cannot withstand the introduction of sexual jealousy with Pierre in the picture. Sexual jealousy may be merely a cover or an alibi, as Evans seems to suggest, but it also emblematizes the breaking of the closed specularity of the early relationship between the two women. Françoise suddenly sees Xavière as Pierre sees her, not as an "insignificant, pathetic little being [petite existence triste]" (20) annexed to her own, but as a separate person, a separate *body*. It is at this point that Françoise reflects upon Xavière's resistance to her—

> a warm, lithe body, not aloof to a man's hands, but one which now confronted Françoise like a rigid suit of armour (240)

—and upon her resistance to Xavière:

> paralysed by the intimidating grace of this beautiful body that she could not even desire [qu'elle ne savait même pas désirer], Françoise was at a loss for a gesture. (251)

It is Xavière the *woman* whom Françoise cannot touch. Furthermore, the virulence of the hatred that eventually comes between the two women is explained in part by the very fact of their being women: "Conversations with Xavière always degenerated at once into hate-ridden confrontations. What appeared in Xavière's tone, in her shifty smiles, was now something far more than a childish and capricious hostility: *a true female hatred* [une vraie haine de femme]" (388, emphasis added). And Françoise's rage against Xavière is likewise vented at one point in terms that descend to a biologistic focus upon gender: "The black pearl, the precious one, the sorceress, the generous one. '*A female*,' she thought, enraged" (395, emphasis added).[30] There is nothing comparable to this struggle in the other triangulated relationships in the novel. The Françoise/Pierre/Gerbert configuration seems basically unproblematic for all three, and even Pierre's jealousy of Xavière's relations with Gerbert does not produce life-threatening or criminal circumstances. Pierre's own identity and existence are never called into question by Xavière's interest in the *other man*. But the challenge of the *other woman* leads to anger, violence, crime.

It is the powerful indifference of the reflection presented by Xavière that reduces Françoise to panic and rage. At a crucial moment in the narrative, Françoise looks at herself in the mirror and sees a face "which said nothing" whereas "Xavière's face . . . was an inexhaustible whispering" (173–174). This comparison, which illustrates Françoise's need to find herself mirrored, also highlights her inability to be, or see herself as, a speaking subject. Xavière seems to have that power, but as a mirror she is not generous.

Françoise cannot find herself in Xavière because, obsessed with seeking that reflection, she is obsessed with Xavière's gaze, Xavière's point of view, Xavière's status as seeing (and therefore whispering) subject (horrifyingly able to reduce Françoise to a seen and silent object—or even worse, to an unseen and therefore nonexistent one). That the gaze of the other in which one seeks affirmation of one's *self* inevitably transforms one from subject to object (and may even then, with the blink of an eye, annihilate that object) is, of course, the existential dilemma. But the other woman not only threatens indifference; as a woman, she is able to *displace* Françoise. At a key point in the narrative, Pierre and Xavière have a rendezvous in a Paris café, and the anguished Françoise is struck by a realization: "Ordinarily, the center of Paris was wherever she happened to be. Today, everything had changed. The center of Paris was the café where Pierre and Xavière were sitting, and Françoise was wandering about in some vague suburb" (119). Even when she was with the other two, "Françoise wondered uncomfortably what she was doing there, witnessing this amorous tête-à-tête. She did not belong here; but where did she belong? Surely nowhere else. At this moment she felt expunged from the face of the world" (286).

This radical displacement shatters the reciprocity that united her securely to Pierre, the reciprocity that Pierre had described so reassuringly: "'The moment you acknowledge my conscience, you know that I acknowledge one in you, too'" (301). At first, although Pierre admitted the obvious, that when he *was* looking at Xavière, he was *not* looking at Françoise (166), Françoise built her security upon the corollary: when Pierre was looking at her, he was *not* looking at Xavière. Their relationship was intact. As Françoise starts looking at Xavière, however, and looking at Xavière and Pierre looking at each other and even at her, she experiences a radical shift. Soon she realizes that it is only through the intermediation of Xavière that she is finding Pierre attractive: "she was too detached from him to be touched by his appearance. It was only through Xavière's smile that she could sense its romantic charm" (288). Indeed, increasingly accustomed to seeing the world through Xavière's eyes, she realizes that "she had reached the point of no longer knowing herself, except through Xavière's feelings for her" (292). In addition, even when Pierre and Xavière break off their relationship, the triangular mediation is still in force. Françoise comes to feel that "it was Xavière whom Pierre continually saw *showing through* her [à travers elle . . . *apercevait par transparence*]" (336, emphasis added). Unable to assert her *self* alone, she has been betrayed by her own *indifference*, her undifferentiated identity as woman and her lack of monstrous egotism. Doubleness comes to represent duplicity. For in doubleness, where no integration is possible, the other shows you where and what you think you are—and where and what you are not.

The Role of Genre

If the philosophical "problem" in *L'Invitée* is complicated by the characters' gender, I would submit that the form of the narrative is equally affected by gender considerations. We earlier examined the "policing" of the text, focusing on some of the ways in which strategies like *style indirect libre* both inscribe and subvert narrative authority. The dilemma of using the language of the law (superpoliced text) to deny the law (existentialist content) is analogous to that of using the language of masculine authority to author(ize) a woman's story. Simone de Beauvoir is engaged in both enterprises. I interpret her reference to the traditional conventions of "the Americans," as well as her justification of her narrative technique on the basis of a theory legitimated by Sartre, as conspicuous bids for some kind of traditional and masculine authorization for her project. Furthermore, questions of *genre* are closely related to the problematic of authority and authorization and therefore, by extension, *gender*.

Interviewers invariably asked Simone de Beauvoir to explain or justify her choice of *genres*, and she seemed always eager to articulate her ideas about the different potentials and drawbacks of the various literary forms she used. One reason for critics' persistent questions about *genre* is that readers have been understandably intrigued by the fact that certain of her fictional works (notably *L'Invitée* and *Les Mandarins*) were admittedly inspired by events and situations in her own life that she also chronicled in some detail in her autobiographical writings. How were the author's motives and motivations different in the novels and in the memoirs? What was the function of this duplication?

These were precisely the questions addressed by Dominique Desanti in a talk delivered at Columbia University in 1985.[31] Setting out to investigate the "degree of truth" in these different versions of the events in the author's life to which they directly or obliquely refer, Desanti concluded that in certain cases "the fictional truth is more truthful than the one expressed in the memoirs." She noted that this might sometimes be attributed to the objectifying and contextualizing mechanisms of historical perspective. "*Les Mandarins*," she pointed out "is literally nourished by posterior factual history." Of course, neither the novelist nor the memorialist has a monopoly on historical perspective. After all, memoirs are *not*, like journals, contemporaneous accounts of the events they describe. The privilege of perspective is more a question of temporal or ideological distance than of *genre*. What Desanti's historical and political examples do, however, suggest, though never fully acknowledge, is that Beauvoir may gain an *ideological* distance in her novels that she could or would not allow herself in some of her autobiographical accounts.

Desanti also attributed the greater truth of fiction in part to the memoir's demands for discretion: a memorialist was very likely to feel the need to edit and thereby alter "the truth" in order to protect other people. Beauvoir was well aware of such necessary constraints on the autobiographical project: "I tried to say everything I could about myself, but I erased incidents or events that could be harmful to other people."[32]

Yet despite the occasional retreats into reticence demanded by a genre too closely bound to the "real world," memoirs seemed to Simone de Beauvoir to offer the ideal and natural place to try to "say everything she could." In her preface to one of the volumes of her memoirs, she declared that she continued to write of her life because in order to "clear up certain misunderstandings, it seems to me worthwhile *to tell the whole truth* about that life."[33] And in a 1984 interview with Hélène Wenzel, she declared that the "truth of autobiography" suited her better than the "lie in the novel."[34]

Desanti was skeptical, and, questioning the good faith of the memorialist who insisted that the memoirs gave the *true* version of her personal experiences, she zeroed in on some of Beauvoir's most interesting self-commentary. She referred, for instance, to a passage in the memoirs where Beauvoir prepares to recount the episode of her affair with Nelson Algren. Beauvoir justifies her decision to tell this story in part by the fact that the depiction of Anne and Lewis in *Les Mandarins* had been a "very inaccurate" account of that episode.[35] The implication, Desanti suggested, is not only that the autobiographical version will be more complete and accurate, but indeed that the fictional depiction *was* a version, however "inaccurate," of the same episode. Desanti next turns to Beauvoir's vehement assertion that *Les Mandarins* is not a "roman à clef" and that although certain aspects of her characters may be "drawn" from real people, the characters themselves are fictions and do not correspond to living counterparts. Of the protagonist Anne, Beauvoir writes: "She was made from me, true [je l'ai tirée de moi, d'accord], but I have explained for what reasons I made her into a woman in whom I do not recognize myself" (*FCir*, 268). And she says of Lewis: "Lewis is the one who approaches closest to a living model . . . I used Algren to invent a character who would exist without reference to the world of real people" (*FCir*, 267). Desanti suggests that Beauvoir seems to want things both ways, first allowing that the novel refers "inaccurately" (at least at some original prefictive moment) to real events and real people (it is drawn from "models") but then categorically denying that referentiality. Refusing any recognition (Anne) or reference (Lewis), Beauvoir abruptly severs any connection between the fiction and the event or person that might have contributed to its creation. There is no duration, no return.

We here see Simone de Beauvoir successfully exploiting the media she is using, capitalizing both on the "truth value" that she locates in the memoirs and on the freedom to invent offered by the fictions. Indeed, the experiences that she recounts in the memoirs serve as a kind of confirmation of her fictional characters' authenticity, while she claims the prerogatives of any writer of fiction who *draws from life* in order to *invent*, asserting her right to enjoy the benefits of reference without the entanglements.

Of course, all artists admittedly draw from *some* experience, whether lived or imagined, but the creative process is not (and cannot be) strictly and transparently representational: the medium is always between. Nor is the artist bound to rules of referentiality to the world beyond the fiction; the created product is autonomous and to see or read it otherwise is to be duped by a "referential fallacy." Beauvoir is adamant that the fictional creation cannot be traced back to or retranslated into the model, yet she does not hesitate to evoke that model as *guarantor* of her authority to create that character. Her novel may not be a key to her life, but her life can, in a limited way and when convenient, be turned to as a key to her novel. In other words, Beauvoir is strictly controlling both the extent and direction of reference, and thereby policing the possible interpretations.

Why did the "truth of autobiography" suit Simone de Beauvoir better than the "lie in the novel"? In her conversations with Deirdre Bair, Beauvoir made a statement about memoir writing that may shed some light on her professed predisposition toward this genre: "The autobiographer has to be like a policemen writing his report: accuracy is paramount."[36] The medium is defined by the necessity for rigorous policing. One who claims to feel most comfortable with this law and order is, very reasonably, coming out for accuracy and "truth." The novel, on the other hand, is a messier and more complicated undertaking from the start, and one about which Beauvoir obviously feels certain ambivalence. When she privileges the novel she is privileging its *freedom*, and in so doing she always exposes the extent to which it will not, for her, remain contained within its own generic boundaries. Not only is it true that fiction, unhampered by the necessary discretion of the memoirs, "allows one to say a lot of things that one cannot say directly about oneself"; it can moreover actually engage, and even perhaps resolve, conflicts from the author's life.[37] In *The Prime of Life*, Beauvoir speaks of the fact that the denouement of *L'Invitée* had a "cathartic value" for her, an idea that she repeats in an interview with Yolanda Patterson:

> Certainly it was a kind of catharsis. I was getting out of my system everything that was disagreeable in a story/affair that moreover/elsewhere became a great friendship [dans une histoire qui par ailleurs est devenue une très grande amitié].[38]

The terms of this catharsis are striking, for the use of the word "histoire" deliberately forces genre boundaries, making the "affair" at the same time already the "story" of the affair. The writing then apparently served to purify this "histoire" and to allow it to develop into "a friendship." Taken literally, this is a rather peculiar transformation, turning stories or histories into relationships. The narrative produces or becomes the event. The affirmation of catharsis thus neatly and effectively obscures definitions of genre, suggesting that the boundary between fiction and "reality" is supremely permeable.

Elaborating upon this process of transforming life through writing, Beauvoir described the composition of *L'Invitée*:

> I exposed myself so dangerously that at times the gap between my emotions and the words to express them seemed insurmountable. . . . If I was to overcome on my own account that solitude into which I had flung Françoise, I had to work my fantasy through to the bitter end, give it substance [lui donner corps] and

not water down my version of it in any way. And indeed, *the identification took place*. . . . [It was] as though I had taken onto my shoulders the burden of a real murder. (*Prime*, 271, emphasis added)

Both of the above commentaries describe a relationship between author and novel whereby the writing is a direct and concrete response to a situation external and anterior to it. The writing is, as Beauvoir described it, "a living activity" (*Prime*, 270), "an act" (*Prime*, 271), and through the successful "identification" of Beauvoir with her projections in the novel, she is able to *experience* and *live through* what she *writes*. The writing act thus takes its place as one more in a series of acts (the author's life) or, in this case, as the final act or resolution of a "real life" drama.

This interpenetration of writing (especially the novel) and life would seem to be in direct contrast with the idea of "the lie in the novel" and with Beauvoir's insistence on nonreferentiality. Indeed, as Beauvoir describes it, the novel is not an isolated fabrication; it is itself emblematic of generic boundaries transgressed. It is interesting that, when she was not prudently preferring "the truth of autobiography," what Beauvoir appreciated about the novel was precisely its indeterminacy and its freedom. On occasion she even held the "truth" and "accuracy" that the autobiographer-policeman guaranteed up to another standard (to which they were found to be unequal), that of "reality," a reality to which some of the indefinite and undefinable aspects of the novel seemed to give privileged access.[39] Beauvoir noted about *L'Invitée* that "in the novel's most successful sequences . . . one achieves an ambiguity of meanings that corresponds to the ambiguity one encounters in real life" (*Prime*, 273). The ambiguity and paradox allowed and fostered by the novel are uniquely able to approach the *real*. The idea that "reality" cannot be transcribed or signified *directly* is also central to Beauvoir's account of the writer's task:

> As for the author himself . . . each of his books says both too much and too little . . . he will never succeed in capturing on paper—any more than in his heart or his physical self—the multitudinous reality that lies all about him. Frequently the effort he makes to achieve this end sets up a sort of dialectical scaffolding within the work itself; this is clearly apparent in my own case. (*Prime*, 479)

In relating this effort to her own fiction, Beauvoir is challenging her readers to read her novels as part of a process, as pieces of a whole. But she is also speaking about "literature" in general, about an author's "oeuvre," and this may give us some insight into her reasons for writing both fiction and memoirs, setting up a dialectic between them in an attempt to approach that "multitudinous reality." Beauvoir invites and challenges her readers to consider her works in context, not to forget that their "truth," a truth clearly distinguished from that of journalistic accuracy, can only begin to be approached and perceived within the dialectic.[40]

This is Nancy K. Miller's point when she says that in order to read the "difference" of autobiographies by women, one must decipher "the inscription of the female subject." This is no easy task since female autobiographers too often attempt to "make sense and thus be susceptible to *universal* reception."[41] For this reason women often fail to acknowledge in their autobiographies the indecorous, messy parts of their experiences, which may then crop up in other guises, in other versions, in other texts. Miller suggests that despite autobiographical "pacts" supposedly limiting and determining proper "identification" of the "I," "the historical truth of a woman writer's life lies in the reader's grasp of her intratext."[42] One needs to engage in "a dialectical practice of reading which would privilege *neither* the autobiography *nor* the fiction, but take the two writings together in their status as text."[43]

As modern critics, we are unquestionably reluctant to allow concerns with "the historical truth of a woman writer's life" to govern our readings. We have been trained to read fictional texts as texts—neither as access to an author's biographical truth nor as extensions of that truth demanding a return to biographical and historical context in order to be "understood" or "read." But Simone de Beauvoir spills into and out of her texts, making each one a context for her, as she is herself a context for each one.[44] It is hard for the reader to respect the laws and limitations of genre, because for every denial of translatability, Beauvoir offers an instance of generic boundaries transgressed. And even if we have doubts about the importance (or the possibility) of arriving at "historical truth," we cannot disregard Beauvoir's belief in and use of this kind of verification: "A book takes on its true meaning only if one knows in what circumstances, from what perspective, and by whom it was written" (*Prime*, 10).

The idea that one might arrive at a "true meaning" in one's reading is very attractive to the Simone de Beauvoir who believes in the "truth of autobiography." But the force of Beauvoir's statement about the autobiographer-as-policeman and her repeated self-justifications concerning discretion demonstrate not only that law and order and propriety have their appeal, but also that this appeal is particularly compelling because there is something potentially very threatening about the writing of memoirs. If policing is a sign of transgression, here the policing author suggests the degree to which autobiography strains at its limits, flirting with lies and indiscretions. The law of "accuracy" is not always easy to observe, and in fact, in certain somewhat apologetic passages, Beauvoir hints at threats posed to this kind of direct and intentional truth. She tends to downplay these areas of vulnerability, affirming the autobiographical project as easy, straightforward, policeable:

> No, I can't say that I have a total understanding of myself, *but I can state that I have told what I believe is the truth* about what I have written.[45]

Still, she carefully defines the limits of the possible "truth of the auto-biography":

> I realize that one can never *know oneself*, one can only *narrate oneself/tell one's story* [je sais qu'on ne peut jamais *se connaître* mais seulement *se raconter*]. (*Prime*, 292, emphasis added)

If one does not, or cannot, undertake to "know oneself," what is the story (the self) one tells? And is one liable for it? Seemingly aware that autobi-ographies automatically pose the question of liability, Beauvoir insists that she is only doing her job ("se raconter") and that her intentions are irre-proachable ("I have told what I believe is the truth"). The vastness and potential threat of that which is excluded from this project are deter-minedly minimized in order that the memoirs may be authorized as a safe and responsible undertaking: "I tried to be completely honest in these *Memoirs* but *what my unconscious was, I don't know myself*, even to this day. I can't express that part of me. But for all I am conscious of, I have taken the responsibility to say everything truthfully that I could about it."[46] Beauvoir's forthright assertion is, however, undeniably haunted by the inadequacy that she makes light of and the challenge that she immedi-ately dismisses. The reader senses a certain defensiveness and overcompen-sation in the author's assumption of limited responsibility.

A number of critics have considered the particularity of women's auto-biographical writings.[47] Nancy K. Miller, for instance, finds female autobi-ography committing a double transgression as it undertakes to justify or apologize for an initial transgression (the woman's life, already deviant if it leads her to presume that it bears recounting): "To justify an unortho-dox life by writing about it . . . is to *reinscribe* the original violation, to reviolate masculine turf."[48] Miller goes on to note that frequently women's autobiographies, "to invoke another literary genre, are a defense and illustration, at once a treatise on overcoming received notions of fem-ininity, and a poetics calling for another, freer text."[49] Speaking of Beauvoir's "not so very hidden agenda," Miller includes her among those to whom she would have this description apply. Beauvoir's memoirs are, however, hardly a treatise on *women*'s autobiography, nor does there ap-pear to be a call for a freer text. If anything, Beauvoir seems to choose to stay within the safe parameters of the genre as defined by male tradition, and she has gone on record questioning the interest and validity of women's autobiographical writings that would justify themselves in those terms alone.[50] Yet "defense"—in two senses of the word, as gesture of protection and as legal argument—would nevertheless seem to be distinctly appropriate and applicable to Beauvoir's autobiographical endeavor.

Beauvoir's gestures of self-protection include a masterful use of camouflage and a tireless adaptability. As an autobiographer, she protects herself first of all by the company she keeps. In the prefaces to two of her early volumes of memoirs she places her autobiography smack in the middle of French male autobiographical tradition, comparing her project to the work of Montaigne, Saint-Simon, and Rousseau, as she borrows their rhetorical gestures.[51] Her autobiographical project does not engage gender concerns; "féminité" is not a subjective element here but another topic to be addressed, as, for instance, when she writes of her evolution as a "feminist" toward the end of *All Said and Done*. Indeed, when the question of the role of gender in her life presented itself, she turned from autobiography to the essay form: "I was so interested in this discovery that I abandoned my project of writing a personal confession in order to give all my attention to finding out about the condition of woman in its broadest terms [dans sa généralité]" (*FCir*, 94–95). The question of gender was not a matter for *confession* (note the guilty traces on this word), but rather one for objective study. This is a particularly telling (and supremely defensive) move if we consider it alongside Beauvoir's explanation as to why she continues writing memoirs: "The study of an individual case is more instructive than abstract and general responses [to the questions one asks writers]: this is what encourages me to examine my own case" (*Prime*, 10).

Another example of Beauvoir's defensive adaptability is her incessant production. This is defense *à la Scheherezade*, the interminable narrative that not only buys time but then wields it, enlisting the temporal in order to give the *process* authority over the *product*. As long as Beauvoir keeps writing, revising, updating, the last word is hers and forever deferred and no final judgment, no final *sentence* can be passed upon her. It is extremely difficult to hold Simone de Beauvoir accountable for the "truth" of any part of her memoirs since that truth is constantly evolving and is furthermore impossible to fix in the interspace of the time of the event, the time of the writing and the time of the reading. Beauvoir had to keep writing: "writing had become for me a demanding occupation. It guaranteed my moral autonomy" (*FCir*, 13). Writing offered her the best protection she could ask, exemption from the moral judgments of others, the freedom of responsibility rather than the imprisonment of guilt.

This moral autonomy is reinforced by some very assertive legal rhetoric. First of all, Beauvoir tends, as I have already suggested, to borrow authorization, to call on character references. In the prologue to *Force of Circumstance*, the authority backing her is the French pronoun "on": "People have generally recognized in my work a quality [On m'a en général reconnu une qualité] that was important to me: a sincerity as far from boastfulness as from masochism" (*FCir*, vi). If her sincerity is generally recognized, her innocence need only be declared. In the prologues of both *The Prime of Life* and *The Force of Circumstance*, Beauvoir insists upon this innocence and furthermore demands the reader's assent and collaboration:

> The present work, at all events, has no moral purpose. . . . I make no a priori assumptions, except that truth in any form can be both interesting and useful. I have no idea [Je l'ignore] what purpose may be served by the truth I am trying to express in the following pages, nor who may benefit from it. I only hope that my readers take up and read these pages with the same innocence [la même innocence]. (*Prime*, 10–11)

> I seem to my own eyes an object, a result, without involving the notions of merit or fault in this estimate. If, in the course of time, an action should seem more or less praiseworthy or regrettable, I am much more concerned, in either case, to understand than to judge it. . . . In short, because I offer no judgment of myself, I feel no resistance to speaking frankly about my life and myself. . . . Like its predecessor, this book asks the reader for his collaboration. . . . [F]or all my care, I will certainly have made a number of mistakes in this book, too. But I repeat that I have never intentionally distorted the truth. (*FCir*, vii)

The reader is charged to follow the author's example, to read with innocence (which Beauvoir, in moving from "Je l'ignore" to "la même innocence," equates with ignorance) and without moral judgment. Beauvoir, anticipating and forestalling her critics, opens her memoirs with this forceful affirmation of a pact that the reader is expected to accept, given Beauvoir's well-known sincerity and evident good faith. The author establishes the rules of the game: her innocence asks only innocence in return; her refusal to judge means that a polite and accommodating reader should follow suit. In a brilliantly offensive defense, she thus answers and effectively silences her critics before they can speak.

While her defensiveness is directed at denying even the *possibility* of transgression, such denials clearly demonstrate that there is some risk here for Simone de Beauvoir. In order to determine the nature of that threat, we need to look more closely at what is being denied, displaced, left out.

In some of Beauvoir's explanations and justifications, we find her repeatedly refusing to assume responsibility for what she does not know or understand about herself. Her ignorance proves and validates her innocence. What is policed out is, however, still inscribed in the text. Parenthetical or qualifying remarks set the parameters for reading an innocent Beauvoir: "I can't say I have a total understanding of myself, but . . .";[52] "one can never know oneself" (*Prime*, 292); "what my unconscious was, I don't know";[53] "Perhaps my image projected in a different world—that of the psychoanalysts—might disconcert or embarrass me. But so long as it is I who paint my own portrait, nothing daunts me" (*FCir*, vii). What she cannot and will not take responsibility for is that unfathomed part of herself, her unconscious, whose relevance to her history she seems determined to deny.

Intertexts and Extratexts

"Introspection is tiring," [said Françoise]
"It's dangerous." (128)

While Beauvoir's autobiographical project apparently seeks to banish unconscious (and therefore irrational and possibly transgressive) desires and motives, these cannot be permanently suppressed. What is policed out of the memoirs is displaced into other areas of her vast text and comes to inform much of her fiction. If her autobiographies are a locus of consciousness and conscience (justification, rationalization, order), her fiction provides an outlet for her unconscious (fears, emotions, disorder). The terms that Beauvoir used to describe her early preference for the novel expose some of her personal investment in fiction and the source of its seductions for her:

> To my mind, this genre surpassed all others. . . . I passionately desired that the public like my work; therefore like George Eliot, who had become confused in my mind with Maggie Tulliver, I would myself become an imaginary character: I would possess the necessity, the beauty, the shimmering transparency [of that character]. It was this metamorphosis that my ambition sought. . . . I dreamed of splitting into two selves, of becoming a shadow that would pierce and haunt people's hearts. There was no point in connecting this phantom with a person of flesh and blood: anonymity would have suited me perfectly. (*Prime*, 290–291)

Her "passionate desire" and her "ambition" appear here both intensely personal and gender-related. George Eliot stands first of all for Beauvoir's *desire* for communion among readers and writers and especially (repeating the primal reading experience) among women. In the free circulation of love associated with those early reading experiences, identities were less important than identification. Indeed, the fact that the author could be known and loved "anonymously" as her heroine led Beauvoir to declare that for herself "anonymity would have suited me perfectly." If the *desire* is for love, however, one would expect the *ambition* to be for recognition. Beauvoir evokes George Eliot's name, after all, and Eliot, with her male pseudonym, would seem to be a perfect emblem of Beauvoir's ambition to have a name of her own in the world of predominantly male authors. Although the reference to Eliot inscribes this ambition, it is never openly acknowledged. Instead, Beauvoir expresses her aspirations in the language of anonymity by which she characterizes her desire.

The dream of "splitting into two selves" ("je rêvais à me dédoubler") is a curious one, not only because it implies identification and interdependence between author and protagonist, but because of the intensity of the desire expressed to have "shimmering transparency," to become "a shadow that would pierce people's hearts." This dream of being *identified* and *known* and perhaps *remembered* (as she is remembering George Eliot) in transparent, haunting, anonymous form, through her novels and characters, would seem to be, for Beauvoir, distinctively a *woman*'s dream. The unspoken problematic is this: how can a woman (author) communicate her experience and thereby achieve historical reality?

We can assert the role of gender in this passage with a certain confidence because of the way Beauvoir herself reacts to what she has written. Her expression of desire and ambition is immediately followed by a gesture of protest and defense. Having revealed her "dream" (albeit safely couched in the French imperfect tense), she abruptly launches into the passage (cited earlier) in which she vehemently denies differential treatment, insisting that her "féminité" has never been either an "embarrassment" or an "alibi."[54] Reading these two passages together, we cannot help but see Beauvoir desperate to readjust her "female alignment" in reaction to what she feels might be read into the description she provides of her relation to her novels and her public. It is almost as if she feels that her first expression of (female) desire has revealed too much.

When she wrote *L'Invitée*, Beauvoir's appreciation of the novel form rested particularly on its ability to produce an almost transcendent communication between author and reader. She never completely abandoned this belief in the novel as a "privileged locus of intersubjectivity,"[55] although she later made it clear that she had no real desire for or illusions about "posterity": "I had wanted to become a legend, like Emily Brontë or George Eliot; but I was too firmly convinced that once my eyes had closed nothing would exist, to cling very tightly to such dreams. . . . I wanted to be widely read in my lifetime, to be esteemed, to be loved. Posterity I didn't give a damn for. Or I almost didn't" (*FCir*, 46). Beauvoir is once again relating her aspirations to the achievements of women authors who preceded her and whom she invokes once again by name. And it is striking that in the paragraph immediately following this avowal of ambition and desire, Beauvoir feels again constrained to address the question of her place in the male world in which she writes. It is here that she sets out to refute those who would call her "la Grande Sartreuse." When Beauvoir writes about her novel writing, she seems to consider herself part of a female tradition and she describes this vocation in terms of her personal ambitions and desires, but in subsequent passages she then hastens to undo any impression she might have left that she has been speaking as a "*woman* writer."

We find Beauvoir in these passages expressing (perhaps despite herself) the problematic discourse of a *woman writing*, especially a desire to transform, *by redefining*, invisibility and anonymity into something shining, haunting, piercing, beautiful, necessary. And we also get a clear picture of the author's stake in the novel and the extent to which writing the novel engages autobiographical concerns. *Beauvoir* wants to be read, to be known, to be loved in, as, and through her fictions.

What emerges from any investigation of Beauvoir's work is a sense of how much she relies upon the juxtaposition and interaction of fiction and nonfiction in order to present herself and her story. My frequent references in this chapter to *The Second Sex* and to the memoirs illustrate the difficulty of considering Beauvoir's work within the limitations of a single genre. She is constantly cross-referencing herself. *L'Invitée* and *Les Mandarins* fictionalize episodes of the author's life, while the memoirs offer a reading and representation not only of that life but also of the writing that is an essential *part* of it. The fact that Beauvoir's fictional and nonfictional works share material is evident not only in the similarity of events and situations recounted, but also in the language and commentary. In the memoirs Beauvoir attributes sentiments to herself and paints pictures of her relations to Sartre and to Olga:

> "[Sartre and I] are as one [On ne fait qu'un]," I declared. This absolute certainty spared me ever having to question my desires. (*Prime*, 118)

> [Olga] did not hold the truth; I was not going to yield up to her that sovereign place that *I* occupied, in the very center of everything. Little by little, however, I capitulated: My need to agree with Sartre on all subjects was too great for me to be able to see Olga through any eyes but his. (*Prime*, 193–194)

The terms are strikingly similar to those she uses to describe the relations among Françoise, Pierre, and Xavière. Yet Beauvoir insists upon the fact that *L'Invitée* is an invention, a distortion, a *departure* from the truth: "To the extent that Olga inspired the character of Xavière in *L'Invitée*, it was *in systematically disfiguring her*" (*Prime*, 194, emphasis added). This "disfigurement" of Olga was, however, based upon her existing "figure." Beauvoir admits that Olga was, like Xavière, impetuous, absolutist, that she did, like Xavière, have "caprices, moods, inconsistencies," but she insists that these were only "the most superficial aspect of her true nature [sa plus superficielle vérité]." There was in reality a generosity in Olga that Xavière lacked. As Beauvoir explains the process of fictional disfigurement: "When I invented Xavière, all I kept of Olga—and even that I darkened in tone—was the myth we had created around her; but her personality would never have attracted us so much, or, consequently, engendered a myth at all, had she not been an infinitely richer character than Xavière" (*Prime*, 194). Nevertheless, this myth not only produced Xavière; it also existed outside of the novel where it disturbed the *actual* relations among Beauvoir, Sartre, and Olga: "instead of peaceably enjoying a normal relationship with Olga, we invented a myth and put it in her place." There is thus no clear-cut distinction between the "lie" in the fiction and the "truth" of the life, for the "myth" of Olga, however fallacious, managed to "disfigure" the "real" Olga in Beauvoir's and Sartre's eyes and to affect the nature of their relationships.

When one reads the novels and the memoirs together, it is clear that the autobiography serves as a gloss, conscientiously policing the reading of the novel and the life behind it. Beauvoir seems to attempt in the memoirs retrospectively to purge the life of the myth, to recuperate Olga (and with her Simone) as generous and moral, and to enclose the dangerous mythical elements (and the anger that they induced) safely in the fiction of Xavière (and Françoise).

Playing the different literary forms against each other, Beauvoir uses the boundaries between genres in different ways. Sometimes they are guarded borders, isolating truth and lies, fact and fiction, serving to protect textual integrity and to resist overinterpretation. Sometimes they are crossing points, giving access to material that could elucidate, authorize, or justify the text. In either case, Beauvoir defines the terms of all border crossings, and while she may herself venture beyond the bounds of a given work, the reader is never authorized to venture freely back and forth. It is Beauvoir who tells us when intertextuality is a valid strategy for our reading and when it is not.

Another effect of the different genres and the ways in which they address each other is that the reader comes to accept a multiplicity of Simone de Beauvoir personae. Not only do we come to know different Beauvoirs autobiographically in the course of the memoirs and fictionally through her protagonists, we also distinguish the novelist, the memorialist, the essayist, the interviewee. Thus, in a pursuit of authority or accountability, the reader is at pains to say which Simone de Beauvoir is ultimately responsible.

Finally, not only do the memoirs provide intertextual references and glosses that attempt to direct and control the reader's interpretations of the novel, the novel itself is a text with an appended gloss—in the form of dedication and epigraph. These two "extratextual" elements are in fact traces of contexts attached to the surface of the text and pressed to serve as commentary upon it. In a gesture of containment and displacement, the dedication ("To Olga Kosakievicz") introduces the "real-life" counterpart of Xavière, but by assigning her the role of recipient and reader, it keeps

THE VOICE OF REASON

her both contingent and external to the text. Just as the dedication introduces but then marginalizes the possibility of considering *L'Invitée* a
"roman à clef," the epigraph from Hegel ("Each conscience seeks the
death of the other one") attaches the novel *externally* to existentialist philosophy and thus effectively introduces and marginalizes the possibility of
considering it a "roman à thèse." Furthermore, the two "extratexts" subvert and illuminate each other, the epigraph calling into question the generosity of the dedication and the dedication asking the gender question of
the epigraph. For Hegel's formula can never fully explain the "crime" at
the end of *L'Invitée*, since it does not account for Françoise's reaction to
Xavière as the *other woman*. But together with the dedication to Olga
Kosakievicz, which addresses and particularizes the gesture (the direction
of pursuit) of the novel, it allows us to begin to be able to read the crime.

Reading the Crime

L'Invitée does *end* with what would appear to be an incontestably criminal
act: Françoise opening the gas valve to bring about Xavière's death. But
although this coolly premeditated and executed murder may be, as
Beauvoir wrote in her memoirs, the *"raison d'être"* of the novel (*Prime*,
271), it fails to explain and justify adequately the "criminal circumstance"
suggested by the five hundred pages that prepare this climax. Indeed,
while it might appear to be the indisputable and *literal* crime to which all
of the preceding "criminal" vocabulary was leading, I intend to show that
the crime committed in *L'Invitée* is in fact far from literal and not at all
where it at first appears to be.
    At the novel's climax, Xavière unlocks Françoise's writing desk and
finds the love letters that Françoise has been receiving from Gerbert.
When Françoise discovers her key missing and then sees the desk open and
the letters from Pierre and Gerbert scattered on the rug, she realizes in an
instant that Xavière now knows about her relationship with Gerbert: "Her
love for Gerbert was there before her, black as treason [noir comme la
trahison]" (399). Horrified, she runs to Xavière's room and the silence
behind the closed door at first makes her think that perhaps the young
woman has killed herself. She considers this possibility with both terror
and a glimmer of hope ("It was one way out, the only imaginable way
out") but no—"Xavière was alive. Françoise's treason lived" (399). In the
pairing of these two sentences ("Xavière vivait. La trahison de Françoise
vivait"), an analogy is suggested between Xavière and Françoise's transgression, that "treason" which, Beauvoir explains in her memoirs,
Françoise "expunged by a murder" (*Prime*, 269). Furthermore, it is
clearly the betrayal, not the murder, that occasions Françoise's guilt. Be-

trayal is the transgression that all the way through the novel threatens to disturb the peace. When, in the first chapter, Françoise turned to leave the quiet square where she had been sitting, she described her return to herself ("strange to become someone again") and her withdrawal from the place that had existed in her "absence" as "desertion, an act of treason" (13). In describing her relationship with Pierre, she makes a similar point: "Neither one nor the other ever withheld the slightest fragment. That would have been the worst, the only possible betrayal [la pire trahison, la seule possible]" (52).

Françoise's dilemma is that, in her view, to choose herself is always to betray something or someone else. Yet such betrayal is basic to Xavière's self-definition. She *always* chooses herself. At one point, Pierre even describes her (his definition of her recalling the "myth" of Olga to which Beauvoir referred in her memoirs): "She's nothing but undiluted coquetry, caprice, and *treachery*" (321, emphasis added). Whereas, in order to avoid betraying, Françoise is willing to sacrifice herself to and for the sake of others, such sacrifices are precisely what Xavière demands of those around her: "Xavière smiled at him. Each time something, more especially someone, was sacrificed for her, a look of angelic sweetness spread over her face" (156).

As the "beautiful trio" begins to fall apart, the question of who will sacrifice whom to whom is raised. Pierre tells Françoise that Xavière "asked nothing less of me than to give you up [te sacrifier]" (348). A little while later, pressured by Pierre to abandon Xavière, Françoise reflects that "she could no longer make up her mind to sacrifice her, even for Pierre's happiness" (349). Once treachery (in the form of Xavière) has been admitted, no peaceful coexistence is possible: one must choose whether to sacrifice others (which Françoise considers "trahison") or oneself. It is not surprising, therefore, that the criminal climax of the novel is related in terms of "trahison" and sacrifice.

When Xavière confronts her with her betrayal, Françoise begs the younger woman to understand that she has not been an antagonist: "'I didn't laugh at you. . . . I only thought more of myself than of you'" (400). But even as she speaks, Françoise realizes that this is not the whole story. The choice not to sacrifice herself was not entirely dispassionate. When she attempts to justify herself further by blaming the other woman ("But you left me very little reason to love you"), Xavière turns on her and vehemently accuses her of the basest motives—jealousy and revenge. Faced with the violence (and the justness?) of this accusation, Françoise is horrified: "[She] contemplated with horror this woman at whom Xavière's flashing eyes were gazing: this woman was herself" (401). In a silent prayer she bargains: "*Let everything be wiped out, and I will give up Gerbert. I no longer love Gerbert, I never loved him, there was no be-*

trayal" (401). She is ready to make a sacrifice of herself and of that self's "truth" (her desire for Gerbert) in order to deny her violent and destructive impulses toward Xavière, and to undo the betrayal. But Xavière refuses her explanations and apologies and angrily tells her to leave. If Xavière refuses to accept her sacrifice, there is no way for Françoise to redeem her treachery. She is alone with the realization: "I did that. It was I" (401). As she reflects on Xavière's hatred of her and pictures the young woman's face day after day "contorted by suffering," Françoise puts a new term into the equation that began "Xavière was alive. Françoise's treason lived [Xavière vivait. La trahison de Françoise vivait]." For now she thinks: "My crime. It would exist now forever [Mon crime. Il existait pour toujours]" (401). In this chain of parallel subjects (Xavière, *trahison*, *crime*), Xavière—who may be conveniently and fittingly represented by the initial *X*—equals, stands for, exists with and as both Françoise's betrayal and her crime.

At this point, Françoise recalls the innocent and pleasurable beginning of her relationship with Gerbert: "This story, too, was true. . . . *How had that innocent love become this sordid betrayal?* " (402, emphasis added). The crime came into existence with Xavière's discovery and recognition of it. Françoise's relationship with Gerbert is criminal only because "Xavière knows." There is no independent sentiment of remorse at having betrayed Xavière's trust; Françoise's guilt and her crime are *embodied* in Xavière:

> One could not defend oneself with timid words and furtive deeds. *Xavière existed; the betrayal existed. My criminal face exists in flesh and bone.* (402, emphasis added)

> [On ne pouvait pas se défendre avec des mots timides et des actes furtifs. *Xavière existait, la trahison existait. Elle existe en chair et en os, ma criminelle figure.*]

Repeating and extending the earlier formula ($X = trahison = crime$), this passage allows the reader to equate Xavière with "trahison" and "criminelle figure."[56]

The move from the imperfect tense of *style indirect libre* to the present tense, and the sudden reappearance of an unmediated first person ("*my* criminal face" [*ma* criminelle figure]) also emphasize the immediacy of Françoise's assumption of the crime, while making it indistinguishable from the immediate flesh-and-blood reality of the other woman. Xavière is "ma criminelle *figure*"—the face, the figure, the illustration of Françoise's crime. The other woman is a criminal reflection of the self. The mirror has captured Françoise and found her guilty. Françoise's dilemma is that once she recognizes the relativity of her position (the threat to her absolute sovereignty posed by other "consciences"), she goes looking for and into mirrors, seeking herself but thereby further substantiating that relativity. Xavière, on the other hand, casting her "blind shadow" upon Françoise's existence, is self-reflecting:

> Xavière was there, existing only for herself, reflected entirely in herself, reducing to nothingness everything that she excluded. . . . she refused to accept any dominance over her, she was absolute separation. (403)

The decision to get rid of Xavière is a decision to break the mirror. X-ing Xavière is not the crime; it is the only way to wipe out the crime. It is the murder *of* the crime, after the fact, the murder *produced* by guilt.

Simone de Beauvoir once wrote: "Death challenges our existence, but it also gives meaning to our lives. It is the instrument of *absolute separation*, but it is also the key to all communication" (*Prime*, 478, emphasis added). Since Xavière was herself described by Beauvoir as "absolute separation," we have further justification for reading her death as a kind of double negative and Françoise's final act as the postcrime gesture of killing death, a complicated process that has more to do with communication than with the death toward which that communication tends. Finally, reading Beauvoir's novel in light of the above statement, we see Xavière, as "absolute separation" emblematic of Françoise's "death," both challenging and empowering Françoise's story. Xavière's death projected at the end of the novel is then what authorizes and opens up the story, giving it direction and *sense*, even as it cuts it off.

Writing the Crime

Françoise's betrayal of Xavière involves not only sexual desire (she slept with Gerbert) but also writing (she corresponded with him secretly). In fact, however forcefully Beauvoir may insist upon its cathartic or purifying properties, writing is unquestionably implicated in the criminal circumstances of Françoise's story. It is no mere coincidence that Françoise's treachery is revealed by letters, and the way in which these letters are described clearly demonstrates that their significance lies not only in the writing that they *contain*, but equally in the writing that they *are*. Strewn across the carpet, they are like black letters on a page, spelling out love and betrayal:

> There were letters from Pierre and from Gerbert lying scattered over the carpet.
> "Xavière knows." . . . Her love for Gerbert was there before her, black as treason. (399)

The status of these letters as text is suggested by Françoise's instantaneous reading of them ("Xavière knows") as well as by the adjective "black," which draws letters, love, and betrayal together into a single image. By making the letters at once a readable sign of Françoise's love for Gerbert and a black mark of her betrayal, Beauvoir's imagery suggests that writing itself not only accuses, but incriminates.

When, at the end of the novel, having already taken her definitive action against Xavière, Françoise returns to her room, gathers up the letters, and burns them in the fireplace, she is not merely destroying evidence; in her mind the letters are, like Xavière, embodiments of the crime itself. Burning the letters is then like murdering Xavière: an attempt to kill the crime.[57]

The relation of writing to crime may only be suggested obliquely within the novel by this reading of the letters, but Beauvoir develops the connection more explicitly in her memoirs where she first associates crime with the pursuit of identity and liberty: "crime figured regularly as an element in my dreams and fantasies. I saw myself in the dock, facing judge, prosecutor, jury, and a crowd of spectators, bearing the weight of *an act in which I recognized myself, and bearing it alone*" (*Prime*, 252, emphasis added). In a criminal act one would *recognize oneself*, and this act would define and secure that self because one would be *solely responsible* for it. Describing her early dependency on Sartre, Beauvoir then goes on to explain that she at one time believed that only a crime could restore her solitude, her autonomy:

> Ever since Sartre and I had met, I had shoved off the responsibility for justifying my existence onto him. I felt that this was an immoral attitude, but I could not envisage any practical way of changing it. The only solution would have been *to accomplish some deed for which I alone, and no one else, must bear the consequences. . . . Nothing, in fact, short of an aggravated crime could bring me true independence.* (*Prime*, 252, emphasis added)

Here, again, in Beauvoir's description of her own criminal impulse, the function of the crime that she imagines seems to be to wipe out another "crime," in this case the "immoral attitude" of having Sartre justify her life for her. The crime she envisages is not, however, directed against that particular transgression, for there is another motive for this crime, another "crime" to be eliminated. The criminal act by which Beauvoir will free herself from Sartre is paradoxically committed both in response to the immorality of her dependency on him (her lack of a separate identity) and in response to the scandal of the other's separate existence: "when I came to realize the existence of other people's consciences/consciousness [la conscience d'autrui], I felt that I was at grips with as shocking and unacceptable a fact as death" (*Prime*, 252). But the paradox is only apparent, since the individual consciousness is equally threatened by absorption (effacement in the other) and difference (displacement by the other). It is not insignificant, however, that it is the scandal of difference rather than that of annexation which provokes the criminal act in *L'Invitée*. The "existential" crime that—as articulated in Hegel's formula of each "conscience" pursuing the other's death—engages both freedom and responsibility does not directly address the other who is not an other. Beauvoir does not, in other words, pursue Sartre's death, for although as the *one* (with whom she is not two but one) he may threaten her autonomy, he is never seen as the scandalous *other*. She even takes complete and sole responsibility for the "immoral attitude" of her dependency on him, thus permitting him to remain intact and essentially unimplicated in her murder of the *other* other.

Beauvoir's treatment of crime in her memoirs at first merely details and explains her preoccupation with the *subject*. Committing a crime and writing about it do not, of course, necessarily engage the same degree of criminal responsibility, and despite her theorizing, Beauvoir is not about to go out and kill anyone. Crime is the theoretical answer to a theoretical dilemma, something to think and write about: "I often amused myself by a more or less close interweaving of these related themes" (*Prime*, 252). In putting the final term to this development, however, Beauvoir identifies her situation with that of Françoise and shows how the crime enters the novel through and as the writing:

> In the first place, by killing Olga on paper I purged every twinge of irritation and resentment I had previously felt toward her, and cleansed our friendship of all the unpleasant memories that lurked among those of a happier nature. But above all, by releasing Françoise, through the agency of a crime, from the dependent position in which her love for Pierre kept her, I regained my own personal autonomy. The paradoxical thing is that to do so did not require any unpardonable action on my part, but merely the description of such an action in a book. For, even if one is attentively encouraged and advised, *writing remains an act for which the responsibility cannot be shared with any other person.* (*Prime*, 270–271, emphasis added)

In this passage, Beauvoir not only telescopes the crime and the writing ("by killing Olga on paper"), she implicates Françoise in criminal activity that corresponds to *Beauvoir's* criminal intent. Françoise turns on the gas and gets rid of Xavière/Olga for Beauvoir. The complicity implied by this crossing of the border between life and fiction means that Simone de Beauvoir, author of this "transgression," shares Françoise's guilt. Both women are involved in killing Olga on paper. Furthermore, as Beauvoir is implicated in the crime of murder, Françoise is in turn implicated in the crime of writing. The crime only needed to be committed *to paper* in order to accomplish its goal; as the murder is subsumed by the narration, the writing is indisputably the scene of the crime.

Within the novel, writing comes to represent the distance between Françoise and Xavière, their different ways of communicating, their different value systems. Françoise is the writer, and while there is no real evidence of her writing in the novel, the fact that she writes still clearly shapes her life and her relationships. Xavière, on the other hand, has no patience with vocations and cannot understand how Françoise can shut herself up in her room every day to write. Scornful of Françoise's conscientious commitment to routine, Xavière reproaches her for turning art into "a task." Xavière believes that writing is something one should indulge in only "when the spirit moves you." One writes for pleasure, not out of duty: "there's something voluptuous about words" (103). When, in one of their last conversations, Françoise refers to Pierre's letters in order to counter something Xavière has been saying, the younger woman makes her position on writing brutally clear, pointing out that not everyone sets as much stock in "writing [écritures]" as does Françoise (396).

If Françoise is the writer, Xavière is the actress for whom writing is just another histrionic act.[58] Whereas Françoise writes to identify herself as a writer, Xavière's writing is used to seduce and disguise. Xavière also writes to expose the inadequacy of Françoise's kind of writing, the static message, and to display the tantalizing and dynamic power of her own. In the apparently desperate note that she leaves for Pierre and Françoise, her "illegible scribbling" is a provocative nonverbal *act*, her indecipherable penmanship a dramatic gesture signifying its own defiance of the conventions of writing and specifically of the constraints of making sense (311).

Xavière is perhaps her most dramatic in the novel at the moment when she silently presses her lit cigarette to the flesh of her left hand, leaving a burn that she later describes using the same adjective she had used to describe words: "There's something *voluptuous* about a burn" (284, emphasis added). With this shocking gesture, Xavière the actress confronts her audience with a scene at once menacing and impenetrable, as she becomes in a sense her own indecipherable text:

> Françoise flinched. Not only did her flesh rise up in revolt, but the wound had injured her more deeply and irrevocably to the very depths of her being. Behind that maniacal grin, *a danger was threatening*. . . . Something was there that hungrily hugged itself, that unquestionably existed on its own account. One could not approach it, even in thought. Just as she seemed to be getting near it the thought dissolved. This was no tangible object; it was an incessant flux, an incessant flight, transparent to itself alone and *forever impenetrable*. (284, emphasis added)

The threat posed by Xavière's action derives both from the passion that motivates the act (as illustrated by the description of her "voluptuous, tortured smile of a woman possessed by secret pleasure [en proie au plaisir]"

[284]) and from its complete lack of sense. In this scene, Xavière is the expression both of woman's desire and of her resistance to interpretation. But Françoise (whose writing entails frequent consultation and collaboration with Pierre) is radically threatened by the existence of this inassimilable text within her story. In some ways, Xavière represents a story that intrigues and repels Françoise, a familiar story that she cannot tell as long as she remains a "collaborator."

At the novel's climax, Xavière confronts Françoise with two scandalous threats (which correspond to the two aspects of Françoise's betrayal): that is, her body and her version of the story. The challenge of Xavière *as flesh* is on several occasions recognized and expressed by Françoise. For instance, when Xavière returns to Paris from Rouen after Pierre has left for the front, Françoise notes: "She had not changed into a docile phantom. It was her presence *in the flesh* that had again to be faced" (385, emphasis added). As this passage makes clear, the challenge of the flesh is also a challenge to narration. Xavière is not a phantom, not a fiction, but a flesh-and-blood presence that defies the fiction-making efforts of the storyteller who wants to contain and domesticate her. In a key passage several pages earlier, Françoise had reflected on this very distinction, imagining the imminent transformation of Xavière from "a memory, an address on an envelope," to a very real threat: "she would see her in the flesh" (382). Flesh and blood will, of course, always challenge and defy the storyteller. Ineluctably inscribing mortality the body becomes an image of death, which both sanctions and radically subverts all narration.[59] But if the body nourishes and defies the text, the text in turn expresses and erases the body. And since, in the instance described above, the corporal challenge is entirely contained *within the text*, one can only ask where and whether the body is. What the novel presents of Olga herself is precisely an address on an envelope since the novel is dedicated, addressed, to her. While the tyranny of the other woman is described repeatedly within the text as "of the flesh," what Beauvoir acts out is her claim that she need only write about the crime in order to free herself from that tyranny. The murder of Olga "on paper" is complicated by the dedication of the novel. Beauvoir pretends to have annihilated Olga with Xavière's murder, but what she accomplishes is more like an elaborate death threat whereby she imprisons and disarms the other woman precisely by returning her to the state of being, forever, an address on an envelope. There *is* no body—not even a dead one.

Xavière poses a challenge to writing and narration not only by being unreadable, indecipherable, but also by being unwritable, unnarratable.[60] Françoise realizes very early that something indefinable in Xavière will always resist her: "Words could bring you nearer the mystery, but without making it any less impenetrable; it only masked the heart in a more chilling shadow" (132–133). The shadow cast by Xavière's presence, however, is not merely one of resistance, since Xavière is also a storyteller. Thus, while Françoise at first feels that she is the true author of Xavière's "romantic story [histoire romanesque]," she comes to realize that the struggle in which she and the other woman are engaged is in fact not for Pierre or Gerbert but for the *story*. Françoise feels keenly Xavière's challenge to her narrative authority, Xavière's competing version of "reality." When she learns from Gerbert that Xavière has been giving him her own account of events, she knows that even if she were now to tell Gerbert the "real" story, "it would be futile. There, the young heroine, the sweet, sacrificial face [figure], would continue to feel in her flesh the noble and intoxicating taste of her life" (394). Heroine of her own story, Xavière is a living contestation of Françoise's story, and the latter imagines her "in her nest of lies" ready to seize Françoise and "force her to become part of her story" (395). Yet as Françoise tries instead to force Xavière into *her* story by confronting her with "the truth," she notes that "the arrogant heroine she was hoping so passionately to vanquish was no longer anywhere; there remained a poor, hunted victim, from whom no vengeance could be exacted" (398). There can be no resolution, no victory. The two versions exclude each other. While Françoise's personal dilemma arises from the fact that contradictory stories may be equally "true" (like the "innocent love" and the "sordid betrayal"), Xavière represents an even more radical subversion of the narrative enterprise. It is not that she refuses to recognize the truth of Françoise's "story." Rather, she calls into question the truth of all narrative: "'Don't you think that in their letters people never tell things as they are? Even if they don't intend to lie?' she added politely. 'Just because they're telling them to someone?'" (396). Associating "telling [raconter]" with "lying [mentir]," Xavière implies that all storytellers are deceptive or deluded. Indeed, Françoise comes quickly to realize that Xavière defines *true* communication as either physical or spiritual but never literary: it occurs either in the *presence* (in the flesh) of people with one another or through "communion of souls over and above words" (398).

Both possibilities threaten Françoise the storyteller with exclusion and annihilation. She can defuse this threat only if she can draw Xavière into communication with her and force her to *proclaim* her defeat: "there could be no possible victory without her admission of defeat [sans son aveu]" (398). Even after Xavière has discovered the incriminating letters in her desk and Françoise is no longer expecting or seeking "victory," she knows that her only hope lies in persuading Xavière to *hear* her confession: "'I have done you a wrong,' said Françoise. 'I don't ask you to forgive me. But *listen to me*, don't make my fault irreparable.' Her voice was trembling with emotion. If only she could convince Xavière . . ." (402–

403, emphasis added, ellipsis in the original). Although Françoise has declared that there can be no victory now, her persistent desire to conquer
the other woman through language is manifest in the sentence "Si seule-
ment elle pouvait *convaincre* Xavière . . . [If only she could *convince*
Xavière . . .]." Since the suspension points suppress any reference to that
which Xavière is to be convinced *of*, the verb "convaincre" acts transitively
and exclusively upon a single object: Xavière. The desire to "convince"
thus becomes an expression of pure power, recalling the Latin word from
which it derives, *convincere*, to overcome thoroughly.[61]

The focus on speaking and hearing once again illustrates the power attributed to the body within the novel. Since it is Xavière in the flesh and
not the literary figment who challenges her, Françoise cannot just write
her off. She must extract from her some acknowledgment of her own
(Françoise's) existence in the flesh. She needs to speak and be *heard*.
Xavière's refusal to *listen*, to be *addressed*, is a devastating refusal of
Françoise's spoken voice. It is this silencing (for an unheard voice is effectively silenced) that precipitates and necessitates the final act, the ultimate
corporal address: murder.

This version of *L'Invitée*'s ending is, however, neatly undermined by its
own narration. Even as telling and writing are thus distinguished and con-
trasted within the text, the text itself, containing *both*, obscures the distinction. The unheard confession is in fact unspoken. Indeed, the moment
of confession, an admission of guilt and perhaps an appeal for forgiveness,
is never reached. What Françoise actually addresses to Xavière is self-
justification and accusation: "'For a long, long time I thought only of
your happiness. You never thought of mine'" (403). Even if a confession
had been articulated, however, it would still have remained part of the
written narrative, unspoken. The murder, the "corporal address," is
equally body-less and literary and unrealized.

When Françoise begs Xavière, "'Don't make my fault irreparable,'" she
is suggesting that the criminal act to which she is driven, the murder of the
other woman, as a logical and inevitable extension of the already existing
crime, will be unpardonable and irreversible, a crime without hope of
atonement or reparation. But this comment recalls Beauvoir's statement
that writing the novel enabled her to *avoid* committing any "unpardonable action." Is Françoise's "irreparable fault" the price and guarantor of
Beauvoir's innocence? It seems that Beauvoir's distinction between the
unpardonable act and the telling of that act allows for a certain hide-and-
seek with guilt within the novel. The boundaries between acting and telling are at once asserted and obscured, as are those between fact and
fiction. Françoise's gesture can then have the force of an "irreparable
fault" but be, according to Beauvoir's escape clause, somehow "pardon-
able," an effective crime that leaves no permanent stain.

Crimes of Passion

There are crimes of passion and crimes of logic.
—Camus, *The Rebel*[62]

"I know, passion is sordid," said Françoise. (308)

Françoise never in fact confesses, but her urgent attempts to make Xavière hear what she has to say follow upon that crisis of "conscience" to which I referred at the beginning of this chapter. Coming at the climax of the novel, this crisis produces something resembling a confession in embryo:

> And now, she had fallen into the trap, she was at the mercy of this voracious conscience [cette conscience vorace] that had been waiting in the shadow for the moment to swallow her up. Jealous, traitorous, guilty [Jalouse, traîtresse, criminelle]. (402)

While the words "jalouse, traîtresse, criminelle," summing up the terms of Françoise's guilt, look remarkably like a mea culpa, there is no identification of the voice that intones them, no subject assuming clear responsibility for the naming, and there is therefore no way here to distinguish confession from accusation. The source of the embryonic confession is unquestionably "cette conscience vorace." Yet in the double signification of the word "conscience," Françoise's conscience (her personal sense of her own goodness or blameworthiness) is assimilated to Xavière's separate consciousness. In moving from the "conscience vorace" to its judgment ("criminelle"), this passage encourages a reading that associates the *other*'s awareness with one's own guilt. "Jalouse, traîtresse, criminelle" therefore reads like a forced confession, an interpretation supported by the language of entrapment and submission ("fallen into the trap" and "at the mercy of").

What is further significant about this crisis of conscience is that the metaphor used to describe it is distinctly corporal. The adjective "voracious" and the verb "to swallow up [engloutir]" conjure up an image of a hungry animal. Françoise's "guilt" is articulated in direct response to the challenge of the body, the overpowering threat of the appetites. This hungry animal, this body, these appetites recall those aspects of Xavière that Françoise found most troubling: Xavière whose "avid tentacles . . . wanted to devour her alive" (293), Xavière, "a female . . . crouching behind the door, in her nest of lies" (395), Xavière and "her presence in the flesh" (385). In fact, the key to understanding the threat of Xavière's body is contained in this confrontation with the "conscience vorace" that threatens to swallow up Françoise. Finding herself reflected in the carnality and desire of the other, Françoise is no longer "a naked conscience in front of the world" (150); she is food, prey. But she is the hungry beast as well, for the "conscience" that accuses her is both Xavière's and her own.

Rejecting the bodiless image of herself "austere and pure as a block of ice," Françoise recognizes that she cannot defend herself "with timid words and furtive deeds" (402). The struggle for survival will be a mortal combat: "It is she or I. It shall be I" (402). The linguistic shift—the move from the epithets that had earlier defined and sheltered Françoise ("self-sacrificing, scorned, clinging obstinately to hollow morality") to the litany of guilt—signals the way in which Françoise has come to resemble Xavière, jealous and treacherous, in order finally to meet her on her own terms. Françoise is hardly comfortable with this resemblance; she has difficulty recognizing those parts of her which are not rational, dispassionate, selfless. The crime of which she stands accused is, however, the crime of passion. Her initial transgression is jealousy, that disruptive and uncontrollable passion which she and Pierre had determined to legislate out of their "beautiful trio." Jealousy leads in turn and directly to the crime of betrayal: "*I was jealous of [Xavière]. I took Gerbert from her*" (401). The significance of this development goes beyond the obvious story of a love triangle. Although Françoise may be jealous of Xavière's relationship with Pierre, she is above all jealous of the other woman's ability to occupy a (jealously guarded) place in the world, to be "a living assertion of herself" (292). In order to stake her rival claim, Françoise must affirm *herself*, but, as we earlier noted, she is uneasy about such self-assertion. The "conscience vorace" that threatens to devour her is not only her own moral judgment and not only the *other*'s consciousness, but also the greedy imperialism of her *own* consciousness.

Since the criminal implications of her own passions are more than she can bear, Françoise seeks to decriminalize or, if necessary, eliminate those passions, first by begging for Xavière's recognition, and finally by murdering her. In her final action, she submits passion to argument and reason. Like the title that Beauvoir originally considered, *Légitime défense* (Self-defense),[63] the ending of the novel emphasizes the logic of the crime, the theoretical (even legal) justifications for killing Xavière.[64] The seemingly dispassionate narration analyzes and scrutinizes the act in philosophical terms and concludes that it is the only possible solution to an impossible situation. The desires and passions whose excesses threatened Françoise are apparently contained and controlled by the cerebral, methodical approach she takes to disposing of Xavière.

It is nevertheless true, as Camus suggests in *The Rebel*, that crimes of passion and crimes of logic may not be easy to distinguish. Françoise's final gesture is, after all, a striking echo of Xavière's "living assertion of herself" that seemed to Françoise so monstrous, so scandalous. In addition, the narrative gestures of containment at the end of *L'Invitée* only attest to the powerful forces being contained. Logic does not really tri-

THE VOICE OF REASON

umph over passion; rather it holds it in check. One senses, for instance, the agitation underlying Françoise's reasoning: "How can I? thought Françoise. But how could there possibly be a conscience that existed and that was not her own? If it were so, then it was she who was not existing. She repeated: 'She or I.' She pulled down the lever" (404). She answers one question with another, and her abrupt conclusion to this dilemma appears to be motivated by the logic of desperation. That the ending of the novel does not, in fact, accomplish the triumph of logic is also evident in the fact that, as we already noted, the logical crime itself is never in fact consummated.[65] But, in this case, the unconsummated crime is surprisingly similar to unconsummated desire—in its lack of completion it endures. The result of the crime's suspension is not to leave the text free and *innocent*, but rather to keep it forever implicated in its desire for violence.

Policing the Ending

The failure of Françoise's carefully premeditated crime to dispose of her criminal passions and thereby exculpate her is evident in the traces of policing and the accompanying residues of guilt in her final reflections:

> Xavière's door was locked on the inside. They would think it was an accident or suicide. "In any case, there will be no proof," she thought. (404)

The "they" ("on") represents Françoise's (albeit minimal) acknowledgment that there exists a monitoring force outside of her own conscience. Although the power of these "police" is decidedly limited—any attempt they make to interpret and judge will be severely hampered by their ignorance—Françoise's uneasiness at the thought that "they" will nevertheless form a judgment of the case is revealed in the way she dismisses them. "In any case" suggests her unspoken anxiety about being found guilty: she reassures herself that "*in any case*, there will be no *proof*" (emphasis added).

In keeping with the logic of her existential crime, Françoise summarily disposes of these policing forces of conventional society. Having suggested that their interpretations must be either incorrect or impossible to substantiate, she places herself outside of their jurisdiction, repeating her contention that her act is hers and hers alone: "Alone. She had acted alone: as alone as in death." But then she adds:

> One day Pierre would know. But even his cognizance of this deed would be merely external. No one could condemn or absolve her. Her act was hers alone. "It is I who will it." It was her own will that was being accomplished, now nothing at all separated her from herself. She had finally chosen. She had chosen herself [Elle s'était choisie]. (404)

The reference to Pierre in this final paragraph of the novel calls into question Françoise's assertions of solitude. Although she defines Pierre by his limited access to her autonomous act (thereby placing him in a position analogous to that of the previous paragraph's "they"), the very fact that she evokes him belies his exclusion, and her certainty and acceptance of his eventual knowledge is suggestive of his continuing influence upon her.

I earlier suggested that the balance of power in Françoise and Pierre's outlaw couple favors Pierre, and that it is, in fact, Pierre who "leaves Françoise free," Pierre who implicitly embodies the law of their society. We find further evidence of this in their artistic collaboration where Pierre is the acknowledged authority. Françoise always submits her work (including her own fiction) to him for final approval. After finishing the manuscript on which she and Gerbert have been working, she exclaims, without even having to *name* the absent Pierre, "Let's hope he likes this" (18).

Françoise was grateful for the opportunity to participate in and contribute to Pierre's work, valuing above all her other "lucky breaks" the one "which gave her the opportunity of collaborating with Pierre" (46). Her singular definition of "collaborate," however, is elucidated by her later reflection about Pierre, that "her every thought was *with* him and *for* him" (113, emphasis added). In Françoise's mind, to work with Pierre is to work *for* him. *He* is the source of both inspiration and approval. A description of Pierre's work further emphasizes the fact that his is the primary role in this "collaboration":

> This was the first time that [Pierre] had put into effect *his aesthetic principles* so systematically, and on such a large scale. He himself had trained all these actors. *Françoise had adapted the play according to his instructions.* Even the stage designer had followed his orders. *If he succeeded he would have asserted decisively his conception of art and the theatre.* (45, emphasis added)

Beauvoir, of course, insists that the collaboration is not all one-sided, that Françoise and Pierre, like herself and Sartre, read, critique, and influence *each other*. This is undoubtedly why she gives Françoise a writing career of her own, apart from the work she does with and for Pierre. Nevertheless, the unhealthy dependency of which Françoise becomes aware relates to her tendency to make Pierre not only her director, reader, and critic, but her *writer* as well:

> Nothing that happened was completely true/real [vrai] until she had recounted it to Pierre; it remained poised, motionless and uncertain, in a kind of limbo. . . . Every moment of her life that she entrusted to him, Pierre gave back to her clear, polished, completed, and they became moments of their shared life. (26)

Pierre, clarifying and verifying Françoise's life for her, essentially appropriates it. *Her* life (which cannot be completely *true* without Pierre's "finishing" touch) becomes *their* life. Pierre is Françoise's *witness*. He sees and he tells. Inasmuch as what he tells is *true* only in his retelling of it, however, he also resembles an author who takes a character's story and articulates it; the true and finished story is both character's and author's.[66]

Although Françoise goes on to say that "she knew that she served the same purpose for [Pierre]" (26), there is little evidence of this. Having come to realize that he is living "for himself [pour son propre compte]" (135), she promptly abandons her idealistic rhetoric about their relationship but never submits the philosophy behind that rhetoric to a thorough investigation; she never permits the radical implications of her disavowal in any way to fix on or infect Pierre. Careful not to consider the possibility that her idealistic picture of the couple (encouraged by Pierre's talk of "not two but one") might have been serving to justify and/or conceal inequality and exploitation, she instead takes all the blame for misinterpreting the terms of their collaboration: "but it wasn't Pierre's fault, he hadn't changed. It was she who for years had made the mistake of looking upon him only as a justification of herself" (135).

What is perhaps most striking at the novel's end is Françoise's blindness to the power that she continues to bestow on Pierre. Despite her declarations that it was wrong to have allowed him to occupy the place of purification and justification for her (the place, that is, of the benevolent law), she never completely wrests that position away from him. Pierre, who has not changed, does not change. In fact, *there he is*, in the final paragraph, the only recognized and anticipated witness of her action. Françoise may protest that his act of witnessing cannot and will not in any way affect her sole possession of her own act, yet one cannot help wondering why, in that case, he is still there. Despite his *literal* absence, he remains at the end of *L'Invitée* a powerful and uninterrogated presence.

Everything we have noted about Pierre's role would seem to provide some justification for reading him as an inscription of "law" in Beauvoir's novel. It is not an accident, moreover, that the criminal denouement occurs between the two women in his absence, nor that Françoise then evokes him in a way that suggests he is still capable to some extent of policing her actions. Even as she declares that no one can now condemn or absolve her, her *naming* of Pierre reaffirms his unchallenged position as an external point of reference (like the law). Her unexamined relationship with him survives unscathed the criminal upheaval of the novel's climax precisely because he occupies this fixed position in her world, and because one of the privileges of the police is to be themselves exempt from interrogation. Françoise can share in this immunity by associating with him.

It was Simone de Beauvoir who placed Pierre in this unassailable position. In her memoirs, she freely acknowledges that it is Pierre "on whom the entire story hinges," and that, in fact, only *Pierre* could plausibly and convincingly have driven Françoise to commit that final criminal act.[67] Why then did she not have Pierre play that role? Beauvoir explains that her "free invention was shackled by a combination of mental blocks and self-criticism [autocensure]," and she admits that, as a result, the character of Pierre "has less depth and less truth" than any of the other protagonists.[68] Indeed, Pierre is hardly a character at all. Beauvoir, in her attempt to shield Sartre from scrutiny, granted Pierre total immunity. There are times in the text when his *actions* or *attitudes* might appear blameworthy (insensitive, opportunistic, selfish, manipulative), but *Pierre* is never portrayed as such because he is never really *portrayed*. He is more of a fixture or a force, a law unto himself. Furthermore, as a deputized agent of his own law, he is above suspicion since his behavior *defines* and *enacts* the law. His role in contributing to a situation that leads Françoise to commit murder is therefore developed in the novel only in order to explain Françoise, never either to pin down or to implicate *him*.[69]

Texts and Pretexts

> *Il aurait tout fallu remettre en question.*[70]

At this chapter's opening I spoke of the need to locate the law and the crime together, to read each in terms of the other. It appears, however, that part of the problem facing *L'Invitée*'s reader may be that law and crime are, in fact, *too* close, *too* intertwined. Having suggested that Pierre serves as a fixed and unchallenged locus of the law, I would now add that the inviolable status of that law is not a given, that it can be maintained only by an intentional displacement of the crime *away from it*. The law seems absolute only because Françoise carries out this displacement so efficiently.

> *She was wrong* to depend so entirely on Pierre: that was a real *mistake*, she ought not to thrust responsibility for herself upon someone else. . . . She would still ask Pierre to sanction the very *censure she inflicted on herself*; her every thought was with him and for him; an act, self-initiated and having no connection with him, an act that bespoke genuine independence, was beyond her imagination. (113, emphasis added)

Pierre has been responsible for Françoise, but he is not responsible for having been responsible. Just like Beauvoir who, while recognizing a certain impermissible dependency in her relationship with Sartre, refused to submit him to critical or criminal judgment, Françoise describes the crime

THE VOICE OF REASON

behind the crime (the fault that the criminal act must efface) but resists in any way implicating Pierre. Although clearly located at the *scene* of the crime, he is just as clearly not liable. His role, as determined by Françoise, is only to add his voice to hers in declaring *her* guilty. By thus shouldering all responsibility for the initial transgression, Françoise displaces the crime before Pierre can even be questioned.

Furthermore, before this *displacement* can be questioned, Françoise throws another "transgression" into the balance. She comments that what is "disturbing" has nothing to do with Pierre's interest in Xavière. He had been involved with other women before and she saw no reason to fault him for it. What disturbs her is "this feeling of rigid hostility that she had discovered in herself" (114). She accepts Pierre's philosophically justifiable actions and focuses her critical judgment entirely on her own troublesome and emotional *re*actions. All fault is now squarely centered on Françoise and on her unacceptable "passions." It is but a short step to carry out a secondary displacement of the crime—to transpose it onto Xavière.

By fixing the "crime" on Xavière, Françoise turns critical attention away from her relationship with Pierre, away, that is, from the uninterrogated (con)*text* of the original transgression. She protects this text both by making it law and by intentionally foregrounding *another* text so that the law will not be read and maybe questioned or tampered with. The "crime" can be shifted so easily from Françoise to Xavière, and can later be reflected back and forth between them, because of what they have in common and how they differ from Pierre. That is, this strategy of shifting the criminal burden first onto Françoise alone and then onto the other woman is so easily accomplished because gender is a convenient and accepted *pretext* for blaming.

The pretext of woman's guilt is inscribed in the tendency toward feminization of the language of *L'Invitée*, and in the way in which this language is then made to express guilt. The feminization is evident, for example, in the title *L'Invitée* and in the fact that (in the French) the word "Françoise" opens the text and the word "choisie" closes it. Granted, in a highly gender-inflected language like French it is tricky to attribute any particular intention to the use of feminine words. It is generally supposed that the language itself is neutral, *neuter*, despite these inflections, and that genders are merely conventional, informational, unremarkable markers which could in no way be charged with criminal intent. I would merely note that to choose the title *L'Invitée* (rather than *L'Hôte* or *L'Autre*, for instance) is to choose consciously to mark the gender of the invited party. The title announces that this is a story about a woman. By the same token, the novel does not conclude as it might have with the penultimate sentence, "Elle avait enfin choisi [She had at last chosen]." The last sentence,

"Elle s'était choisie," not only elaborates upon Françoise's choice, it literally *inscribes her* in her action, in the word "choisi*e*." The sentence thus performs what it declares, and the appended *e* sums up and represents that performance. In this way the text subtly gives the difference of gender the last word.

If we look closely at Françoise's "confessional" sentence ("jealous, traitorous, criminal" [402]), we may further note that her "crimes" of passion and betrayal are subtly gender-*infected* by the gender-inflected language used to describe her. The feminine endings (jalou*se*, traître*sse*, criminel*le*), may claim the neutrality of established forms, yet they cannot help but address and accuse the gender of the criminal. She is not merely jealous, betrayer, criminal; she is *female* jealous, *female* betrayer, *female* criminal.[71] This accusation of gender serves as an effective pretext for allowing the text to remain neutral and unsullied.

The final paragraph of *L'Invitée*, like the endings of the novels we shall study in the next three chapters, focuses upon the female protagonist and leaves us with the image of a woman's solitude, separateness, survival.[72] Françoise is portrayed as solely responsible for her act, autonomous, alone. Yet although her final self-affirmation might appear to be a stronger and more triumphant gesture than those of the other protagonists, it is actually more constrained. While the other three women do not assert or name themselves, they are powerful and disconcerting presences at the end of their novels. There is something tremendous or scandalous about Elizabeth Rolland at her dying husband's bedside, Clarissa Dalloway appearing on the stairs, Lol V. Stein sleeping in the ryefield. Despite Françoise's declaration of selfhood and independence and her dramatic final act, she does not attain this stature, for the ending of *L'Invitée* attempts to domesticate passions and to reason away monstrosity. In the final analysis, Beauvoir proves to be the most vigilant police figure of all. Both in the novel and in the memoirs we note her strict stylistic control over Françoise's criminal passions. Even as Françoise speaks her thought in the novel's last paragraph ("'It is I who will it [C'est moi qui le veux]'" [404]), the utterance has little force. It is contained by quotation marks that imply narrational control; the I is reduced to an object pronoun ("moi"); and the desires are expressed at a distance from their subject ("qui le veux"). This sentence epitomizes the measured tones in these last paragraphs where the prose expresses no strong feeling, no relief, joy, pleasure, panic—only logic and determination. Desires have been reduced to reasons. In the same way, in the final sentence ("Elle s'était choisie"), we find the narrator policing the protagonist. "Elle" (she) subverts all claims of subjectivity, effectively masking or suppressing the "je" (I), which is proclaimed but never given a voice. Likewise, in the memoirs, referring to the murder of Xavière as the "*raison* d'être" of the novel,

Beauvoir emphasizes that the crime is reasonable, within her control, part of her thesis.

Unlike the final images of the other three novels, which, as we shall see, seem to resist closure, *L'Invitée* ends in an attempt to read itself. Its definitive reading—"Elle s'était choisie"—is therefore, despite what it *says*, a more obedient and less courageous ending than the others. The aggressive self-definition that pretends to be daring is much like the earlier "confession": a defensive strategy designed to foreclose the readings and judgments of others.

Ultimately *L'Invitée* is a novel resisting its own criminal passions and its own crime story. Playing to the absent police (represented by Pierre on the last page), it maintains complicity with the male reader. Though there is something about her crime that Pierre will not be able to penetrate and understand, Françoise is unwilling to consider a dangerous possibility: what that male reader cannot read might be radically unacceptable to him if he could. She claims her act as her own, but she leaves it, like her unconscious, safely uninvestigated. We are left with the impression of Beauvoir writing *against* herself. In fact, one might conclude that just as the crime *in* the novel was to wipe out crime, the novel itself may be an attempt to expunge the very crime it represents (that of a woman writing). The more radical crime, that of questioning the law, or even naming the law the crime, is not committed. I would contend, however, that Françoise's crime of logic is almost unreadable unless her passion is also read into it, and that the unarticulated struggle between reason and passion points to where that radical crime would be.

Two

Cries and Lies:
Le ravissement de Lol V. Stein

Analytic Space

Marguerite Duras's *Le ravissement de Lol V. Stein* seems at first glance an odd place to look for "crime."[1] Although it touches upon traditional themes of love, deception, betrayal, and jealousy, this novel has none of the apparent qualities of "confessional" genres where crime and guilt (however subjective or ill-defined) serve as points of departure. Nor does it burn with the heat of those melodramas where crime and passion are messily entangled. Recounted in the often dispassionate prose of a seemingly reasonable (and analytical) narrator, Jacques Hold, *Lol V. Stein* is, if anything, disturbingly cool, distant, even banal.[2] One might, of course, read in the title a suggestion of a crime—the "ravishing" of someone called Lol Stein. But in its linguistic ambiguity (rape or rapture? Is Lol ravished? ravishing? ravisher?) the title in fact merely prepares us for the elusive nature of the entire novel. If there *is* a crime here, its detection is continually frustrated, hampered by the absence of corpus delicti, an absence provocatively inscribed as and through Lol and her story.

It is nevertheless this very elusiveness that first arouses our suspicions. In *Lol V. Stein* the stage is set for criminal investigation by the establishment of what Viviane Forrester calls "an analytic space." When Forrester declares that Duras opens up an analytic space in her writing, she is not implying an author/analyst and a text/analysand. What is produced is not an *analysis* but an open space, with Duras, "brutally conscious [sauvagement avertie] of what makes/looks like a symptom, knowing [savante] about what the analysis is tracking."[3] Indeed, of all Duras's novels, *Lol V. Stein* may be the one that most insistently incites and resists analysis, as dozens of critics feel compelled to say something (but never, they all concede, enough) about Lol V. Stein.

In and around *Lol V. Stein* the analytic space is indeed wide open, for there is no pinning down this subject. What is a "ravishing," after all, but a violent act of displacement, a dramatic figure of absence where presence was? The "ravishing" in this novel is not easily located at any fixed point. It cannot be contained by the primal event to which on one level it apparently refers (the night of the dance at T. Beach when Lol watched her fiancé Michael Richardson dance until dawn with Anne-Marie Stretter and finally go off with her, leaving Lol behind); the "ravishing" does not stop there: it is repeatedly suggested in the endless process of memory, evocation, and narration that tracks Lol through the story in an attempt to locate what cannot be located, and to know what cannot be known.

The first revelation of Lol as a case, the first symptom of her difference and of the impossibility of placing her, is given at the novel's very beginning by Tatiana Karl, who had been her schoolmate: "In school, she says, and she wasn't the only one to think so, there was already something lacking in Lol, something which kept her from being—Tatiana says, 'there'" (3).[4] Jacques Hold, Tatiana's lover and Lol's narrator, is equally lucid about the impossibility of his undertaking. He knows (or says he knows) that what he knows is that he knows nothing: "That was my initial discovery about her: to know nothing about Lol was already to know her. One could, it seemed to me, know even less about her, less and less about Lol V. Stein" (72).

As Lol invites or eludes analysis *within* the novel, so the novel itself circles Lol's "lack" compulsively until she becomes the expression of symptoms that no reader/analyst can resist. Even Jacques Lacan, who devoted few essays wholly to literature and for whom the gesture of writing about a contemporary work was uncharacteristic, was drawn or driven to speak into the space left by Lol's "ravissement," but his "Hommage fait à Marguerite Duras du Ravissement de Lol V. Stein," although presented as an appreciative interpretation of the novel, nevertheless at the same time steadfastly refuses (or maintains the impossibility of) interpretation.[5] Probably the most celebrated sentence in Lacan's "hommage" is his declaration that in *Lol V. Stein* Marguerite Duras "shows she knows, without me, what I am teaching [s'avère savoir sans moi ce que j'enseigne]." Lacan's assessment echoes Forrester's portrayal of Marguerite Duras as "knowing [savante]"—but Lacan stresses the fact that Duras knows without knowing. This is not the analytical knowledge of logic and dissection but a kind of symptomatic knowledge, a knowledge of whole spaces (represented as coincidence with, rather than as penetration of, the object *known*). Lacan will not try to fill the space that Duras opens, for in paying homage to Duras, Lacan notes,

> The only advantage that a psychoanalyst has the right to take from his position, if his position be recognized as such, is to recall with Freud that the artist, in his subject matter, always precedes the psychoanalyst who therefore does not need to play the psychologist there where the artist is paving the way for him.[6]

The "symptom" Marguerite Duras/Lol V. Stein is to some extent immune to analysis. But although *Lol V. Stein* confounds analysis (the product), it at the same time depends upon it (the process). For the novel is structured around the premise that "something happened," and the work of Jacques Hold's narrative seems to be to struggle to reconstruct (and/or invent) that "something" in the past in an endless attempt to comprehend, construct, and possess "something" in the present.

When the psychoanalytic process is engaged, however, it brings a lot of criminal baggage (usually in the form of guilt) along with it. The systematic unearthing of the past (and particularly of early significant—and possibly violent—experiences) and the accession to that past in part through scattered "clues" which leave a trail that can only lead back to some crucial "moment of truth": this is a model common to both psychoanalytic and criminal proceedings.[7] Furthermore, thematic configurations that recall the Oedipal triangle necessarily introduce a history of crime as well as of desire (and the desire for crime as well as the crime of desire).[8]

It is significant, however, that the criminal circumstance of *Lol V. Stein* extends beyond the thematic level into the novel's textual strategies.[9] Implicit references to a primal scene arouse suspicion precisely as they are repeatedly evoked and deferred through processes of forgetting or anticipation. In similar fashion, Lol is not merely an evasive (and therefore suspicious) "character"—her relationship to language (and specifically to that language used to narrate her) further enacts that evasiveness.

Surveillance

Described by Tatiana Karl as having been particularly adept in school at avoiding the supervision of the school monitors ("les surveillantes" [85]),[10] Lol, first on the night of the dance at T. Beach and again ten years later upon her return to S. Tahla, becomes herself a "surveillante," a watcher. Yet although we, and Jacques Hold, watch her watching, we never see *through her eyes.* Hold time and again carefully locates and names her look, her gaze, but in so doing he only objectifies her watching. It is Jacques Hold, not Lol V. Stein, who puts into words what Lol supposedly sees. Indeed, it is Jacques Hold, not Lol V. Stein, who *sees,* for it is Jacques Hold whose narration *follows* Lol's daily walks,[11] and it is Jacques Hold who (inventing, he readily admits) interprets them: "No, Lol must have given herself the credit for passing unperceived in S. Tahla. . . . Each day, following her walk, she must have felt all the more reassured: if she willed it, people scarcely saw her, she was almost invisible" (31–32). The narrator would have us know that essential to Lol's surveillance of S. Tahla is her own "*incognito,*" that she even becomes herself an emblem of the anonymous and pervasive power of policing, able to define the terms of her own recognition: "It seems to her as if she's been poured into an undefined identity that could be called by a number of indeterminately different names, an identity whose visibility depends on her" (fr 41). But of course, it is Jacques Hold who casts Lol in this role, and might we not question his motives? Does he insist upon Lol's enigmatic authority in order to mask his own policing? in order to try to understand her as a reflection of his own desires? his own will to power? Jacques Hold speaks for the silent watcher, Lol V. Stein, and the terms in which he describes her surveillance anticipate and reveal something about his and our own surveillance of her:

> She recognized S. Tahla, continually recognized it both from having known it earlier in her life and from having known it the day before, but without S. Tahla reflecting back any confirmation, each time, a bullet whose impact would always have been the same. All by herself, she began to recognize less, then differently, she began to return day after day, step by step, toward her ignorance of S. Tahla. (33)

Recognition approaching ignorance. The terms are strikingly similar to those in which Jacques Hold later describes his own approach to and growing ignorance of Lol V. Stein. As Hold's portrait of Lol slides with alarming ease into self-portrait, his attempts to empower her tend rather only to reveal *his* preoccupations with power.

Our access to Lol is both assured and just as decisively blocked by her narrator, as he alternately claims authority ("I invent, I see"; "I'm not mistaken") and denies it ("I don't know"; "I'm mistaken"). While he at times allows Lol a certain degree of self-actualization ("Then one day this infirm body stirs in the belly of God" [41]), even giving her a will of her own ("One can neither get close to her nor move away from her. You have to wait until she comes in search of you, until she wants to" [95]), he just as surely undermines his own observations as he admits that "to please her [*à sa convenance*], I would invent God if I had to" (123). This last so apparently generous gesture is especially revealing in the light of the way Jacques Hold has defined Lol's relationship to God. Suggesting that Lol wanders around S. Tahla in order to be able to think about the dance at T. Beach, Jacques Hold situates her in an endless repetition of that past precisely because she is powerless to change anything of that past, "She is not God. She is no one" (47).

When, two pages later, Jacques Hold repeats, "But Lol is still not (not yet) God, not anyone [Lol n'est encore ni Dieu ni personne]," he goes beyond the earlier definition of Lol as what she is not. Still neither creator nor created, Lol is now (through the narrator's use of "still [encore]") a figure of "virtuality."[12] She is here defined as what she has *not yet been or become*. This is also a deceptively generous gesture on Jacques Hold's part, for two pages later it becomes clear that while Lol may be beginning to become someone, or at least some *thing*, there is no question of her being God: "this infirm body stirs in the belly of God." God is what/who contains her.[13] How arrogant then for Jacques Hold to presume to be able to invent God for Lol V. Stein! Yet his arrogance is veiled—not only by the magnanimity of his gesture ("to please her"), but equally because he throws up "God" as a verbal smoke screen (not *naming* his own role and thus dissimulating the fact that he proposes to play God to God).

Doubling Narrators

God yet not God—this is symptomatic of what Béatrice Didier describes as "the basically elusive narrative essence" of the novel, a narrative structure in which "there had to be a narrator, but a narrator of absence." Didier points out that there is no single, unified narrator but rather a "double narrator who in turn splits in two."[14] Another way of putting this would be to say that Hold the narrator lacks "integrity," and the narrative strategy that he represents is certainly well illustrated by his tendency to hedge his bets, by his talent for playing both sides against the middle. Another example of Hold's hedging occurs in the "chapter" immediately following his definition of Lol as "this infirm body."[15] Describing the first time Lol followed Jacques Hold and witnessed his meeting with Tatiana Karl, Hold the narrator boldly recounts the action simultaneously from his and from Lol's point of view. Speaking for Lol in the third person, he flaunts his omniscience: "Lol decided," "[Lol] thought," "she feels," "[Lol] knew." What is striking about these pages is that Jacques Hold the narrator renders Jacques Hold the character more or less opaque, making him a pure function of *Lol*'s insight. The narrator, exercising his narrative prerogative, creates a transparent Lol. Nor does he hide the mechanism; he readily admits: "I invent, I see." He then allows Lol in turn to repeat his gesture, that is, to expose what transparency there is to be revealed in the Jacques Hold she follows and mentally analyzes: "Not one of them [women] escaped his glance, imagined Lol [Lol inventait], not one who might possibly have suited his fancy [qui aurait pu être éventuellement *à sa convenance*] or, if need be, someone else's fancy, why not?" (47). Jacques Hold inventing Lol inventing Jacques Hold—God inventing God. And does not the repetition of "à sa convenance" reinforce this association?

At times Jacques Hold might have us believe that he is inventing Lol's story, that he is inventing God, for *her* sake. Yet his personal stake in the narration of Lol's history is evident almost from the start. Despite a rational and more or less methodical approach, he is admittedly doing more than merely detailing what he has and has not seen and heard. He is editing, and in justifying his editorial choices, he reveals to just what extent his undertaking is *not* disinterested: "the presence of her adolescence in this story might tend somehow to detract, in the eyes of the reader, from the crushing actuality/presence of this woman *in my life*" (4, emphasis added). Furthermore, as this passage makes clear, the narrator not only has a relationship with Lol, he is also and at the same time in the process of establishing a relationship with a *reader*. Both relationships constrain and motivate him.

Significantly, Hold's relationship with his reader seems to be based upon a shared stake in Lol as "unknowable." If Lol is unknowable, Jacques Hold is free to invent; fiction is justified as the closest possible approximation of a truth that is not directly representable. Furthermore, the reader is free to read; the reader's credulity is also validated. When Jacques Hold the analyst, in complicity with the reader, systematically engages in a reification of his own ignorance, he is striving to secure his own (and by extension, the reader's) authority. Thus, he makes no attempt to deny, to correct, or to conceal the self-deconstructing elements of his narration that continually cast doubt upon his motives and intentions. Part of Hold's powerful abdication of power lies in his acknowledgment of and/or contribution to this deconstructive process. He readily admits his lies after he tells them. He uses rhetorical devices such as apophasis, saying what he will not say: "It will never be a question of Lol's blondness, nor of her eyes, never" (70). His discourse is a tissue of irreconcilables: "I know; I know nothing"; "one trace remains . . . no trace." Indeed, while he hastens on the one hand to substantiate his story with facts, with names, he is moved on the other repeatedly to raise the question of his own fallibility. Taking the measure of his narrative performance with comments such as "I'm mistaken," "I was mistaken," "I'm not mistaken," Hold acts as if by bringing lucidity to bear upon the blind spots he might belie their blinding power.

Jacques Hold further subverts his own narration by making specific references to details only to undermine their referentiality. If we look closely at one example of this, we see that Jacques Hold's failed attempts at referentiality may be precisely the point that he is trying to make. For instance, he describes meeting Tatiana Karl in the Hôtel des Bois on a Tuesday. The next chapter then begins: "The following day . . . it's Thursday" (116). What has happened to Wednesday? A clue may lie in an earlier conversation that anticipated the events of these days. Jacques Hold addresses Lol V. Stein:

"I won't leave Tatiana Karl."
"I know. You're supposed to see her again."
"On Tuesday."

> The violin stops. It withdraws, leaving behind it open craters of immediate memory. I am frightened, appalled by all other people but Lol.
> "And you? When will I see you?"
> She tells me Wednesday, sets a time and place. (108)

But "Wednesday" has disappeared from Jacques Hold's narration. Intentional suppression? Or a careless oversight, a misnomer? In either case the narrative logic is flawed. What did we expect? In a story where temporal dimensions are anything but fixed and linear, where one approaches past and future simultaneously and in equal measure, and where the present (*presence*) is generally inexpressible—

> now, the present, the present alone, which turns round and round, whirls in the dust and at last alights in the cry, the soft cry with broken wings, and Lol is the only person to notice the break in it (65)

—in a story caught in the interstices of *forgetting* and *remembering*, Jacques Hold's naming of days seems overzealous and incongruous. It is a construction set up to be knocked down.

To locate the responsibility for these manipulations solely with the narrator is, of course, to overlook the fact that Jacques Hold is both more and less than Lol's narrator. Someone has bothered to invent this ignorant and fallible God for us. Wednesday's disappearance may effectively remind us that knowing the present by naming the day is impossible and beside the point, but it also suggests another scenario and another Jacques Hold, one whose lies are symptomatic not of ignorance but rather of some repressed knowledge. One suspects that it might be *important* that it was *Wednesday* (the day, place, and hour fixed by Lol V. Stein for the next meeting with Jacques Hold) that has disappeared from the chronology. Jacques Hold suddenly commands our interest and attention. His motives are open to interpretation; he shows himself to be in need of or subject to analysis. But then, it is not easy to subject Jacques Hold to analysis. He is, in his own way, as evasive as Lol. On those rare occasions when he might be said to present something incongruous and therefore analyzable, the reader must confront the very real possibility that it is all a case of projection, misreading, or mistaken identity.

Furthermore, when analyzing a text's incongruities one must consider the possibility that these are merely the result of an author's carelessness, although this is probably *not* the case of the days of the week in *Lol V. Stein*—Duras is not one to dispense gratuitous detail. Another passage in the novel that at first reading seems "wrong" *could* similarly be due to a typographical error, but might equally well be intentional and therefore further evidence of Jacques Hold's textual acrobatics. The textual incongruity occurs in the description of Lol's arrival at Tatiana's house and of the encounter that will culminate in Lol's meeting Jacques Hold (a crucial meeting for Hold since he can at this point assume his place as the story's narrator, as "he" and "I" come at least momentarily into focus: "Tatiana introduces . . . Jacques Hold, a friend of theirs—the distance is covered—me"). Lol advances slowly toward the group: "hydrangeas are withering in the shade of the trees. They are already turning purple, is probably her only thought. The hydrangeas, Tatiana's hydrangeas, at the same time as Tatiana now, she who from one moment to the next is going to cry out *my name*" (64). The first person pronoun is elsewhere used outside of direct discourse only to designate Jacques Hold the narrator. If this is Hold's transcription of Lol's *thought*, it is a startling departure from the rest of his narration. We expect to read "her name," if he is referring to Lol. "My name" has the feeling of a Freudian slip. Either Jacques Hold so identifies with Lol at this moment that her thoughts become, without his mediation, *directly*, his words (an event in itself significant), *or* he is anticipating his own entry into the story. Tatiana Karl will cry out Lol's name—but Jacques Hold is preoccupied with the fast approaching moment when he *himself* will be *recognized*. "My name" cries out the egocentrism of the first-person narrator. Of course, in keeping with the text's subversion of all bids for authoritative position, "my name" not only inserts the first person into this critical moment, it also very effectively suppresses him. For no *name* is named. "My name" remains stubbornly ambiguous. Indeed the very structure of the expression in French, "mon nom," a perfect palindrome, illustrates the problem, suggesting as it does a double mirror in which the name itself should be but is not reflected. In this suggestive mirroring, identity slips away.

All of this adds up to the fact that in some ways, if "God" was a smoke screen for Jacques Hold, Jacques Hold is himself a smoke screen. On those rare occasions when Hold slips into focus, we realize how readily we have been willing to forget that Marguerite Duras is also establishing a relationship with the reader in which the shared stakes may be the "unknowability" of the narrator Jacques Hold.

Jacques Hold himself at one point suggests that it is not only Lol but he himself who may be the subject of his growing ignorance: "But of what about myself am I to this degree ignorant, [what do I not know] that she summons me to know? who will be there, at that moment, beside her?" (96). Through the use of the interrogative and by attaching the concepts of ignorance and knowledge to the two people whose encounter is being related ("I do not know" and "she summons me to know"), this passage questions the relationship of ignorance and knowledge. As he implies that one does not displace the other, that in fact they grow *together*, the narrator subtly but clearly establishes a parallel between his situation and that of Lol V. Stein. When he asks, "Who will be there?" he anticipates the cry at the heart of Lol's crisis: "Who is there?" This shared identity crisis makes clear that what one asks of the other is the unanswerable question of one's own identity—that *being there* is always defined by or in relation to the other.[16]

Inventors and Forgers

Lol V. Stein plays with this idea of reflexivity (especially well illustrated in the novel's elaborate *jeux du regard*), and as a result there is far more emphasis placed on the role of error (*se tromper*) than on that of deception (*tromper*). If error is to be the inevitable price of being or constituting an other (for there is room *in the passage* between one and the other for one to *be mistaken*), it is likewise the price of narration, or at least of that narration which mimes the interpersonal scenario as it attempts to bridge gaps. In a kind of apology for his narrative enterprise, Jacques Hold clearly outlines the choice as he sees it: "To level the terrain, to dig down into it, to open tombs wherein Lol is playing dead [fait la morte], seems to me fairer—given the necessity of inventing the links I'm missing in Lol's story—than to fabricate mountains, erect obstacles, accidents" (27).

The distinction between invention and fabrication here is the distinction between an interpretive approximation and the assertive erection of a monument, both in the place of absence. The approximation is inevitably subject to error, while the erection has much more to do with outright lies (*tromper*) than with mistakes. Fabrication may be able to cover what is missing, thereby explaining its absence and effectively exculpating the narrator, but it is (from Jacques Hold's point of view) the reification of an *obstacle*. It substitutes one "truth" for another and as such it must betray its history. The dead are not only left dead, they are pinned to their resting places by elaborate narrative headstones.

The only way to connect the narrating present to the narrated past is to attempt to cross that distance, to level the terrain, open the tombs, invent, and err. This process is not about *facts*. Clearly the erection of a monument is more stable, more "factual," more historically prudent. It is about *interpretations*. The "mistakes" are not factual incongruities; they are signs of erring interpretation. They do not lie about the past; they reflect upon their own failings—for the invention is not *meant* to represent something that was but rather to work in the spaces left by that passing.

In *The Archaeology of Knowledge*, Michel Foucault draws a distinction between two kinds of history: the traditional form that "undertook to 'memorize' the *monuments* of the past, transform them into *documents*," and a contemporary history that "transforms *documents* into *monuments*." The text as document demands a "historical reading" dependent upon translation and interpretation, whereas an "archaeological reading" is brought to bear on that text which stands as a monument to its own textuality and temporality.[17] Jacques Hold's self-defined narrative project reveals Lol's narrator to be a historical reader of the past who in turn expects to create a *text as document* that must be read *historically*. While acknowledging the inherent problems of referentiality and verification in such an approach (since "Lol never said a word to anyone," there are no firsthand accounts, no direct access, only "monuments of the past" to work with), the narrator nevertheless establishes his "inventing" as intimately bound to a process of memory: "So, since I, for my part, seem also to remember something, let me go on" (28).

Insofar as Jacques Hold treats Lol V. Stein as a document "in need of translation," he must acknowledge and accept the inevitability of error. As we have already noted, the narrator's ongoing self-critique serves to incorporate the error into the narrative strategy. It is, however, when Lol articulates an instance of Jacques Hold's error that the reader fully realizes both the advantages and the insufficiencies of Hold's kind of narrative. In the train on the way to T. Beach, Lol has expressed her need to tell Jacques Hold what she is feeling. What she then discloses—"I don't love you, yet I love you, you know what I mean [vous me comprenez]"— is emblematic of Lol as paradox. Furthermore, the tag "vous me comprenez" (literally "you understand me") is equally ambiguous. Is it affirmation, explanation, or supplication? Apparently incapable of interpreting Lol's statement, Hold replies with questions: "Why don't you kill yourself? Why haven't you already killed yourself?" And as if to complete the symmetry of her "I don't love you/I love you" paradox, Lol answers Jacques Hold with the antithesis of "vous me comprenez": "No, you're mistaken [vous vous trompez], that's not it" (159). Lol's reply performs two seemingly contradictory functions. In responding to Jacques Hold's questions, Lol associates the narrator's error with his interpretive attempts (specifically his attempt to interpret her past: "Why haven't you already killed yourself?") and with his failure to respond appropriately to the text that she has presented and that in a sense she embodies. As if the document itself were accusing the translator's error, Lol confronts Jacques Hold: "That's not it." On the other hand, by completing the oxymoron "You understand me/you are mistaken," Lol at the same time repeats her initial message; she re-presents herself. She offers Jacques Hold another chance. His error becomes part of her definition.

It is significant that the narrator has made no attempt to quiet his text. Lol is allowed, even perhaps encouraged, to confront him with his lack of authority—probably because he has no desire to occupy that uncomfortably assailable position of defending some authoritative version. The narrator's strategy is one of evasion and co-option. With all due modesty, he muses on Lol's judgment:

> She says it without any trace of sadness. If I am mistaken, I'm less *gravely* [*moins gravement*] mistaken than the others. I can only be *profoundly* mistaken about her [Je ne peux me tromper sur elle que *profondément*]. She knows it. She says:
> "It's the first time you've been mistaken."
> "Does it please you?"
> "Yes. Especially in that way. You are so close to
> She tells of the happiness of loving, concretely. (159–160, emphasis added)[18]

Confirmed by Lol's knowledge ("She knows it") and her pleasure ("Does it please you?" "Yes"), Jacques Hold is able to reify his ignorance and redeem the error. This recuperative process is exemplified by his use of the words "gravement" and "profondément." Though these words are not synonyms, their semantic fields do intersect. Both express a weightiness, seriousness, extremity. Yet once their resemblance has been noted, their differences become all the more significant. To be *gravely* mistaken implies danger, tragedy, fatality. To be *profoundly* mistaken implies penetration, intensity, depth. "Gravement" seems to lead to death, the dead end, the lying monument. "Profondément" suggests the opening of a tomb, power, the possibility of a beyond. Jacques Hold's error is not "grave" but it is, in keeping with his narrative strategy of opening the tombs where Lol "is playing dead," profound.

Again the narrator has subtly claimed Lol's support for his enterprise. When first describing the choice between tomb smashing and mountain building, he had noted, "And, knowing this woman, I believe she would have preferred me to compensate in this way for the shortage of facts about her life" (27). At that moment he based his assumption of Lol's approval on a knowledge of her that he elsewhere admitted to be far from complete. In similar fashion, Hold's interpretation is selective when he once again assumes that Lol supports his handling of her story. Comparing his errors with the "grave errors" made by others, he essentially overlooks her critique. He completely fails to consider that what pleases Lol might be not the error but the fact that this is the "first time" he has been mistaken; he presumes that Lol's pleasure is a validation of his narrative. He seems to have no scruples about leaving her direct discourse abruptly suspended ("'You are so close to") as he takes over and sums her up indirectly ("She tells of the happiness of loving . . .").

Yet the price of Jacques Hold's antiauthoritarian bid for power is that the text must be free to reflect upon him and his narrative strategies. Immediately after he has come into focus, attained his place, and introduced himself, he introduces Lol as her own narrator:

> From the moment Lol entered the house, she never so much as glanced at me again.
> She immediately began talking to Tatiana. (66–67)

Yet he denies her direct narration and, having enumerated her topics of conversation, he sums her up with comments upon her narrative style: "Lol didn't speak much but she spoke clearly enough to reassure anyone who might have been concerned about her present condition—but not her, not Tatiana" (67). Tatiana, unlike the other listeners, is uneasy and accuses Lol of talking about her life "like a book." Only Tatiana senses the extent to which what Lol is fabricating is creating "obstacles" and "accidents." The "book" of her life is *reassuring* "about her present condition," but Tatiana refuses to read Lol that way. She has a stake in the past and she will not accept the turning of the document (the scraps and traces of Lol V. Stein) into a monument, even or especially by Lol herself: "One should never recover completely from passion. And besides, Lol's passion had been ineffable" (67).

Tatiana pleads with Lol to open up the text, to make room for her, Tatiana Karl, to enter into it: "Tell me something, you do know what, when we were young" (68). But Lol can find no detail to recount that might allow her listener access to their shared past; instead she presents her critique. She does not narrate; she reads. And what she has to say is not about the *matter* (events, emotions) which made up that past, but rather about the *manner* by which her *story* has been constituted. She does not dispute the facts but the interpretations:

> "If you want my opinion, I think they were mistaken." (68)

> "About the reasons. They were mistaken about the reasons." (69)

However much Jacques Hold may try to establish his complicity with Lol through their shared acknowledgment of error, Lol's challenge to his interpretive and narrative enterprises stands. While her commentary on storytelling (that of Jacques Hold as well as of the others) signals the inevitable error in interpretation, when she herself "narrates" (as Jacques Hold's commentary on *her* story-telling reveals) something different happens:

> "The light went on in your room, and I saw Tatiana walk in front of the light. She was naked beneath her black hair."
> She does not move, her eyes staring out into the garden, waiting. She has just said that Tatiana is naked beneath her black hair. That sentence is still the last

to have been uttered. I hear: "naked beneath her black hair, naked, naked, black hair." The last two words especially sound with a strange and equal intensity. It's true that Tatiana was as Lol has just described her, naked beneath her black hair. She was that way in the closed room, for her lover. The intensity of the sentence suddenly increases, the air around it has been rent, *the sentence explodes, it blows the meaning apart*. I hear it, a deafening force, and I fail to understand it, *I no longer even understand that it means nothing*. (105–106, emphasis added)

For Jacques Hold, Lol's narration has given way to the semiotic play of the moment. Hold at first marvels at the narrative's accuracy, for *it is true* that Tatiana *was* just as Lol describes her. But just as quickly the sentence ceases to describe what Tatiana was, in the closed room, for her lover. The words themselves are charged and the intensity of the sentence gathers and builds until it explodes, like a clap of thunder, and empties of all meaning, all reference. Lol's sentence does not *document* the past of Tatiana—it has no history—it is rather a *monument* of the present, designating absence:

> The void is statue. The pedestal is there: the sentence. The void is Tatiana naked beneath her black hair, the fact. It is transformed, poured out lavishly, the fact no longer contains the fact, Tatiana emerges from herself, spills through the open windows out over the town, the roads, mire, liquid, tide of nudity. Here she is, Tatiana Karl, naked beneath her hair, suddenly, between Lol V. Stein and me. *The sentence has just died away* [*La phrase vient de mourir*], I can no longer hear anything, only silence, the sentence is dead at Lol's feet, *Tatiana is in her/its place* [*Tatiana est à sa place*]. I reach out and touch, like a blind man, and I fail to recognize anything I have already touched. (106, emphasis added)

Tatiana comes to take the place of the sentence, *her place*, in an equivalence that goes beyond reference. Indeed, she comes to occupy her place not through a process of signification but in unprecedented immediacy out of the death of language. When Jacques Hold touches *this* Tatiana, he does not recognize any Tatiana he has touched before. Lol's words have created her from nothing, from "the void" that is posed on the pedestal of Lol's sentence. When this void begins to move and grow, to transform, to expand, no longer to contain itself, one is reminded of "[the] infirm body [that] stirs in the belly of God."[19] But whereas originally Lol V. Stein was the "infirm body of the other," watching the undressing of another woman, Anne-Marie Stretter, by Michael Richardson ("a God wearied by this undressing") and able to react only by producing a vain and inarticulate cry,[20] in this reenactment and recasting of the scene of undressing, Lol has uttered a sentence that, "dying at her feet," has left Tatiana *à sa place* (in the sentence's place, Anne-Marie Stretter's place, Lol's place). Lol has created a circumstance.

Jacques Hold, though he tends to portray Lol as "not God, not any-one," on occasion nevertheless seems to suggest another Lol *behind it all*, a Lol who makes or lets her story happen and who, in her detachment, resembles God. Jacques Hold first suggested this role for Lol when he detailed the stages of her approach to Tatiana Karl's villa and to the mo-ment when her encounter with Tatiana and with Jacques Hold would trigger both action and narration. In a modified *style indirect libre*, Hold shows Lol forging her own destiny:

> These people, as yet unaware that their peace and tranquility are about to be shattered forever, must not see even the slightest hint of [her impatience]. . . . She had to succeed. For these people, the next few days are going to be—more specifically than a more distant future would be—*what she will make of them*, she, Lol V. Stein. *She will fabricate the necessary circumstances, then she will open the doors that have to be opened: they will pass through.* (62–63, emphasis added)

This Lol, "fabricator," is also the Lol who forges the sentence-pedestal described above. At such moments she reveals herself to be a completely different kind of narrator from Jacques Hold. She is a monument-builder. Her text demands to be read archaeologically, or as Denis Donoghue would put it, graphically.[21] But Hold is what Donoghue calls an epireader, committed to historical interpretation. Even when he recognizes what Lol's narration is *doing*, he resists the implications for his own reading. Rather than read and assume his failure in response to her assessment that he is mistaken, he comforts himself with her pleasure and with the knowl-edge that he is *so close*. He does not dwell on the fact that he is incapable of transcribing *what* he is so close to.

We have noted the extent to which Jacques Hold tries to turn his inad-equacies to his own narrative advantage. It would, however, be inaccurate to portray him as a complacent manipulator. On one occasion in particular he expresses the anguish he feels in confronting the unnarratable chal-lenge of Lol V. Stein. In a self-contained chapter he describes noticing Lol in the ryefield as he stands at the window of the Hôtel des Bois waiting for Tatiana Karl:

> I thought I could discern, between the hotel and the foot of the hill, a gray form, a woman, her ash blond hair unmistakable in among the stalks of rye, I had a violent reaction, although I had been prepared for anything, a very violent reaction I could not immediately define, between terror and disbelief, the temp-tation to cry out some warning, to offer help, to thrust away for good or be caught for good, for all of Lol V. Stein, in/by love. I stifled a cry, prayed to God

for help, ran out of the room, retraced my steps, paced round the floor, too alone to love or to no longer love, suffering, *suffering from the disgraceful inadequacy of my being to know that event.* (109–110, emphasis added)

It is true that the narration of this crisis (two long and emotional sentences) is directly followed by a gesture of containment:

Then my emotion abated somewhat, gathered itself together, I was able to contain it. (110)

And it is then partially retracted by the two short and composed sentences that close the chapter:

I'm lying. I did not move from the window, confirmed to the verge of tears [confirmé jusqu'aux larmes]. (110)

But these attempts at control hardly erase the impression left by the original outburst. This short chapter clearly illustrates Jacques Hold's struggle to "know that event" which is Lol, "a gray form, a woman," watched and watching. That the event defies comprehension (knowledge and containment) is underscored by the fact that this same scene (Lol in the ryefield, Jacques Hold in the Hôtel des Bois) is repeated without explication at the very end of the novel.

On the Subject

But what does suffering without a subject mean?
(fr 23)

Like Jacques Hold, other witnesses—her mother, Tatiana Karl, Jean Bedford—try to recall or to recount Lol V. Stein, and like Jacques Hold, they can find her only in her exclusion; they can find her only displaced and watching the closed *regard* of the couple Michael Richardson and Anne-Marie Stretter on the night of the dance at T. Beach, or ten years later lying in a ryefield watching the hotel window behind which Jacques Hold is embracing Tatiana Karl. Yet despite her displacement everywhere in the novel, Lol is *central* to it: she is everywhere its subject and the object of all efforts at narration.

From the very beginning, the problem of Lol is defined as the problem of the subject. Though her prostration is "marked by signs of suffering," she is "not there" to suffer. Without a subject, the "signs" of suffering cannot signify. The verb cannot be conjugated. Lol's silence expresses not only her failure to occupy the place of the subject "I," but also the degree to which her failure is part of the order of discourse.[22] She is "interdite" in both senses of the French word: *dumb*founded and prohibited. The silent, forbidden woman in the story points to language's law and inscribes its transgression.[23]

As I have noted, however, Lol V. Stein is, despite the interdiction, the *subject* of *Lol V. Stein*; all efforts at narration and reading are about, are *on the subject of*, Lol. The two locutions, "about" and "on the subject of," here used synonymously, both illustrate the problematic of locating the subject. The first stresses that circling activity which describes but does not really touch the *center*, while the second makes "subject" the *object* of a preposition, thus illustrating the slippery lexical and grammatical ground of the concept. Not only does "on the subject" turn the subject into an object, but "subject of" likewise articulates a double reading of "subject" in terms of both subjectivity (as the subject of a sentence) and subjection (as, for instance, the subject of analysis). With the help of this unstable concept, our subject, Lol, is constantly shifting.[24] While her access to the status of subject might appear to be realizable only through her subjection, she nonetheless refuses to stay put long enough to allow us to subject her to our analysis.[25]

The act of reading Lol as unlocatable *locus* can find some confirmation in the place names in the novel. Lol was born in S. Tahla; she was abandoned by her fiancé at the Casino in T. Beach; she married Jean Bedford and they lived in U. Bridge during a ten-year hiatus before moving back to S. Tahla where Lol reencounters Tatiana Karl, where Jacques Hold meets Lol, and where Lol's story is begun. The names are strange: S. Tahla, T. Beach, U. Bridge. Unfortunately, their obviously English resonances within the French text misled Richard Seaver, in his translation of the novel into English, to render them as South Tahla, Town Beach, and Uxbridge. These translations obscure the fact that these indefinite and therefore unlocalizable geographical signs use initials (*S T U*) that do not immediately signify and that furthermore establish an alphabetic progression into which Lol *V*. Stein fits neatly and naturally.[26] Though we are told that the V. in her name stands for Valérie, as Lol is short for Lola, we are also told at two important moments in the story that Lol V. Stein was what she called herself: when she pronounced her name during her madness after the dance and when she gave herself two names (Tatiana Karl and Lol V. Stein) during her "crisis" at the novel's end. By taking her *place* with the other cryptic locations in the novel, she becomes another unlocatable locus of her own experience—and in the *progression* of her experience. Lol's "absence of subject" was at one point described in terms of algebra: "it seemed that suffering had failed to find any chink in her armor through which to slip, that she had forgotten the ancient algebra of the sorrows of love" (9). *S*, *T*, *U*, and *V* look like algebraic terms, unknown quantities in unresolved relationships inviting *solution*.

Geoffrey Hartman once wrote that "to solve a crime . . . means to give it an exact location."[27] This statement might also help to establish the importance of Lol as elusive location in a reading of the criminal circumstances suggested in the novel. The question is whether we can locate Lol at the scene of a crime.

The Crisis and the Crime

Much of the action of *Lol V. Stein* revolves around "la crise de Lol," which is used to refer to the night of the dance at T. Beach (with its aftermath) and later to the climactic episode that finds Jacques Hold and Lol V. Stein in a hotel room in T. Beach ten years later.[28] In the novel's early pages, before any description of the events that transpired during the dance, the narrator notes that Tatiana Karl "believed that this crisis and Lol were but one and the same, and always had been" (4). But it is Lol herself who recognizes in this crisis the possibility of something criminal. At one point when she and Tatiana are reconstructing the past, the night of the dance, through a question-and-answer dialogue, Jacques Hold asks Tatiana something about Michael Richardson, and Lol immediately says, "What about the police, why did the police come?" Tatiana answers, "No, your mother mentioned the police, but they never came" (92). This is the first and only mention of the possibility that the police might have been called. In the narrator's version in which Jacques Hold presents "in full, and all mixed together, both that false impression that Tatiana Karl relates and what I have been able to imagine [ce que j'invente] about the night of the T. Beach Casino" (4), the police play no part. Yet it is Lol's memory that the police had (inexplicably) been there.

   Lol's question ("What about the police, why did the police come?") is, nevertheless, strangely and significantly resonant of the questions that, in the narrator's version, accompanied the unexpected arrival of Lol's mother:

> It was at this point that a woman well along in years, Lol's mother, had entered the ballroom. . . .
>
>   Who could have informed Lol's mother about what was taking place that night at the T. Beach Casino? It could not have been Tatiana Karl, Tatiana Karl had not left Lol's side. Had she come on her own? (11)

Unlike Lol's father who was immediately defined by the narrator in terms of a concrete referent (he is a professor at the university), Lol's mother was essentially suppressed in the book's first paragraph. After three short sentences in which Lol, her father, and her brother were briefly presented came the final sentence in which Lol's mother was buried: "Her parents are dead" (1). Lol's father has links to a world beyond the text (*"her father was originally from Germany"* [93]), but her mother is only defined in terms of the closed fantasmatic world of *Lol V. Stein*: all we really learn about her is that she is "well along in years" (11) and that she comes from S. Tahla (93). These two pieces of information locate her in a space and time that are indefinite and relative. Nevertheless (and this is not surprising since, as the narrative switch immediately following the first paragraph shows, the external referents could never produce a narrative of Lol V. Stein), Lol's father is the absent parent of the story. Beyond the narrator's almost apostrophic mention of his profession, national origin, and decease he has no role. In fact, he is so utterly absent that even his death is not again remarked upon (whereas the mother's *is* noted, if only in terms of Lol's indifference to it).

Lol's mother, on the other hand, clearly has a place within the world of *Lol V. Stein*, though that place is *outside* Lol. Mme Stein represents the *outside* world for Lol V. Stein, a decentered and decentering position that is illustrated in a number of different ways: by the fact that she witnesses and testifies to Lol's breakdown after the dance, by the fact that she serves as intermediary, informing Lol of Jean Bedford's marriage proposal, and not least of all by her unexplained and unsolicited presence at the scene of Lol's *ravissement*. Lol's mother stands between Lol and S. Tahla and that link means either that she acts as "go-between" or that she *comes between*. When Lol's mother bursts upon the scene of the dance, she reintroduces the world where there had been only the interminable and inescapable moment. She breaks the spell, her insults and her cries filling the silence, her touch waking Lol from suspended animation. As she steps between Lol and the couple on the dance floor, she reintroduces time and space, the inevitability of change, the inexorability of an *ending*:

> The screen her mother formed between them and her was the very first sign [that something was drawing to a close]. With a powerful shove of her hand, she knocked [this screen] down. The vague, emotion-filled wail ceased.
> Lol cried out for the first time. (12)

It is the mother's cry that unleashes the daughter's cry, the mother's violent intrusion that provokes her daughter's violent reaction. Yet Lol makes no reference to her mother's arrival at the Casino when she and Tatiana reconstruct that night ten years later. We have only two hints of this scene's possible significance for Lol. One is her indifference to her mother's death:

> The death of her mother—Lol had wished to see her as seldom as possible after her marriage—left her dry-eyed. (23)

The other is her question about the police. When Tatiana assures Lol that the police had not been there on the night at T. Beach, Lol responds: "That's strange, I thought they had. And he really had to leave?" (92). Michael Richardson's departure is associated for her with an externally imposed imperative. From the moment that he *changed*, adds Lol, he had to leave. We must return to the earlier narrative to determine that the moment when everything changed was when Mme Stein stood between Lol and the couple, that the changes were dictated by the inevitable and perpetual evolution toward an ending of which Lol's mother was a *sign*. The fact that Lol has apparently discounted, forgotten, or repressed her mother's presence only makes more significant her bewildered recollection of *police on the scene*.

IN THE LAST chapter of the novel, Lol's crisis is again (or finally) reached. Lol V. Stein and Jacques Hold have traveled to T. Beach together. They have visited the Casino. They have rented a room. It is in this room, in this action, that the repetition compulsion of Lol's story reaches its culmination: "Lol dreams of another time when the same thing that is going to happen would happen differently. In another way. A thousand times. Everywhere. Elsewhere" (177).

But Lol does not move. She does not know "who is there [qui est là] in the bed":

> Who is it? The crisis is here [La crise est là]. Our situation at this moment, in this room where we are alone, she and I, has triggered it.
> "The police are downstairs [La police est en bas]."
> I don't contradict her.
> "They are beating people on the stairway [On bat des gens dans l'escalier]."
> I don't contradict her. (178)

The complete identification of the displaced Lol with the crisis (*"Qui est là dans le lit? Qui est-ce? La crise est là"*) is thus marked for and in Lol by the statement "The police are downstairs." Why do the police appear at the very moment of crisis? What do they represent for Lol? Why must she invent them? Or were they there all along?

At the center of Lol's crisis, this nameless, faceless force of law and order makes its appearance. The anonymous power of the police is furthermore suggested by the contiguity of Lol's two statements: "The police are downstairs" and "They are beating people [On bat des gens] on the stairway." A relationship is forged between the police and the impersonal French "on": *they, one,* a concept that carries a great deal of authority without ever naming or defining the source. In addition, in the symmetrical presentation of Lol's two statements (and through a kind of homophonically produced metonymy based on the near homophones "en bas" and "on bat"), the police are associated with violence.[29] They also come to be associated with male domination, for Jacques Hold quickly recognizes and borrows their power:

> She doesn't recognize me, not at all anymore.
> "I don't know anymore, who is it?"
> Then she recognizes me vaguely.
> "We'll go away [On va s'en aller]."
> I say that the police would catch us. (178)

Inasmuch as the police introduce and represent violence and male domination, they target Lol's fear of both, fear of the violence of being there in her body, fear of the man's ability to violate, fear of the *ravissement*. But why are the police there? Where is the crime?

When Lol says "la police est en bas" (the police are downstairs, down below), she is in part saying quite literally: "We are above the law." But to be above or beyond the law is to be, in the eyes of that law, criminal. And Lol's statement shows that she is well aware of the eyes of that law. When Lol names the police, she *assumes a place* in relation to their law, the law of the world beyond the room, the law of social intercourse. She establishes the parameters of transgression.

When Lol was already ravished, already not there, she could not be prosecuted or found guilty. But when she has *placed herself* in the dangerous situation of being no longer the *voyeuse*, of being there *in the flesh* with Jacques Hold, something like guilt comes close to attaching itself to her.

Finally in the position of being the (sexual) object of Jacques Hold's attentions, replacing Tatiana, his lover, the other woman, she begins to know the magnitude of the female subject's dilemma. As subjected object, the other woman's other, what *place* is rightfully hers? But as she is accused by the presence of the police, as she lies naked before her narrator, her crisis displaces her again. Asking again, "Who is it?" she demands that Jacques Hold answer, "Tatiana Karl, for example." And when it is all over, she raves and begs, flees and returns, and in Jacques's words, "there was no longer any difference between her and Tatiana Karl except in her eyes, free of remorse, and in the way she referred to herself . . . and in the two names she gave herself: Tatiana Karl and Lol V. Stein" (179).

Yet even as it becomes apparent that criminal circumstances surround and color Lol's crisis, the novel deftly subverts any suggestion of Lol's (or, by extension, woman's) guilt. It accomplishes this in two ways—by questioning the authorities, particularly in the person of narrator Jacques Hold, and by refusing to let Lol *stand for* woman or women. There is no way to *pin a crime on Lol* for there is constant displacement: there is no way, no *place*, to make an accusation stick.

In the Place of Lol V. Stein

There's a place to be taken.
(fr 60)

Characterized by a "lack" that marks her absence, Lol is engaged in a constant process of displacement; she is effectively *not there*. As Monique Schneider describes the novel, "Everything will be played out within a phenomenon of disparity [écart]: in the gap between a primordial event and the echo in which one awaits its reverberation."[30] So we attempt to read Lol, seeking her always in the gap between her history and her story.

Displacement is not, however, the final term of *Lol V. Stein*. There is an equally strong tendency toward *replacement*, for if one is not in one's place, another may be there *in stead*. Anne-Marie Stretter takes Lol's place at the dance. Later, Tatiana Karl and Jacques Hold take the place of Anne-Marie Stretter and Michael Richardson. Finally, Lol briefly takes Tatiana Karl's place with Jacques Hold and then withdraws, allowing Tatiana to take hers. The place occupied by Lol, Anne-Marie Stretter, and Tatiana Karl is, in a certain sense, *a single place*, and the replacement of each woman by another is accomplished through identification and doubling. One cannot read *Lol V. Stein* without wondering what purpose is served by this doubling and what it means for Lol. Is it a means of escape or just another trap? Does it subject her or give her transcendence? Does it produce simple repetition or change?

Before considering the implications of this "female doubling," however, I would note that while one might say that the men, too, occupy *a single place*, the "replacement" of Michael Richardson by Jacques Hold functions differently. There is no doubling. Since Richardson and Hold never meet, since they occupy two distinct moments in the chronology of Lol's story, they engage in no direct confrontation, no struggle for place. Indeed, Lol insists that she has not chosen Jacques Hold because of any resemblance to Michael Richardson (43, 105). It appears that she has chosen him rather because he is Tatiana Karl's lover.

Lol first stirred from her ten-year "slumber" after witnessing a man and a woman passing in front of her house. At this moment, the narrator suggests, a memory may have been stirred in Lol by the lovers' furtive kiss, for shortly thereafter Lol begins to wander the streets of S. Tahla. Several weeks later, seeing the man again, Lol quietly observes him, watches him watching other women, and recognizes, in the indiscriminate nature of his "*regard*," his desire: it is the man's (any man's) desire for "the other woman" (all other women) that attracts her attention.

Choosing to follow this man (Jacques Hold), Lol is in fact following his desire. Hold the narrator reflects that it is Tatiana Karl whom Lol is really following "through this man from S. Tahla" (44), as Hold the character furthermore perceives that his lack of resemblance to Michael Richardson is an indication not of Lol's recognizing him as a unique individual, but rather of her *indifference*. She has no need to compare the two men. Her choice is "free from any preference." Jacques Hold is "the man from S. Tahla" as Michael Richardson was "the man from T. Beach": he does not *replace* the other man—he *continues* him:

> Just as my hands touch Lol, the memory of an unknown man, now dead, comes back to me: he will serve as *the eternal Richardson*, the man from T. Beach, *we will be mingled with him*, willy-nilly, all together, *we shall no longer be able to recognize one from the other*, neither before, nor after, nor during, we shall lose sight of one another, forget our names, in this way we shall die for having forgotten—piece by piece, moment by moment, name by name—death. (103, emphasis added)[31]

If Michael Richardson and Jacques Hold offer the seamless continuity of a single, eternal man, Tatiana Karl, in contrast, figures rupture and doubling. We cannot read Tatiana as a perpetuation of Anne-Marie Stretter. Unlike Hold, whose absence from Lol's past allows him to slide into her present, Tatiana shared Lol's past, with a place of her own on the night of the dance: that of the silent and unremarked witness at Lol's side. Thus when she becomes the focus of Lol's attention in the present, a shift is implied. Tatiana is not blending into an "eternal" Anne-Marie Stretter; she is doubling her and at the same time taking her place. Taking over for Anne-Marie Stretter, Tatiana demonstrates that the two women are interchangeable, yet irreducible to a single term.

The singularity of the man and the doubling of the women are repeated within the novel's triangular configurations in which one woman is posited in exclusion, looking at the other always in relation to the third term (a man), seeing herself as, in, replaced by that "other woman." Just as in *L'Invitée*, the triangles in *Lol V. Stein* describe a woman's displacement and replacement, thereby illustrating the (female) subject's dilemma. As she recognizes her desire in the other woman and the other woman in her place, she acknowledges her radical absence from (and as) the scene of her desire. In many ways, Duras seems here to be reworking—from the *other woman*'s perspective—the triangulated relationship depicted in *L'Invitée*.[32] When Lol speaks to Jacques Hold about the scene of her ravishing, she evokes both displacement and replacement:

> "From the first moment that woman walked into the room, I no longer loved my fiancé." . . .
> "When I say that I no longer loved him, I mean to say that you have no idea to what lengths one can go in the absence of love." . . .
> "It's a *substitute*." . . .

"Yes. *I was no longer in my place.* They took me with them. I later found myself
with them gone." . . .

"I don't understand *who is in my place.*" (126–127, emphasis added)[33]

Replacement by the other woman effected the absence of love, but Lol
shows this absence to be a motivating force in the trajectory of her desire
("'you have no idea to what lengths one can go'"). She is not only replaced and displaced, but *transported*: "'They took me with them.'" Absence of love *prolongs* the desire of absence.[34]

Madeleine Borgomano has noted quite appropriately that the desire is
not to replace but to *be replaced*. She also stresses that this is no symbolic
substitution: the replacement is "in the body itself."[35] When Jacques Hold
recounts Lol's desire to be present at the disrobing of the other woman,
he describes a physical desire, the necessity of being "flesh to flesh, form
to form" with this gesture, "her eyes riveted on its corpse [son cadavre]"
(39).[36] The other woman's identity is a matter of indifference to Lol, yet
both her *otherness* and her *corporality* are vital. When Lol and Jacques
Hold sit alone on the train and Lol tells Jacques that her memory of
T. Beach now depends upon him, she still insists upon evoking the absent
Tatiana so that, as Jacques Hold relates it:

> Tatiana is there, like another [comme une autre], Tatiana for example, mired
> within us, the Tatiana of yesterday and the one of tomorrow, whoever she may
> be. I plunge myself deep into her warm and muzzled body, an idle hour for Lol,
> the resplendent hour of her forgetting/oblivion, I graft myself upon her, I
> pump Tatiana's blood. Tatiana is there, so that I can there forget Lol V. Stein.
> She slowly becomes bloodless beneath me. (157–158)

Tatiana "for example," Tatiana "there, like another," reenacts the doubling whereby Lol may witness her own physical replacement. This description of Tatiana as an *other body* recalls Jacques Hold's earlier attempt
to imagine or invent Lol's desire in relation to Anne-Marie Stretter:

> The tall, thin body of the other woman would have appeared little by little. And,
> in a strictly parallel and reverse progression, Lol would have been replaced by
> her at the side of the man from T. Beach. Replaced by that woman, almost to
> her very breath. Lol holds her breath: as the woman's body appears to this man,
> her own fades [s'efface], fades, voluptuous, from the world. (40)

Hold imagines Lol transfixed by an unresolved desire to witness the undressing of the other woman although the complete revelation of that
other body could only exclude her and destroy the triangle. If that strip-
ping process were consummated, Lol's gaze would be lost in the transparency. There would be no *place* for the specular (and no need for *specula-
tion*) in the man's final "knowledge" of the other woman. The woman
wholly revealed, utterly *there*, could have no double. As the man came

into full visual possession of that other body, Lol's own body would fade, voluptuous/voluptuousness, be erased from the world ("s'efface[r], volupté, du monde").

Of course, as the word "volupté" makes clear, the final erasure is the ultimate transport.[37] The desire to be replaced (and to see oneself replaced) in the flesh is the paradoxical desire to know one's own death. The strength of this desire doubtless lies in the fact that only death can guarantee life was ever there, that even as it negates, death confirms existence. In the same way, death both incites and kills desire.

The complete and final nakedness of the other woman is, however, always deferred: "That very slow divesting of Anne-Marie Stretter's dress, that velvet annihilation of her own person, Lol never succeeded in bringing this to its conclusion" (40).

In much the same way, Lol's description of Tatiana "naked beneath her black hair" establishes the incomplete nudity of that other woman, for the last veil (the hair) is never lifted. As long as the desire for revelation and annihilation is not brought to term, death continues to hang on to its mystery and the triangular configuration is undisturbed.

Both desire and crime are inscribed within this triangle. In much of Duras's work the inscription of crime is closely related to that of desire, and while no crime is clearly named or placed in *Lol V. Stein*, the idea is indisputably in circulation. The emphasis on *bodies*, for instance, and the kind of imagery surrounding them suggest both sex and death, "corporal love" and corpses. Probably the most striking instance of this is Jacques Hold's description of making love to Tatiana as he covers her head with a sheet: "He hides Tatiana's face beneath the sheets and thus has *her headless body* [*son corps décapité*] there at hand, at his entire disposal" (123, emphasis added).

In order to consider the ways in which crime circulates with desire, let me first modify my assertion that "no crime is clearly named": the word "crime" does appear three times in the novel, but a reading of these occasions only further substantiates the crime's elusive nature. When the replacement that helps to constitute the triangle and that serves to hold it together is explicitly associated with crime, the location of that crime is systematically undermined by the terms of that association:

> Lol was thus married, without having wanted to be, in the way that she wished, without having to resort to the brutality of a choice, without having to plagiarize *the crime that it would have been*, in some people's eyes, *to have replaced* the man from T. Beach who had jilted her with some unique being. (21)

First of all, the crime referred to here is purely hypothetical (expressed by a conditional mood): it never occurred. Furthermore, it is significant that it is not Lol who makes the association between replacement and crime. The replacement of Michael Richardson by another unique being would have been criminal "in some people's eyes." If Lol *had* been guilty of such an act she would merely have been "plagiarizing" the crime. But what crime? Where is the original for this plagiarism? In a curious textual twist, the original is defined as the *interpretation* that some people would have given to the act that never occurred. In these terms, crime seems to be "in the eyes of the beholder" and nowhere else.

The only crime actually confessed to in the novel is that referred to twice by Jacques Hold when he declares that he has "committed the crime" of forgetting Tatiana Karl and of dancing with and talking to Lol V. Stein:

> I have forgotten Tatiana Karl, I have committed this crime. (fr 157)

> I danced with the woman from U. Bridge, yes, and talked to her, I committed this crime as well, with relief, I committed it. (fr 158)[38]

The concept of crime seems to arise for Jacques Hold as a consequence of his having replaced Tatiana with Lol. The shift of his attention from one woman to the other constitutes for him a kind of "criminal" betrayal. It is not the woman's gesture of taking another's place that is criminal, but rather the man's complicity in defining that place and in *recognizing her there* that enacts the "crime." The crime occurs precisely because there is a *triangle*.

Although Jacques Hold explicitly names and assumes "crime" in the novel, we cannot merely accept his definition. We cannot merely take his *word* for it. After all, since Hold never succeeds in comprehending Lol and since personal motives help to determine his narration, his is never an authoritative account. Furthermore, his crime of *forgetting* in no way explains the pervasive and suspicious uneasiness, the hint of "crime" that seems to attend Lol's "crises" (and, of course, insofar as Jacques Hold narrates these crises, he has a role in sowing the seeds of suspicion). In order to read the crime in *Lol V. Stein*, we must take into account both Jacques's definition and Lol's experience. Unfortunately, these two readings fail to intersect neatly; instead they resist all attempts to place the crime squarely within the context of Lol's story. The crime that is hinted at refuses finally to resemble the crime that Jacques Hold has named. Granted, both versions implicate the triangle, but the triangle turns out to be a far from simple configuration.

On the one hand, the triangle enacts the crime of betrayal. Shifting focus, removing one's gaze, forgetting—for Jacques Hold the crime lies here, within the triangle's dynamic tensions. As long as there are three terms struggling to occupy two places (in the reciprocity of the "regard" that is the object of desire), the brutal exclusion of one term is inevitable. And the price of displacement is guilt. Furthermore, as the triangle entails this betrayal, the process of forgetting perpetuates the triangle. The forgotten, betrayed, excluded is essential to the act.

On the other hand, on the night of the dance at T. Beach, the stable, specular triangle of Lol V. Stein, Anne-Marie Stretter, and Michael Richardson seems to Lol utterly devoid of criminal complications. It is only with the dawn, with the intrusion of time and change (implying the possibility of death), that crime becomes an issue. Crime is suggested to Lol not by the couple that excludes her but by the collapse of their triangle. The world (reintroduced by her mother's touch) tells her that she has been displaced and that this is criminal. It is this revelation that provokes Lol's crisis.

In a sense, then, the triangle always both introduces and defers the crime. The triangle's criminal potential may apparently commit the crime, but it at the same time destroys it (or at least destroys the evidence of it). Crime in *Lol V. Stein* is a persistent but elusive suggestion within the free-flowing dynamics of the triangle.

In Flight from Apprehension

Trying to read Lol for the crime is like trying to locate her desire: Lol is first and foremost a problem in location (a problem she poses for her readers, for Jacques Hold, for herself). From the moment she begins to move ("this infirm body stirs in the belly of God"), Lol resists placement although Jacques Hold wants more than anything to put her in her place within his world and his story. As they travel to T. Beach in the train, he holds her very tightly ("I have to hold her forever, not let her go") and speaks to her of his frustrated attempts to situate his world in relation to hers:

> I in turn tell her about what happened two nights before in my room: I had studied my room closely, and I had moved various objects around, as though surreptitiously, according to the vision she would have had of them if she had come, and also *according to her place among them*, Lol moving among the unmoving objects. I pictured them being moved about into so many different positions that I was overcome by a feeling of suffering, it was as though some sort of unhappiness came and lodged in my hands because of my inability to decide what the exact position of these objects should be in relation to her life. I gave up the game, gave up trying to fit her, alive, into the death of things. (162, emphasis added)

The suffering aroused in Jacques Hold by the need to keep displacing the objects in his room recalls to Lol the object of her own "suffering":

> What I have been saying about the objects in my room has happened to her body, that makes her think of it. She has taken it for walks through town. But

that's no longer enough. She is still asking herself *where this body ought to be, where exactly to put it*, so that it will stop complaining. (162–163, emphasis added)

It was said of Lol that she did not suffer, yet her body, separate from her and unable to find its proper place, will not stop complaining. The radical dislocation of the body, emblematic of Lol's lack of presence to herself (a lack that is in turn emblematic of her desire), is elaborately played out in the scene that follows. Jacques Hold hears Lol saying that she is approaching the *place* of her body's happiness: "'I'm a little closer to knowing [where to put my body] than I was before. For a long time I used to put it somewhere else than where it ought to have been. Now I think I'm getting closer to the place where it will be happy'" (163). Hold's response is more in keeping with his physical hold on her ("I don't let go of her") than with what he has supposedly learned about Lol ("I gave up trying to fit her, alive, into the death of things"). He touches her "with his open hand, more and more urgently, roughly" and in so doing exacts a response. But as Jacques's description makes clear, "the pleasure of love" that shows on her face seems to occur far from any place where "the body would be happy." Indeed, rather than put her "alive, into the death of things," Jacques Hold seems to have succeeded in putting Lol dying, into life: "The full warmth of her breath burned my mouth. *Her eyes are dead* and when they open again I also have on me the first gaze of *someone who has lost consciousness. She moans weakly.* The gaze has come up from its dive and rests on me, *sad and empty*" (163, emphasis added).

To escape from this unlivable place, this deathly embrace, Lol invokes the name of Tatiana. Reestablishing the triangle and thus loosening Hold's hold on her, "she begins to recall specific places"; she reestablishes a geography within which she can distance, even lose herself. Her return from her "dive" into death and oblivion brings with it language ("a somewhat incoherent monologue") and memories ("successive recognitions of places, of things"). These new perspectives and dimensions permit and signal her dislocation. She is suddenly far from Jacques Hold: "This is the first time she has deserted me so completely [qu'elle s'absente si fort de moi]."

In speaking the name of the other woman, Lol thus displaces and replaces her body's desire. She later repeats this process in the hotel room at T. Beach. To her question "Who is it?" Lol insists that Jacques Hold reply, "Tatiana Karl, for example," and in the midst of the crisis she calls herself both Lol V. Stein and Tatiana Karl, doubling Tatiana to the point of interchangeability: at these moments she slips out of place and again escapes Jacques Hold's embrace and comprehension.[39]

The next morning Lol reminds Jacques Hold that he has a date to meet

Tatiana that evening at the Hôtel des Bois. As Hold remarks, she has forgotten a lot of things but not this rendezvous. When he tries to convince
her to stay longer with him, telling her that Tatiana can wait, she does not
understand his urgency: "Why tonight?" (180–181). In a sense, resisting
Jacques's desire to prolong their tête-à-tête, Lol is affirming the two
women's interchangeability for *him* as well as her own indifference. When
she sends Jacques back to Tatiana and returns to her "place" in the field
of rye, she reconstitutes the triangle and with it her own desire (to be
replaced, to *witness* that replacement). Indeed, Lol is constantly resisting
the shift from three to two. The triangle, which on the one hand appears
to be responsible for bringing on the crisis, is paradoxically Lol's only
means of holding the crisis in check.

When, at the very end of the novel, Jacques Hold returns to the Hôtel
des Bois to meet Tatiana Karl, Lol is already there:

> Lol had arrived there ahead of us. She was sleeping in the field of rye, worn out,
> worn out by our trip. (181)

With these words, Hold portrays the fixed triangular configuration to
which they have returned. The subtle shift from "us" (which equals Jacques Hold and Tatiana Karl) to "our" (which equals Jacques Hold and
Lol V. Stein) illustrates that triangle's dyadic terms but seems finally to
indicate balance rather than tension between them. In fact, while the final
configuration recalls former triangles (the night of the dance and Lol's
earlier vigils in the field of rye), this scene feels different. For one thing,
Lol is not *watching* from the sidelines. Asleep, she is no longer regarding
that which (he or they who) regards her. She has retreated—or ad-
vanced—into sleep. But does this move represent repetition or change?
Paralysis or potential? Is desire sated or just momentarily forgotten? Is Lol
finally, quietly, in her place? Or has she once again slipped away, beyond
Jacques Hold's and our own reach?

Jacques Hold had earlier noted that Lol came to the ryefield to rest,
to sleep. On one previous occasion he had arrived at the hotel to find
Lol already sleeping in the field (152), and even the very first time he
noticed her there, her surveillance had resembled a kind of sleep, close to
death:

> Living, dying [Vivante, mourante], she breathes deeply, tonight the air is like
> honey, cloyingly sweet. She does not even question the source of the wonderful
> weakness which has brought her to lie in this field. She lets it act upon her, fill
> her to the point of suffocation, lets it lull her roughly, pitilessly, until Lol V.
> Stein is fast asleep [jusqu'au sommeil de Lol V. Stein]. (53–54)

But on that first occasion Lol was also there to "*feed on, to devour* this
non-existent, invisible spectacle, the light of a room where others are"

(54, emphasis added). The association of sleep and hunger is repeated toward the novel's end. Having visited the Casino ballroom where Lol had ten years earlier witnessed her own abandonment, Jacques Hold and Lol V. Stein emerge into the daylight. Lol yawns, saying, "I got up so early this morning I'm sleepy" (172). She then lies down on the sand, saying, "Let's go and get something to eat, I'm hungry," and immediately falls asleep. At this moment her hunger and her fatigue are indistinguishable. When Lol wakes, she drags Jacques Hold to a restaurant she knows. "She is famished [Elle meurt de faim]. . . . Lol is eating, gathering sustenance [elle se nourrit]" (174). The juxtaposition in the French of "elle meurt de faim" and "elle se nourrit" echoes the "living, dying" imagery used to describe Lol sleeping when Jacques first saw her in the ryefield.

In addition to Lol's deathlike sleep and ravenous appetite (a figure of her desire) in that first scene, one also encounters memory: "In the distance, with fairy-like fingers, the recollection of a certain memory flits past" (54). Memory is also an essential element in the later scene. When, after leaving the Casino ballroom with Jacques Hold, Lol is overcome by sleep, Hold determines not to try to "struggle against the deadly monotony of Lol V. Stein's memory" (172). He sleeps at her side, and when they awaken it is to "rediscover our current memory, marvelous, fresh with the morning" (174).

Clearly Lol's final slumber in the ryefield is no radical departure: she has been sleeping and forgetting all along. What makes the ending different may be the fact that *it ends there*. Lol is set to sleep through the scene of her own replacement, and as the imperfect tense of the verb in the last sentence ("she was sleeping") refuses to close and define the novel, she is left endlessly sleeping in the narrative past.

Furthermore, the *gaze* and the desire that would normally circulate in the triangle appear to have ceded to this *sleep* and *"oubli"* (forgetting/oblivion). It is thus impossible to know for certain how to read this last sleep. Is this a static (and crime-free) moment suspended between memory and expectation, recalling the eternity of the night of the dance before the world intruded? Or is it a dynamic moment charged with all that is being suspended, forgotten?

AT THE FARTHEST limit of *oubli*, forgetting ceases to know itself as forgetting, presence and absence telescope, triangles collapse. At their farthest limits, crime cannot be committed, desire cannot be satisfied—for crime and desire depend upon potentiality, the doubling of the body there and the body not there around a "place to be taken." As the farthest limit, death cannot be known. And so we must ask: Is the end the farthest limit? Is Lol's story over? Have desire and crime and death been elided in one final *oubli*?

Traces

> I refuse to admit the end [je nie la fin] which is probably going to come separate
> us, its ease, its distressing simplicity, because the moment I refuse to accept it,
> to accept this end, I accept the other, the one which has still to be invented, the
> one I do not know, that no one has yet invented: the endless end, the endless
> beginning of Lol V. Stein. (174–175)

Is the end that Jacques Hold narrates Lol's final evasion, the untellable
story of an irrecuperable past? Is it the simple and inexorable conclusion
that he earlier denied? Or is it "the other, the one which has still to be
invented"? Even as Lol's final sleep confirms her enigmatic difference,
shutting Jacques out, denying him access, in its permanent refusal to signify it also represents resistance to that separation which Jacques Hold
could not accept.[40] For in the final oblivion there is no way of *knowing*
whether there has been any change, any integration of the self. One cannot close the chapter on *Lol V. Stein*. The ending must be forever "still to
be invented."

Even if Lol's sleep is read as ultimate *ravissement*, unquestionably figuring death, we are still left with the *image* of the sleeper, for although Lol
is not described in this last scene, we nonetheless *see* her there. Lol has
been seen and described in the ryefield before—"the dark spot in the rye"
(56), "a gray form" (109)—and as the final scene evokes the earlier
scenes, these earlier descriptions resonate through our reading, tracing the
missing image. This unarticulated image of Lol leaves a dark spot, a
smudge in the ryefield, and as long as the impression of that blot remains,
like a fingerprint or a scrap of text, there is no ending. Neither crime nor
narration has attained its dying limit.

One of the stories that *Lol V. Stein* tells (and perhaps that all stories
tell?) is about the inevitability of traces (criminal, desiring, textual). The
sleeping body of Lol V. Stein in the field of rye is a metaphor of a trace;
and indeed it is doubly a trace, for inasmuch as it presupposes a replacement of one referent by another, a metaphor is a trace.[41] The problematics
of time and place surrounding Lol, however, clearly discourage us from
any attempt to understand this "trace" as a residue or a fragment of a
greater unified past. The trace is not "of the past"; it is another dimension
of the present.

Duras has frequently commented on her forgetfulness and the vital role
it plays in her writing. Identity between and consistency of past and present are not a mark of "truth" for her: sometimes what is "truest" is precisely what has been forgotten. Furthermore, for Duras the remembered
is always something new. The trace, therefore, does not stand for what

was, but rather for what is and is not. As such its creative potential is enormous. In *Woman to Woman*, Duras noted that "they help me get away from being disgusted with myself sometimes, these traces that you leave behind and don't recognize most of the time."[42] I would propose that the trace in *Lol V. Stein* recalls in thematic and criminal terms Derrida's conception of "trace" in "every process of signification": "Nothing, neither among the elements, nor within the system, is anywhere ever simply present or absent. There are only, everywhere, differences and traces of traces."[43]

Manifesting the dynamics of absence and presence, the trace is the opposite of death. In the face of death, any trace is the mark of survival, the deferral of the final annihilating gesture. Death must be the absence of all trace. Yet just as desire and crime must continually approach their own limits, so does the trace depend upon the death that would negate it. Thematically and textually, *Lol V. Stein* portrays a striving toward an end that cannot be realized, toward a limit which, as it defines the desire, is to be continually confronted but never crossed.

In *Lol V. Stein* it is the evocation of death that literally *scares up* the trace which is Lol. Lol twice overhears the suggestion of her own death. As she relates it later to Tatiana Karl, the first occasion was on the night of the dance at T. Beach:

> "Did you notice, Tatiana, at the end, while they were dancing, they said something to each other?"
> "I did notice but I didn't hear."
> "I heard: *maybe she will die*."
> "No. You stayed there next to me the whole time, behind the green plants, at the end of the room. You couldn't have heard." (95, emphasis added)

The other occasion, recounted by the narrator earlier in the novel, took place when Lol and her husband Jean Bedford had moved back to S. Tahla. By the narrator's own admission, the story is based upon hearsay (the governess remembers *a little*) and upon his own partial recollection ("I, for my part, seem also to remember something"). Nevertheless, describing the passage of a young couple and their furtive kiss secretly observed by Lol, the narrator also suggests that Lol witnessed more than the kiss:

> They had exchanged a few words which, in spite of the quiet street, Lol had not been able to catch, except for the isolated phrase, spoken by the woman:
> "*Dead maybe* [*Morte peut-être*]." (28, emphasis added)

The similarity between these two scenes of aural witnessing is striking, and the parallel between the two *accounts* is no less significant. In both cases, the critical moment is presented within a narration where the teller's authority is called into question. Tatiana forcefully contradicts Lol's recollection of the night of the dance; and the episode of the passing lovers is related within the immediate context of the narrator's justification for "inventing missing links." Of course, if Tatiana was indeed the woman overheard on the second occasion, then her haste to dispute Lol's version of the first might be explained as a self-interested attempt to discredit Lol's memory. Uncertainties about Tatiana's motives, however, cannot alone serve to authenticate Lol's story. Similarly, although further reading in the novel may permit a tentative, retrospective identification of the second episode's narrator with Jacques Hold and of the couple with Tatiana Karl and Jacques Hold, one cannot forget that such identifications are expressly withheld in the original narration which remains essentially uncorroborated.

Were the crucial words in fact spoken? Could Lol really have overheard them? These unanswerable questions are an important part of reading these two episodes, for the indeterminate status of the narration reflects the equivocal nature of the narrative itself. Neither the utterances nor that to which they refer can be verified. Each overheard fragment contains the mark of its own reluctance to affirm: the word "maybe [peut-être]."

The limits of narrative authority are further exposed by the fact that the event to which both accounts refer is temporally displaced, not only from the time of the narration (part of the nature of narratives) but from the time of the narrative as well. The future implied in the first episode ("she is going to die [elle va mourir]") and the past in the second ("she has died [(elle est) morte]") essentially point to and frame an absent, elided present, the unnarrated ten-year hiatus between the two "signs." When the narrator speaks of opening "tombs wherein Lol is playing dead," he is in a sense treating Lol's ten-year absence from her own story as that death foretold and memorialized. This unnarrated absence is an appropriate figure for death since the ultimate limit of narrative authority, the final silencer, is, of course, death. But is this really death? However appropriate the references may be, they point in vain: death is not something you can figure. Just as both framing statements were tempered by the equivocation of "maybe," so this attempt to refer directly to the place of death itself (marked by the tomb) is couched in terms suggesting that this death is also another *act* (she is *playing* dead [elle *fait* la morte]). Thus while they unquestionably introduce "death" into the narration, erecting a monument over stasis, absence, lack, and silence, the two statements Lol overhears at the same time displace that death. Indeed, while professing death, the utterances actually produce quite the opposite effect: movement.

The first "rumor" is associated (if not causally then perhaps through contiguity) with the undoing of the static triangle.[44] Hearing herself objectified and excluded by the words of the other woman, Lol is also in a sense reading her death in the "text" of the other woman. As long as she is hearing and reading, however, the death is deferred. When, with the dawn and through her mother's intervention, she sees the triangle coming apart, as she begins to recognize the beginning of the end, Lol moves from passivity to crisis. The violence of her passage is marked by her cry.

The second "rumor" likewise marks the end of stasis and, in this case, the narrator clearly attributes Lol's sudden activity to the words she has overheard:

> As for the connection between these excursions and the passage of the couple, I see it less in the glimmer of recognition Lol had for the woman she had happened to see than in the words that the woman had let slip in an offhand way and that, in all probability, Lol had heard.
>
> Lol stirred, she turned over in her sleep. Lol went out for walks through the streets. (29)

Whereas in the first instance Lol's death was evoked as a future possibility, in the second what she overhears resembles an (albeit tentative) obituary. Yet it is precisely this evocation that seems to resurrect her, just as the elusive Lol is repeatedly reinscribed in the aftermath and debris of her own ravishing.

The death that the rumors introduce into the story is, certainly, a paradoxical death, a death that is *narratable*. Lol cannot know her death, except as she hears it *recounted*, and by virtue of this narration she is both dead and not dead. Inasmuch as words try (and fail) to name and point to death, it is there to be named; but, at the same time, since to hear the story of one's death is to *live* it, to survive it, the story one hears is always of its absence.

Jacques Hold acknowledges this paradox when he describes Lol's return to the ballroom and recalls and recounts once again (in telegraphic form) the events of the night of the dance. As, with an abrupt shift into the present tense, Hold eternalizes that *ravissement*, he reproduces the paradox of death and survival (the paradox of Lol and the paradox of his own narration): "The vast, dark prairie of dawn arrives. A monumental calm covers everything, engulfs everything. *One trace remains, one.* A single, indelible trace, at first we know not where. What? We don't know where? *No trace, none*, all has been buried, and Lol with it" (170–171, emphasis added). Even as it narrates the absence of all trace, this passage leaves a trace. Even if everything has been buried, including Lol, a trace remains, the trace of no trace. This is storytelling: the rumor of death that is also always the rumor of survival.

We have already suggested that the paradoxical interimplication of death and survival is closely tied to the problem of knowing Lol and to the related problems of narrating and reading her story. When Jacques Hold characterizes Lol as "abyss and sister" (156), he expresses perfectly the difficulties that Lol poses for him. As her lover and her narrator, he is torn between alienation and intimacy. Lol is at once most distant and nearest, utterly absent and strangely familiar. She is the inexorability of death and the hesitant promise of survival.

Just as these figures of rupture and connection express the paradox of Lol, the "hole-word" that the narrator evokes as a figure of Lol's desire exemplifies the paradox of the narrative enterprise. The narrator describes Lol's obsession with the moment on the night of the dance when "dawn arrives with incredible brutality and separates her from the couple" (36–37). It is this precise moment that contains Lol's desire and its failure. This was the moment to stop the dawn, to penetrate into the eternity of the triangle: "she should have entered it . . . it would have been forever, for her mind and for her body, their greatest sorrow and their greatest joy blended even into what would be their unique definition, but unnameable for lack of a word" (38). The narrator likes to believe that, for a split second, Lol thought this word could exist, and as he goes on to describe it, his own desire quickly becomes indistinguishable from hers:

> It would have been an absence-word, a hole-word, whose center would have been hollowed out into a hole, this hole in which all the other words would have been buried. One would not have been able to say it but one could have made it resound. Immense, endless, an empty gong, it would have held back those who were wanting to leave . . . in one fell swoop it would have named the future and the moment themselves. Missing, this word ruins all the others, contaminates them. . . . How were the others found? Hand-me-downs from God knows how many love affairs like Lol's affairs nipped in the bud, trampled upon, and from massacres, oh! you've no idea how many there are, how many bloodstained failures . . . and, among them, this word, that doesn't exist, yet is there: it waits for you just around the corner of language. (38–39)

By the end of the passage we no longer hear the voice of Lol's desire, for it has been drowned out by the narrator's urgency and anguish on his own behalf: if the missing word with the power to name contaminates all the others, what is this story he is telling but another "blood-stained failure"? Like Lol (abyss and sister), the word that does not exist *is there*—it beckons and defies, entices and eludes you just around the corner of language. The "hole-word" is a very *present* absence with all of the force of one's desire for it.

The "abyss and sister" and the "hole-word" both tell the story of "trace/no trace." They are analogous figures of the paradox in and of *Lol V. Stein,* a paradox that permeates the figures themselves since, of course, one will always fail to figure "abyss" and "hole." Such failure is the heart of *Lol V. Stein*, for even the traces, as we have seen, are inevitably traces of no trace. Yet as that failure is inscribed, it suggests, if only for a split second, what *would* be traced there in its absence. Somewhere in the compounding of negatives is a hint, an idea, a suggestion of creative potential.

This potential, immobilized by conditions and retractions, is the basis for a passage in which the narrator tries to capture the essence of Lol's desire, an erotic and narrative desire that again seems to mirror the narrator's own:

> One would have had to wall in the ball, make of it this ship of light [navire de lumière] on which each afternoon Lol embarks but which stays there, in this impossible port, forever anchored and ready to sail away, with its three passengers, to leave this whole future in which Lol V. Stein now stands. There are times when it has, in Lol's eyes, the same élan as on the first day, the same fabulous force. (39)

This passage is a tightly woven fabric of tensions and contradictions. The entire vision is presented as part of an unrealized condition: "One would have had to wall in the ball [Il aurait fallu murer le bal]." But a series of demonstratives ("*this* ship of light," "*this* impossible port," "*this* whole future") then affirms a present and a presence. This present is, however, riddled with irreconcilables: the ship of light on which Lol *embarks* each afternoon remains *anchored* in the "impossible port"; the impossible port is further defined as "*this whole future* in which Lol V. Stein *now* stands." In an oxymoronic twist, the *future is now*, immutable, impossible, while the past is forever poised, ready to take off. The "ship of light" in the "impossible port" is that vital past bound to the barren present. Yet is it bound? Sometimes it seems to Lol to have the same "élan," the same "fabulous force" that it had on the first day. Even the barrenness is undercut, for no one moment of this story is ever sovereign. The dream may be impossible but every narrative failure leaves a trace of the dream.

If we read the end of *Lol V. Stein* in light of this passage, we find the narrator at his most penetrating, his most inspired. In fact, this might be the closest he comes to his subject, for the desire that he imagines for Lol may be none other than his own desire to be (or to create) the ship of light with a fabulous force—to hold all of Lol within a comprehensive vision, to possess the energy and fabulous power of fiction making, to make (and complete) the journey with her. Keeping all of this in mind, one begins to suspect that Jacques Hold's reference to "our trip [notre voyage]" at the very end of the novel is saying far more than it lets on. Of course, *what* the ending is saying rests, like Lol, eternally indeterminate—the "ship of light" in the "impossible port"—although it may on occasion, in the reader's eyes, appear to take on a certain "fabulous/story-making force."

Narrative strategy is the complex business of finding and leaving traces. The trace, in the "scene of writing," is the power to trace over, the potent mark of oblivion.[45] At the end of *Lol V. Stein*, the black letters on the white page are traced over the black mark of Lol in the field and over Jacques Hold's narrative voice, as these two already absent traces in turn mark the vast and inscrutable expanses of Lol's sleep and Hold's voyage. The trace of Lol is no inanimate residue, no archaeological artifact: it contains the "fabulous force" of all of its possible readings.

The point is not that the unreadable ending must not be read. On the contrary, the "fabulous force" of the trace is in its interminable repetition. Reading is the opposite of ending. Like narrators, readers and critics engage in "narrative strategies," tracing more traces over the traces that they find.

At two apparently inconsequential moments in *Lol V. Stein*, characters make judgments that might serve as metaphoric examples of "meta-writing" or, more specifically, "metacritique"—critical comments upon the critical process itself. It is easy to read the first remark as a defense of traces, a testament to the desires that motivate and the (small but significant) satisfactions that reward (Lol's) critics: "Tatiana still maintains that Lol V. Stein was beautiful, that they fought over her at school because even though she slipped through one's fingers like water, *the little bit one managed to retain of her was worth the effort*" (3, emphasis added).

In the second remark, we might read a declaration of Lol's resistance to reading and criticism. Her offhand statement could even be interpreted as a caveat to readers and critics about the dangers and inevitability of misreading, a kind of *défi* reminding us of the importance of proceeding with caution, delicacy, and respect. In the context of dinner-party conversation, Lol has been inquiring into changes in the U. Bridge house that she and Jean Bedford left behind when they moved back to S. Tahla. She is surprised and shocked to learn that some of the plants she had set in the garden have been removed, and she declares: "One ought to destroy a house after one's departure. There are people who do it" (134) ("On doit détruire les maisons après son passage. Des gens le font" [145]). It would be better not to leave traces, says Lol, for those who come after, destroy.[46] The woman to whom she has been speaking comes to the defense of traces, pointing out "with subtle irony that other people might have need of the houses one left behind" (134).

Whatever our needs as critics and readers, as we persist in reading the traces of Lol, this exchange tells us to remember that Lol is forever anticipating and resisting the destruction we bring. Our satisfactions, the traces of traces of her that we hold on to, are not to be had without some measure of guilt. In an uneasy flash of critical self-awareness, who can help wondering whether, reading Lol, one is not just like Jacques Hold, just like the people who move into houses left empty. Is the reader just an-other violent intruder? When Lol says, "The police are down below," when she flees from apprehension, does she mean us, too? What are we doing, sifting through the traces? Who are we looking for? It is unfortu-nately common to assume that the presence of police is evidence of a crime and that only the guilty flee. Without stopping to face any trumped-up charges, Lol asks us to reexamine these assumptions.

Three

Bearing Witness: *Kamouraska*

Out of the Past/Into the Past

Of the novels considered in this study, Anne Hébert's *Kamouraska* is probably most clearly and *literally* centered upon a crime. In fact, a historically documented crime that occurred in 1839 served as the basis for Hébert's fictional creation. Through and within the convolutions of memory, resistance, and reconstruction that make up the narrative, one discerns a plot: Elisabeth d'Aulnières-Tassy-Rolland, attending her dying husband, Jérôme Rolland, is increasingly possessed by and forced to relive her past. Twenty-one years earlier she had conspired with her lover, George Nelson, to murder her first husband, Antoine Tassy. After the failure of an initial attempt by Elisabeth's servant Aurélie Caron, Nelson ventured alone across the icy expanse of eastern Québec to Kamouraska to accomplish the deed. Following the murder, Nelson fled across the border to Vermont. Elisabeth, accompanied by one of her aunts, tried to follow him, but was captured and jailed. She was subsequently tried and released, while Aurélie Caron served two years in prison.

In *Kamouraska*, the impending death of Jérôme Rolland triggers the recapitulation of long-past events. Struggling to keep her hold on the present, Elisabeth is forcibly confronted by a past whose crimes persist in telling on her. From the very first, the past crime, indirectly evoked, is relentlessly and powerfully present. As Elisabeth steadfastly maintains her innocence, virtue, and honor, as she resists or attempts to control the memories, she is driven back, steadily and inexorably, toward the scene of the crime. An examination of the novel's opening paragraphs shows how the criminal past insinuates itself into the desperately blameless present.

Something criminal is first hinted at when the story fails to achieve the objectivity implied by a third-person narration. In the first paragraph of the novel there is an obvious attempt to establish the authority of an uninvolved and uncompromised narrator. This paragraph is a model of narrative propriety: uncluttered, informative, reassuringly maintaining, through the use of the French past historic tense (*passé simple*), a decent distance from the scene that is being recounted.

The summer went by from beginning to end. Unlike in other years, Madame Rolland didn't leave her house on Rue du Parloir. It was very fair, very warm. But neither Madame Rolland nor the children went to the country that summer.

[L'été passa en entier. Mme Rolland, contre son habitude, ne quitta pas sa maison de la rue du Parloir. Il fit très beau et très chaud. Mais ni Mme Rolland, ni les enfants n'allèrent à la campagne, cet été-là.][1]

The woman is safely defined in and by her married name. References to her habits, her house, and children further establish her within a secure and appropriate context and time frame. Even the name of the street, la rue du Parloir, reflects the bourgeois nature of her situation (though "parloir" also serves to place Madame Rolland in a "speaking room" where the heretofore unspoken will finally be articulated).

In the second paragraph, the omniscient narrator begins to describe Madame Rolland's state of mind: "Her husband was going to die and she felt a great calm." Almost immediately, however, one is aware of an undertone of apology. The wife's "great calm" must be justified by the easy and discreet way in which her husband is dying: "That man was slipping away ever so gently, without too much suffering, and with admirable tact." The formula then used to describe the woman, "dutiful and above reproach," seems weighted with the overzealous protestations of denial: against what unspoken reproach is this defense erected? Finally, the "great calm" is abruptly undercut and succeeded by an acknowledged agitation that must itself in turn be justified: "If she felt a pang in her heart from time to time, it was because it seemed to her that this waiting state was bound to assume distressing proportions." The woman's serenity is suddenly suspect: "That peaceful sense of being free, ready for anything—that feeling that surged through her, down to her very fingertips—could bode no good. Everything seemed bent on taking place as if the meaning itself of her real expectation/waiting [le sens même de son attente réelle] would soon be revealed to her." By the end of the paragraph, the calm declaration of the first sentence has been completely overturned: "But even now grief was working its protective defenses. She clung to it as if hanging on to a railing. Anything was better than that awful calm."

Strong emotions subtend this narrative revolution. The omniscient narrator loses control. As the last sentence of this second paragraph resonates with the submerged first person of the *style indirect libre*, it opens the text for the emergence of a startling subjectivity in paragraph three.

The first three sentences of this third paragraph still waver between third- and first-person narration: "One ought to have left Québec. Not to have stayed here. Alone in the desert of the month of July" (fr 7). The word "here" marks the point at which the past tense falters. The slip is

decisive and irreversible. With the appearance of "I" in the following sentence, the narrator's commitment to distance and objectivity is abandoned. Suddenly the verbs are in the present tense; the woman speaker
exists, and exists alone: "There's no one I know left in town." With the
sudden sense of isolation (unleashed by the first-person pronoun) come
hints of paranoia and guilt. Immediately following the narrator's accession
to subjectivity, she sees herself as objectified by others who watch and
follow her:

> When I go out, they stare at me [on me regarde] as if at some strange beast.
> Like those two hooligans looking me up and down this morning, on my way
> back from the market. For a long time they followed me [ils m'ont suivie] with
> their eyes. I shouldn't go out alone. . . . They are watching me. They are spying
> on me. They are following me. They are squeezing closer to me. They are walk-
> ing right behind me. [On m'observe. On m'épie. On me suit. On me serre de
> près. On marche derrière moi.]

Among these nameless others ("on" or "ils") in a kind of vertiginous
chain of guilty associations, Madame Rolland recognizes a woman: "That
woman, yesterday, following me so closely. I felt her there right on my
heels with her steady, deliberate step, her determined walk. And when I
turned around, she hid herself in a doorway. Yes, I saw her disappear inside, quick and nimble like nobody in the world, except . . . That's what's
clutching at my heart, scaring me to death; quick and nimble like nobody
. . ." (ellipses in the original). Pursued by "that creature," "that stubborn
follower," and by whatever aspect of the past she represents, Madame
Rolland keeps walking, as though to embed herself ever more deeply in
the present: "Walking, always walking. They turn and stare as I go by.
That's my real life" (emphasis added). It is, however, precisely here that
there occurs the first evocation of the past, and with it, the first mention
of police: "That's my real life. To feel the world divide into two lines to
watch me pass. The Red Sea that splits in two to let the holy army cross.
That's the world, life in the world, *my* life. One day, it's between two
policemen that I had to face this cursed world." Although this is not the
first appearance of the past tense in the novel, it is the first encounter with
the *true* past of the story. The *passé simple* of the first paragraph was
merely an attempt to bury the crime so deeply, in the past of the past, that
it might never have to be recounted or reckoned with.

A Crime Committed—to Memory

Kamouraska is a gradual, cumulative, and repetitive recapitulation of bits
and pieces of an obsessional history that cannot be suppressed. Significantly, the first "piece" that is presented is not the chronological begin-

ning of the story but the end: the drama of apprehension, the arrest of Elisabeth. In the beginning, the crime lies beyond the story's boundaries. We are led quickly from the arrest to the outcome: the extradition of the lover will never take place; Elisabeth remarries and "honor is reestablished"; "poor, little Aurélie Caron," abandoned by her mistress, serves two years in prison. But justice cannot obscure the crime. The assertion of an ending will not undo what preceded it. Addressing herself to the lover who abandoned her, Elisabeth speaks of the future: "Never more your dear face. And age bearing down on me." Yet in that future she sees as well the inevitable inscription of the past: "I am still untouched, or nearly. Two fine little lines from the sides of the nose to the corners of my mouth. The daily effort of virtue, no doubt. My good days are numbered, though. *The fine slaughter still to come* [*le beau massacre à venir*]" (emphasis added). She is, by force of the language she uses, still "safe and sound" ("since I tell you that I am safe and sound"). She declares herself "incorruptible flesh." The ravages of age and the ravages of the past have yet to meet in her. Thus she speaks of slow combustion ("la salamandre," a slow-combustion stove), suggesting that she is still, though not forever, unscathed by the violent crime that was committed in the past. The implied and inevitable conflagration takes on the character of apotheosis, a bringing together of scattered and incendiary elements of the story, and of the storyteller.

The first chapters of *Kamouraska* are especially marked by tension between past and present. The name Madame Rolland, constantly repeated, illustrates the woman's terrible determination to maintain a distance from her history. The effort to maintain a front (for what is behind it entails the reanimation of the past) is tremendous.

> Oh, how I love to walk through the streets, with the image of my virtue just a few steps ahead! Never out of my sight, not for a second. Watching like a galley-master. That image, always that image. The Sacred Host in the holy procession. And me, following right behind, like a silly goose. That's what a decent woman is: a silly goose who struts along, captivated by what she imagines her honor to be.

Madame Rolland's increasing anxiety in the face of the foreboding past and the impending future is marked in every way by pursuit. Story and crime dog her heels as she is haunted by memories of having been pursued and arrested. Her references to the more distant past are cryptic and formulaic; the crime is neatly linguistically elided. She refers to the time "after the misfortune of Kamouraska [le malheur de Kamouraska]. Upon my love's return from Kamouraska."

In this first retelling of the tale, the crucial event was not the murder of Antoine Tassy, the "misfortune of Kamouraska," but George Nelson's flight and Elisabeth's arrest. A haunted narrator, Elisabeth seeks sanctuary in the period of time between the murder and the arrest, a time when there had been (at least in her fantasies of that period) the chance of happiness. In thus abridging the story, Elisabeth not only refuses to return to the scene of the crime, she also displaces the transgression. Her apprehension by the police is not treated as a response to an accomplished violation, the inevitable first step in punishment for a crime already committed. Rather it appears more an act of prevention, keeping her from "crossing the border" (a transgressive act she would have committed in the name of love). That the lost and yearned-for past should here be situated after the murder serves to emphasize Elisabeth's persistent denial of criminal responsibility. The murder, ancient and impersonal history, predates her story.

In the second chapter of *Kamouraska*, Elisabeth is obsessed with pursuit. The opening description of "Madame Rolland," "very upright," standing at the window, is minutely detailed:

> Hands motionless on her crinoline skirt, [Madame Rolland] bends near the shutters, glances sharply between the slats, lends an ear, hidden by smooth coils of hair. A warm, wet gust rises from the street. The gutter is overflowing and makes a deafening noise. In the bedroom full of thick velvet and English furniture, a man's voice rasps and mumbles something incomprehensible about the gutter. (6)

Once again, despite the present tense, the narration, in its descriptive narrativity, is making a bid for distance. The second paragraph opens with the same, almost somnolent, descriptive tone: "One hears, in the distance, a horse's heavy gait." With "one's" awareness of an approaching cart, however, an uneasiness sets in that quickly gives way to panic:

> What can that wagon be doing out now, in this empty, deserted night? For a while now someone's been prowling about the town. The wagon is approaching. Rue Saint-Louis, rue des Jardins, rue Donacona. Silence. My God! The iron-rimmed wheels are turning the corner, the heavy, tired hooves are approaching.
>
> Any minute now, the horse and carriage will be pulling up under my window. It's me they're after! I'm sure it's me. One day, a carriage, no, a sleigh. It's winter. (6)

The transition is swift and complete: with the repetition of "one day" (a linguistic sign of recollection or anticipation, the very locution that signaled the violent return of the past in the first chapter), Elisabeth is thrown back from the summer night, rue du Parloir, to her winter flight from the police: "Behind me the noise of the runners on the hardened snow. They're chasing after me and my aunt Adélaïde. The team of horses, galloping hard. They are trying to catch me. Oh no! . . . The police. They arrest me" (6–7).

Always, in these early chapters, the crime is held off. Elisabeth refers to "the misfortune of Kamouraska," to "the sacrifice celebrated on the snow": "In the cove of Kamouraska frozen over to a dry, powdery field. Murderous love. Shameful love. Deadly love. . . . The madness of love" (5). But all of this is naming crime from a distance, calling it misfortune or sacrifice, calling it love, and leaving it there, at that distance, *on ice*. Troubling the austere and virtuous surface of the present, images of police and pursuit are insistent, for it is not the crime that first haunts Elisabeth; it is the punishment. Indeed, the crime seems to lie buried at the most frozen, wintry heart of the story, on the snow-covered cove of Kamouraska—understandably last to yield to the slow-burning, backward gaze of the present.

Dead Letter

Along with the frustration and indignity of having been arrested before she could rejoin her lover, Elisabeth is haunted by another troubling possibility: her lover's complicity with the police. She cannot decide whether to cast her lover as a lonely and pitiable victim like herself ("Poor sweet love, how he suffered! How cold he was all the way to Kamouraska, all alone, in winter") or as one of those responsible for her own suffering: "Love, love, how you have hurt me! Why would I pity you? You ran away like a coward, you left me behind, all alone to face that pack of judges" (3). She vacillates between communion with and alienation from her lover. Their communion lies in their shared plight: they are separated by the border and by circumstances beyond their control; they are at the mercy of the judges. A letter from George Nelson to Elisabeth, undelivered because "intercepted by the judges," is emblematic of Elisabeth's fantasy of their communion. Seeking to undo the apparent abandonment implied by George's flight to the States, Elisabeth evokes her lover's last letter:

> *In a while you'll leave Canada, won't you? Only tell me that. Tell me how I can write you. . . .*
>
> *Please tell me how you are and how the poor child is doing.* (3 and 5, emphasis in the original)

A voice calling out for an answering voice ("*tell me*"), the letter might be read as an attempt to establish writing as a means of transcending borders. Unfortunately the letter did not reach its destination. Thus, intercepted and undelivered, when the letter appears in all its literality in the first chapter of *Kamouraska*, it can only be the desperate inscription of Elisabeth's desire. How can she quote an intercepted letter?

In a vertiginous return to the decisive episode of the novel's first two chapters, Elisabeth finds herself, in the book's penultimate chapter, once again on the point of being abandoned: "two policemen appear at Doctor Nelson's house with a warrant for his arrest. . . . It's too late! What am I doing here? Doctor Nelson has escaped. He's run away. . . . Quick, the American border, in a new sleigh, drawn by a brand-new horse. The police on his heels" (240). The police are after him, but so is Elisabeth: "Run away. But where to look for him? In the vastness of the woods and forests? That man is lost. I am lost. We are followed, my aunt Adelaide and I. The police!" (241). Her flight toward and after George Nelson quickly becomes a flight away from the police. The seeker is sought, the hunter hunted. Elisabeth again relives her arrest and imprisonment, the finale that started the entire recapitulation, the lockup that first liberated memory. And now once again phrases from the lost letter surface to combat the terror of silence and abandonment:

> *You'll leave Canada, won't you? You'll come, Elisabeth, only tell me that. You'll come? You'll come? Tell me?* . . . (242, emphasis and ellipsis in original)

But the undelivered missive cannot now be delivered to bring comfort and redemption to the past: "I didn't receive that letter. Worse than prison, abandonment. Your endless silence. Your writing seized. The sound of your voice intercepted. Your call, your plea lost somewhere in justice's endless piles of papers. Lord, I am damning myself! . . . I'm going to kill myself" (242).[2] Although up until this point Elisabeth's efforts to receive and read the letter kept it essentially a phantom text through which she attempted to fill George Nelson's absence, in the final chapter evidence is presented that the desired letter actually existed. It is authenticated too late, however, both in the narration and in the events themselves. By the time the real letter arrives it has already done its damage.

> Only the expectation of a certain letter still beats in my veins.
> I am waiting for a letter that will be intercepted, *that will never reach me, or rather, yes it will, but much too late*, years after, having been lost in the piles of papers on the magistrates' desks, too late, too late . . . (245, emphasis added, ellipsis in the original)

The letter's eventual arrival cannot erase its nonarrival. This letter, finally received, can in no way exculpate the lover and reestablish the desperately desired communion. There can be no response to a dead letter.

Furthermore, this letter, even had it arrived on time, could scarcely have stood as a declaration of George Nelson's true intent. It is a mere sounding, a series of *appeals*, offering nothing of Nelson but his desire for Elisabeth's response. The only direct statement left by the lover remains the fact of his absence.

Running through the novel, counterpointing Elisabeth's attempt to deliver the undelivered letter and thus to trick the past into being other than what it was, there is Elisabeth's response to the letter's absence, a clear response, for the abandonment did reach its mark. In a key passage near the beginning of the novel, Elisabeth attempts to plot her story's diverse elements, and she expresses this *plot* in terms of a complicity that excludes her:

> My husband is dying once again. Peacefully, in his bed. The first time it was in violence, blood and snow. Not two husbands replacing one another, following one another, in the marriage registers, but a single man endlessly reborn from his ashes. One long snake, always the same, endlessly reforming itself in its coils. *The eternal man who takes me and then abandons me.* His first face, cruel. . . . Dirty swine! Antoine Tassy, squire of Kamouraska. Then comes the somber radiance of love. . . . Black love. Doctor Nelson, I'm sick and will never see you again. What a pretty triptych! The third face is so gentle, so dull, Jerome. (26, emphasis added)

Where she had begun only by relating Jérôme Rolland's death to that of her first husband, Elisabeth cannot avoid inserting George Nelson into this triptych of men who abandon her. This vision of the eternal man clearly underlines what she perceives as Nelson's complicity with the others *against* her.

If the dead letter would have been a piece of evidence for communion and forgiveness, there exists another piece of evidence that was at Elisabeth's disposal much earlier but that, in the course of reconstructing the past, she successfully represses until its climactic emergence in the final chapter. This piece of evidence is the testimony of a young medical student who claimed to have been the last person with whom George Nelson spoke before he fled the country. Nelson's parting words, as repeated by this witness, constitute a rival version of the good doctor. Spoken (and repeated) in English, these are the words that George Nelson supposedly uttered: "It is that damned woman that has ruined me" (247).

Is damning hearsay to be accorded greater weight than a written document? Would not a reported remark, in a foreign language, inevitably be subject to distortion and misinterpretation? Would not the letter, written later in the doctor's own hand, actually have been the most recent, the most accurate version of his feelings—something in the nature of an affidavit? What is there about the letter that undermines its own authority, that robs it of the ability to stand up to the destructive force of a malicious and idle rumor?

As has already been suggested, the delayed letter, arriving too late, has rendered itself unreadable. It does not arrive to challenge the accusations of the medical student's story. If it arrives too late to answer or to be answered, it might as well not have arrived at all, for the intercourse is broken. The letter's authority is also subtly undercut because it is written in French. French was a language that the lovers shared, but it was not George Nelson's native tongue. Does one perhaps lie more easily, or more inevitably, in a borrowed tongue?

When one speaks of letters, however, one is not speaking of mouths and tongues. In weighing the evidence, one must also consider the relative "truth values" of the spoken and the written word. This novel has a great deal to say about what can and cannot, must and must not, be written and spoken. While it demonstrates the power of the written word, it also calls its "truth" into question. The novel is filled with signed depositions, legally admissible testimony representing the language of the law. Does the testimony, once inscribed and with a signature affixed, have the weight of truth? The folly of such an assumption is clearly demonstrated by the juxtaposition of Elisabeth's last literal evocation of the letter (*"You'll come? Tell me? . . . "*) and the passage that follows: "I'm going to kill myself. The walls oozing saltpeter. All night long Aunt Adélaïde writing a letter to the judge" (242). George Nelson's letter leads into Adélaïde's letter, which appears in full in the text and in the very first sentence of which (in the best legal language possible), Elisabeth's aunt perjures herself: "The party in question, Elisabeth d'Aulnières, always treated her husband, the late Antoine Tassy, with nothing but kindness and respect." How can Elisabeth put her faith in the integrity of George Nelson's letter when she knows the very real potential of letters to bear false witness?[3] Furthermore, as I have already suggested, even if Elisabeth wanted to believe in the veracity of a signed statement, she could find little evidence of such a statement in George's letter. What is there in its series of unanswered appeals to match the declarative force of the statement "It is that damned woman that has ruined me"?

Love's Law and Death's Law

Doubts about George Nelson shadowed the story from the beginning. Nevertheless, no unsympathetic assessment of the doctor ever succeeds in replacing the more generous one that Elisabeth persists in trying to enter-

tain. There is never actually a climax where Elisabeth's doubts about her
lover are conclusively borne out and shown to represent the truth about
George Nelson. The novel is not about Elisabeth's delusion, but about
contradictions. Elisabeth is caught in a duplicitous world where different
truths, and different real lives, are in constant interplay and tension.

Elisabeth's identification with George is based upon shared transgression and a common place at the margins. Retreating into a private world
of unavowable and murderous desire, a secret world of adultery and plotting, they become (as all lovers must to some extent become) outsiders—
foreigners and outlaws.[4] Separating themselves from the rest of the world,
they are united by love's law.

Yet the forces that alienate Elisabeth from George are very strong. The
language difference epitomizes the many ways in which they occupy separate worlds. Though they begin to forge a common destiny through their
complicity, boundaries always seem to fall between them. Nelson, American expatriate, raised a Protestant, can never be other than an exile in
French Catholic Canada, a world to which Elisabeth, firmly established in
one of the "old families," can never wholly cease to belong. The aunts will
always be there either to save her or to damn themselves with her; her
childhood home will always take her in. Furthermore, and by a curious
twist of perspective, George Nelson, having been sent to Canada because
of his father's Loyalist sympathies (following the American Revolution),
must always to some degree represent the English, the colonizing power
whose language and laws reduce the French to the status of exiles in their
own country. Ironically, from either point of view, whether George Nelson be oppressed or oppressor, Elisabeth must align herself with those on
the opposite side of the division.

In addition, the dividing line of gender seems determined to keep the
two apart, for just as surely as Elisabeth belongs to a world of women
(aunts, mother, servants), George claims a place in a world of men that,
from Elisabeth's point of view, is bound to exclude her. Encounters between these two worlds are shown, in the novel, to be volatile, marked by
the play of desire, the need for and danger of recognition, and the constant potential for violence. A grave drama is established, the term of
which must almost inevitably be death. Elisabeth's alienation from
George is based upon death's law.

Elisabeth's widowed mother understands that death's law rules the
love between man and woman. As Elisabeth prepares to marry Antoine
Tassy, "Madame d'Aulnières bursts into sobs. Dreads having to explain
to her daughter the mysteries—for her inseparable—of marriage and
death" (64).

Elisabeth and George also recognize that love's law and death's law are inextricably bound. When they meet in the pine forest and "it is still not dark enough to . . . ," they play dead, pretending to be "tombstone figures":

> Make absolute emptiness. Everything that is not us must be stripped from us, like mushrooms that you scrape off a rock with a knife (an old school friend, an unfortunate husband). Any link to anything beyond the two of us must be severed [doit mourir]. The body freezes. The heart drains. Silence. Dizziness.
>
> You touch my hand. The blood comes surging back through my veins. Purified, relieved of the entire world, only desire inhabits us, like a flame. (148)

If the price of togetherness is death, the conquest of death comes about through the desire that binds the lovers. They try desperately to assert their identification over and against the forces of alienation, to fall on the same side when the toll is taken. So playing dead constitutes a kind of foreplay for them, after which "the blood comes surging back," for their desire is to escape death, the ultimate separator and alienator, and to live.

Throughout the novel, the imperative is to live. Faced with Antoine Tassy's murderous and suicidal impulses, Elisabeth resolves: "To keep that man from hanging himself. From destroying me along with him. To live. To give birth to a second child" (86). Life is clearly a choice that must constantly be made in the face of the threat of or necessity for death. When George Nelson and Elisabeth begin to fantasize about eliminating Antoine from the face of the earth, Elisabeth imagines a duel between her husband and her lover. A duel would be a prototypical life/death choice, but the stakes are too clear:

> What if, by some misfortune, the heart ripped open by a bullet were yours, my love? I would die.
>
> But one day won't we have to make up our minds to put an end to chance? To stop dreaming. If we want to live. (146)

The choice between life and death is not something to be left to fate. When George's sister Cathy, an Ursuline nun, dies faithless and crying out, "It's too late now to pray! Doctor, save me!" (168), George returns to Elisabeth filled with "the urgency of being happy" (167). From this point on, survival becomes his supreme mission: "Now that death has come and gone. Get back to Elisabeth as quickly as possible. Just one thing matters now: to live. Whatever the price. But live!" (167).

At the same time, it is clear that life and death, love and death are hopelessly intertwined and interimplicated. Elisabeth articulates this in the following terms: "Yes, now's the time to compromise ourselves for good. To cause a scandal. To accept once and for all that they accuse us and point at us. Both of us bound together in a single necessity. Having broken with the world. . . . Justice reestablished. The reign of blessed savagery. That's what will save us" (155–156). The implacable life energy becomes invested in Elisabeth, and is then spoken in a voice that includes but is at the same time larger than her personal voice. This voice that addresses George Nelson is the voice of the law of their desire:

> But I am here, I want you to live and him to die! I have chosen you, George Nelson. *I am life and death inextricably linked.* See how bitter-sweet I am. (162, emphasis added)

> I'll use Cathy's voice if I have to. The selfsame voice of every threatened life that wants to live. Save me, Doctor Nelson! Save yourself with me! Not with prayers. Not with some righteous, abstract alchemy. But with all your flesh of a living man, with all my flesh of a living woman. Your name to give your wife, Doctor Nelson, in exchange for a hated one. Your heart, your soul to offer, all. A man to be killed, there's no other way. *I am love and life, my demand is as imperious and absolute as death itself.* (168, emphasis added)

There is an underlying connection between Elisabeth's fear that George could be conspiring against her and the idea that pursues her of the complicity among the laws and forces of love and life and death. In a key passage, Elisabeth's recognition of Antoine's complicity in his own death leads her to doubt George's role:

> What if each of them, both at once, were to wear the same fraternal face? Two men, with faces racked and transfigured by something strange and dreadful sweeping over them: the taste of death. And what if, somehow, I were to see it all happen? There in the cove at Kamouraska, the very moment when a loaded pistol is aimed at a young man's temple. A young man, much too fat, and rotten to the core—I would die! I'm sure I would die! I'm just the opposite of death. I'm love. Love and life. Life and death. I want to live! I want you to live! (200)

Even as Elisabeth tries to exclude death from her side of the equation ("I'm just the opposite of death"), that death proclaims itself still and already there ("Love and life. Life and death"). She is left with only the voice of her desire to cry out against that ultimate complicity ("I want to live! I want you to live!").

At the very end of the novel, Elisabeth, still wavering between alienation and communion, between rejection of and reconciliation with George Nelson, articulates her dream desire:

> And what if he were waiting for a letter from me, there in his prison in Burlington? Oh, were I certain of that, I would die of joy! My God, to be able to run to him. Beg them to hitch up the horses and take me to the border. Find

him alive. Fling myself into his arms. Say to him: Look, it's me, Elisabeth. Hear him answer: Look, it's me, George. The two of us together for life. (248)

The emphasis in Elisabeth's fantasy is on living, on mutual recognition, on the ability to speak, to hear, to name oneself. In this vision, letters are expected, questions are answerable and answered, two "I"s are able to declare themselves "we" for life. Yet even this vision of uninterrupted communion is expressed (however figuratively) with reference to, and in terms of, death: "*I would die* of joy." The use of this expression is not accidental. It occurs with some frequency in the novel, usually spoken by Elisabeth. Earlier, Elisabeth had declared, "Aurélie, I can't live like this, separated from my love. I will die, Aurélie" (179); separation could not be survived. Now at the novel's end it appears that union cannot be survived either.

Witnessing for the Prosecution

The police who appear in *Kamouraska* are not mere cogs in the anonymous machinery of the law. In Elisabeth's imagination, those who pursue not only have the arresting power of police, they also have a personal stake in the game, for the policing role is most often claimed by witnesses. Near the end of the novel the two "agents de police" who have been tailing George Nelson are identified as James Wood, an innkeeper, and Robert Dunham, a servant at the manor in Kamouraska, deputized because of their ability to recognize the fugitive. Analogies between police and witnesses are repeatedly demonstrated in parallels and substitutions on the narrative level. For instance, as Elisabeth at one point feels herself forced to confront and reexperience her past "flanked by two policemen," the imagery shifts and she finds herself flanked instead by the servant girls, Aurélie Caron and Justine Latour, who are prepared not only to restrain her but to accuse her and testify against her (53).

Elisabeth most fears the powers of recognition and naming of the witnesses who fill the novel. The dreaded and inevitable future is one in which the guilt will be pinned on her: "Every alibi, gone flat. Every escape, blocked off. Destiny will cling to my bones. I'll be *recognized as* guilty [*reconnue* coupable], guilty before the world" (17, emphasis added). In the face of this threat, her only recourse is somehow to delay the day when "reality and its imagined double are going to be one and the same. No difference at all between them" (17). And her only means of doing this is to "state/refuse her name [décliner son nom]. To name herself Elisabeth d'Aulnières forever." In other words, she states (*décline*) her maiden name, while she refuses (*décline*) any other name that might incriminate her. The emphasis is clearly judicial (the first act of a defendant in court is to state his/her name). Nelson has left her to face "the pack of judges"; the police are incidental—it is the judges and witnesses who gather in packs to pursue her.

In *Kamouraska*, Elisabeth is pursued or confronted and temporarily *apprehended* by the deputized police, by the many witnesses, by Aurélie Caron, by Jérôme Rolland, by Antoine Tassy, by Madame mère Tassy, and indirectly by George Nelson. The varied nature of police pursuit inevitably opens up questions of jurisdiction in terms of which policing is no longer merely a matter of arrest and imprisonment, but one of conscience, playing on the border of legal and other crimes. The most strident and persistent of the witnesses pursuing Elisabeth are women. If she is haunted by the specter of her lover's alienation from her in complicity with the masculine world of the police, she is likewise haunted by the specter of her alienation from those other *women* who rise up to testify against her.[5] Her most dogged pursuer is Aurélie Caron with whom (as with George Nelson) she is engaged in a drama of mutual complicity and betrayal. The consciousness that binds Elisabeth and Aurélie, however, is fatally dependent upon a third term:

I really must have a talk with you, Aurélie. What do I do? I would like to know . . . boys . . . boys . . . (61, ellipses in the original)

That girl taunts me and makes me green with envy [mourir de jalousie]. At fifteen she knows as much about life as the dead themselves. (55)

"Your love affair is killing me, Madame . . ." [—Vos amours me font mourir, Madame . . .] (179, ellipsis in the original)

Each woman feels seduced and yet ultimately excluded by the other's carnal knowledge of men. A subtle triangular energy draws them together yet ultimately splits them apart. In the drama of love and death that they enact, Aurélie is friend, sister, lover—and enemy to Elisabeth. Thus Aurélie's pursuit of Elisabeth stands for consciousness and conscience of something criminal, but the crime is not Antoine Tassy's murder. It is a crime of betrayal committed within the Aurélie-Elisabeth-George triangle and a crime of abandonment repeated in Elisabeth's retreat into the redemptive sanctuary of her class privilege.

When Elisabeth accuses Aurélie, saying: "You're not my friend anymore, Aurélie. I told you to give false testimony, anything rather than to betray us" (241), she again acts out the tension between union and separation that informed her relations with George Nelson. Her attitudes toward Aurélie throughout the novel participate in the confusion of pursuer and pursued, torturer and victim, that make crime and guilt so hard to pin down. Aurélie is a traitor because she failed to bear false witness.

In *Kamouraska*, in the tensions between reconstructing and refuting, interpreting and deferring, remembering and forgetting, we may read a struggle for narrative control that is at the same time a struggle for the authority to produce or prevent a definitive reading of the crime. Both criminal and narrative processes realize the inherent antinomy between plea and verdict, between testimony and sentence, between the still-developing and the irrevocable. Both criminal and narrative processes imply the preexistence of some kind of law. Thus in order to locate the crime and the criminal, one must inevitably interrogate the law.

A Question of Jurisdiction and the Letter of the Law

Law has to do with establishing and enforcing acceptable behavior within a given context, within a given society. Law is a way of mapping and policing a territory, a *jurisdiction*. If the spatial component of law is evident in the ways in which we refer to it (we say: *within* the law, *above* the law, *under* the law, *out*law), the linguistic implications of the concept of jurisdiction are likewise clear: as the "diction" of "jurisdiction" indicates, a law must be articulated in order to be exercised, and this articulation occurs through language. Evidence of the role of language in defining jurisdictions may be found at the beginning of *Kamouraska*, where there seem to be two distinct territories articulated by two different languages. The language of the Law is the "Queen's English" of the "acte d'accusation [bill of indictment]." The language of the "crime" (or at least of the "criminal") is the French narrative itself.[6] The first appearance of English in the text occurs on the second page and is remarkable not only for the way in which the italicized English makes its stand against the surrounding French (one fragment in a series of fragments, it is distinguished from the others precisely by the shift into English), but also for the very clear opposition that it establishes internally between the English queen and the French woman accused of some as yet unspecified crime:

> The indictment. Court of King's Bench. Session of September 1840. *The queen against Elisabeth D'Aulnières-Tassy.* My wild youth. Interrogations. (2, emphasis added)

> [L'acte d'accusation. Cour du Banc du Roi. Terme de septembre 1840. *The queen against Elisabeth D'Aulnières-Tassy.* Ma folle jeunesse. Les interrogatoires. (8)]

Any clear-cut opposition between law and lawbreaker, authority and subject, English and French, is, however, almost immediately complicated and undermined in the text. The queen may be against Elisabeth, but

Elisabeth attempts to undo that powerful opposition by stressing precisely
her *resemblance* to the other: "The Queen, against Elisabeth d'Aulnières.
Absurd. How dare one accuse me of offending the Queen? When it's obvious that I resemble her, like a sister, with all my children around me. I
look like the Queen of England. I act like the Queen of England. I'm
fascinated by the image of Victoria and her children. Profound mimicry.
Who will find me guilty of any wrong?" (29). Even when she is forced by
circumstance to acknowledge that this identification is a "false representation" and that she can only offer "the backside of Victoria's image [l'en-
vers de l'image]," she has already established herself in relationship to the
queen.[7] However calculated it may be shown to be, the defensive gesture
of *rapprochement* (through sisterly resemblance, profound mimicry), is
never entirely undone. Elisabeth maintains her "haughty bearing of an
offended queen" (17). Furthermore, George Nelson refers to her later in
the novel in terms that make her the queen in a metaphorical chess game
between him and her husband: "I'll take his queen. I'll take his wife. It has
to be" (124).[8] Elisabeth's admittedly problematic identification with the
English queen thus serves to displace that authority by suggesting other
possible allegiances and jurisdictions.

There are many different ways of dividing up the world, and there are
naturally as many conflicting allegiances in this novel as there are interfer-
ing national and linguistic norms. These conflicting allegiances make it
impossible to read the crime simply through the binary perspective originally evoked of a judicial authority responding to a transgression. First of
all, it is clear from the start that since an *English* authority is condemning
a *French Canadian* transgression, any law-abiding citizen's allegiance to
that authority might understandably be weakened in response to the "colonizing" nature of British rule. As Elisabeth herself puts it: "The Queen!
Always the Queen! Couldn't you just die laughing? As if it could make the
slightest difference to Victoria-beyond-the-seas! What does she care if
there's adultery and murder committed way out there on a few acres of
snowy waste that France gave up to England?" (39).[9] But the complexities
of the transgressive situation go beyond even the problem of a distant and
hostile authority. There are codes other than the British legal code being
applied in this story—several of them quite as powerful as and certainly
more deeply ingrained in the fabric of Québécois life than that of the
Crown. The ways in which both religion and class realign affiliations cannot be overlooked.

A vocabulary of Christian moral law is widely evident in *Kamouraska*:
in persistent references to salvation, damnation, and absolution, to sins
and sacraments; in devil imagery and George Nelson's preoccupation with
sainthood; in descriptions of Elisabeth as an "adorable" virgin "above the
ordinary laws of men" (43); and in the emphasis upon Judas's crime, *be-*

trayal ("Which one of us betrayed the other first? I'm innocent!" [247]). In Québec society, the Church creates strong allegiances and poses a very powerful challenge to secular authority, but even so, this alternative authority is not portrayed as a unifying or centralizing force in the novel. Rather, it leads to further divided allegiances. Elisabeth is jealous of the closed Catholic school world that Antoine and George had shared as boys, a world from which she was and must always be excluded: "I would like to erase from you forever that time when I don't exist, that closed world of boys, masses and Latin" (146–147).[10] At the same time, Elisabeth is herself born into an exclusive Catholic society of pious bourgeois women who will close ranks to save family honor. Even as these two closed worlds illustrate an essential division within the Church between patriarchal and matriarchal spheres, however, the nature of George's and Elisabeth's adherence to these worlds is in turn questioned in the novel.[11] George Nelson and Antoine Tassy were bound together in school not because they shared a faith and a community, but because (each of them being alienated in his own way from the rest of the schoolboys) they had together created their own world, a complicitous, symbiotic relationship of torturer and victim. Likewise, Elisabeth was from the beginning in open rebellion against her aunts' gentle devotion: "She has *the devil* in her. You'll never succeed in bringing her under control!" (emphasis added).[12] In fact, it was their niece's *un*assimilated presence in their respectable world that drove the aunts, in their attempts to save her, into confrontation with Christian moral law: "The child is damning herself! And we're damning ourselves along with her!" (44).

Such language is not at all unusual in *Kamouraska* where a vocabulary of salvation and damnation repeatedly undermines the charges of the secular authorities. When Elisabeth was declaring her sisterly resemblance to the queen, she asked literally, "Who will convict me of any *sin*? [Qui me convaincra de *péché*?]" (emphasis added)—as though crime and sin were interchangeable, and legal and moral interdictions one and the same. Yet it is one of the novel's most striking paradoxes that while *original sin* is assumed by the religious context (and Elisabeth's early dream of returning to an "early innocence" [46] is summarily shown to be, of course, impossible), still, as Elisabeth notes, "according to the English law of this conquered land, we are innocent until proved guilty" (193). As long as the law and jurisdiction to which the discourse of transgression refers are undermined or subject to changing interpretation, *guilt* cannot be proved.[13] Clearly judgment of transgression within the novel is impaired by the tendency within the telling to conflate the religious and the secular. If in secular, legal terms one is "innocent until proved guilty," in Catholic terms the evidence of original sin (as desire and sexuality) is indisputable and introduces transgression into Elisabeth's story long before she ever contemplates killing her husband. Describing her marriage with Antoine, Elisabeth acknowledges that "at night, I again become Antoine's accomplice. To the point where I am disgusted to my very core" (96). The night is "drunkenness, blasphemy, violence, love, derision." And from the point of view of the three aunts (who "are wide awake, crossing themselves and trembling all over"): "Sometimes, at night, the child will moan and groan. In pain or pleasure. The crime is the same" (95).

"Langue étrangère"

The most obvious obstacle to any attempt to fix or define the guilt in *Kamouraska* is the fact that English represents the language of the Law and French that of the "crime." Judgment is further frustrated in the novel, however, by the varied and complex roles played by these two languages. French is the language of love in which George and Elisabeth communicate, yet they are not speaking the same language when they do so. Hastened out of the United States by his Loyalist father in order that he might escape the contamination of American Independence and rest faithful to the British Crown, George quickly adopted the ways of his country of exile. He converted to Roman Catholicism and was soon speaking fluent French. But French, Elisabeth's *langue maternelle*, would always remain for him a foreign language, a *langue étrangère*. In this novel where the theme of the *étranger* is so central, the importance of *langue étrangère* is indisputable and worthy of further investigation. But first a word about *langue maternelle*.

Elisabeth's *mother tongue* (the language she is born to, the language of the mother) is for her also a *widow* tongue: "My mother, deep in mourning, carrying me in her womb. . . . They're taking my father's coffin out of the house" (47). The young widow swoons, and the baby inside her kicks: "Such a long and frightening faint could kill us both!" (47). And then the voice of the mother is heard and narrated:

> "What a wicked little girl!" [—Quelle petite fille malfaisante!]
> Is that the first voice in the world to reach my ears? (46)

The mother language, language of love and death, is also the language that first accuses Elisabeth, branding her with something close to original guilt. Elisabeth will come into the world already *malfaisante*.

In contrast, George Nelson's mother tongue is the English of the *father* who chased him from the family home, and inasmuch as he carries this language with him, we might call it an *orphan* tongue.[14] Yet it is the same English of the *acte d'accusation*; it is the Queen's English, too. Elisabeth recognizes the inevitable tension in this connection: "Elisabeth d'Aulnières, widow Tassy. Do you hear? It's in a foreign tongue that they accuse you and charge you. That language is the language of my love" (39). The shift in point of view from "they accuse *you*" to "*my* love" and the ambiguity of the phrase "my love" (English is her lover's language but also, in part, necessarily that of her *love*) illustrate the paradox and the potentially divisive power of the *langue étrangère*. Each one's language, known but foreign to the other, is the language both of their love and of their alienation. Though the language of their communication and communion is French, their relationship can only ever be bilingual and some aspect of their shared language will always be a *langue étrangère*.

It is the wedge of the *langue étrangère* that finally makes Elisabeth and George strangers to one another, for when we read backwards into the novel from the ending, we come to see just how profoundly George's curse ("*It is that damned woman that has ruined me*") has infected the entire narrative. If the source of Elisabeth's wickedness (*malfaisance*) was the mother tongue, the source of Elisabeth's *malédiction* was the *damning* judgment of her own lover. Elisabeth herself provides the translation into French: "Je suis innocente! Voyez comme George Nelson me charge? Maudite, il m'a appelée maudite" (248) ("I'm innocent! See how George Nelson accuses me? Damned, that's what he called me, damned" [247]).

This piece of hearsay produces a devastating realignment of affiliations. Returning to his "foreign" tongue, the same one that brings the *acte d'accusation* against Elisabeth, George Nelson has retreated into a private male complicity that excludes her and makes of her "that damned woman." Paradoxically, there is abundant textual evidence of Nelson's "damning" well in advance of its narrative inscription. The words *maudit* and *damné* appear frequently in the novel. The reader does not, however, recognize them as *translations* until the *original*, suppressed utterance finally breaks into the text. The French narration presents George Nelson as the one who is originally *damné*. The taunts of the schoolboys ("Tous les protestants sont des damnés!" [125] ["All Protestants are damned!"]) are transformed in Nelson's nightmare into the accusing cries of an angry crowd: "Tous les étrangers sont des damnés!" (156) ("All foreigners are damned!").[15] But Elisabeth has clearly declared her desire to share this exile and this damnation, to be "étrangère" alongside George, "étrangère à tout ce qui n'est pas vous" (123) ("a stranger to all that is not you" [120]). It is only when the letter cannot arrive, when the abandonment cannot be denied, that she assumes the exile and damnation for herself alone: "Your appeal, your call lost somewhere in justice's endless pile of papers. Oh Lord, I am lost/I damn myself [je me damne]!" (242). When, in the narration, the words of George Nelson's betrayal of Elisabeth to the medical student can no longer be silenced or deferred, Elisabeth redefines the border: "You're talking in a foreign tongue [en langue étrangère],

Doctor Nelson" (247). He has become a foreigner and a stranger, and he has left her, alone—both damned and "étrangère."

Here, finally, we may perhaps best understand the significance of the chess game. Elisabeth had always perceived the ultimate threat to her own existence posed by the fraternity underlying the sadomasochistic relationship between her husband and her lover. Complicitous even in their deadly rivalry, they were two men engaged in something like a chess game, and the woman, the queen, was never anything but another fancy pawn. Elisabeth needed to receive George's letter in order to combat such suspicions, in order to refute the statement he made by leaving. He finally speaks, however, not *to* her but *of* her, to another man. His language is foreign not just because it is the English of the lawmakers and judges, but also, and perhaps more significantly, because it is the *language of men*.[16] Taking him at his word, Elisabeth can only curse him in return: "Let him return then, anathema, to his native land. After thirty years' absence. Henceforth banished in/into his own country. A stranger/foreigner wherever he goes, to the end of his days" (247).

In Pursuit

Elisabeth's curse, however, neither resolves the tension between allegiance and alienation nor arrests the movement of the narrative. Immediately after repudiating George in this way, Elisabeth describes herself in terms that emphasize the persistence of her connection to him: "Myself a stranger and possessed [étrangère et possédée], pretending to belong to the land of the living. Traitorous Elisabeth, here you are rejecting your deepest allegiance" (247). The lack of resolution is no accident. *Kamouraska* is characterized by the language and imagery of circularity and reciprocity. Reciprocal configurations are used repeatedly to describe the relationship of Elisabeth and George: "I provoke him, I bedevil him. As he provokes and bedevils me" (124); "I haunt and torment this man. As he haunts and torments me" (154); "And I'm haunting you, as you haunt me" (221).

Images of circularity are equally evident. The relentless rhythms of coming and going, of *aller et retour* (like the repeated voyage out to Kamouraska and back), punctuate the story. As a result, circularity problematizes reciprocity. If one considers two models for a reciprocal relationship—"an eye for an eye" and "do unto others as you would have others do unto you"—one realizes that the difference lies in where the cycle begins. In these terms, it is the story's inability clearly to begin and end, to have a before and after, that makes it hard to locate the crime and to assign responsibility.

Circular patterns in the novel often reflect the pursuit of the criminal by the Law that seeks to make an *arrest*. Much of *Kamouraska*'s narrative force is derived from the dynamics of propulsion and pursuit—Elisabeth driving and driven toward the edge of the world, pursuing the crime and pursued by it. It comes as no surprise, then, that the image of the hunt (*la chasse*) is central in the novel, creating a kind of perpetual hide-and-seek with guilt. As long as the "chase" goes on, crime and guilt are not fully *apprehended*. The chase produces a gap in which justice is suspended.

Very early in the novel, Elisabeth locates a similar gap within herself: "My musty, mildewed soul is somewhere else. Held prisoner, some-where, far away" (8). The separation of body and soul allows Elisabeth to skirt the crime. As long as her soul is somewhere else, Elisabeth's body can play the faultless role of devoted wife: "What a devoted and attentive creature! Truly a saint, Monsieur Rolland . . . age, misfortune, crime—none of them touches your wife. They all roll off her like water off a duck's back" (9).

Just as Elisabeth's body and soul play hide-and-seek with each other, thus frustrating the assignment of criminal responsibility, so also temporal manipulations in the novel allow the crime to be misplaced. The crucial moment that Elisabeth fears and cannot help pursuing is repeatedly lost in the labyrinth of "too late" and "not yet," of "one day" (past) and "one day" (future). Elisabeth's reconstructive method suggests that the crime must be located in the linearity of history (at some moment crime is com-mitted and once committed it cannot be undone), but the time games obscure that linearity so that it is not the criminal but the crime that threatens to escape.

Further, the language itself of the narrative plays hide-and-seek. Elisa-beth is a woman of many different names. She can easily lose or hide her-self behind an objectifying pronoun: "Thinking of yourself in the third person. Pretending detachment. Not identifying with the young bride" (67). Recapitulating her own history, "the way you tell a story, with-out really believing it too much" (67), she can persistently refuse to in-criminate herself: "No, I won't admit the total complicity that binds me to this fair-haired man" (68). Wherever the language games leave even temporary gaps, they provide her escape routes, deferring the moment of judgment.

The hunt is not interminable, however. Elisabeth knows and fears the outcome when she first acknowledges the dream that has come to torment her: "No use deluding oneself, one day reality and its imaginary double will coincide. . . . I will be recognized as *guilty*" (17, emphasis added). The alternative is equally horrifying. At the very end of the novel, Elisa-beth recognizes that the game of innocence may imprison her as surely as the guilt she had been trying to avoid, that she may finally be "condemn[ed] . . . to wear the icy mask of innocence" (235), playing out the "tedious comedy" day after day until "the perfect resemblance sticks to my skin" (248).

In keeping with the problematics of circularity, the chase is again and again shown to be not merely a result but just as importantly a cause of what happens in *Kamouraska*. When, at the beginning of the sixth chapter, Elisabeth is sent off to the governess's room, she sees her situation in these terms: "Chased! I am chased out of the bedroom we shared. Chased out of my bed" (25). Her imposed separation from her dying husband might have been an innocent banishment intended to provide her some much-needed rest, or it might have been a weightier one, evidence that her husband never fully believed in her innocence. The language she uses to describe that banishment, however, metonymically suggests both the tracked beast pursued by the hunter and the damned sinner driven from Paradise. Thus is Elisabeth easily delivered into the hands of nightmares in which she is rejected, hunted, and damned.

The hunt was instrumental in bringing Elisabeth and Antoine Tassy together in the first place, and it was the shared pleasure of that diversion which made inevitable their fatal marriage. Both were implicated in the hunt: "You're on my trail, Antoine Tassy, stalking me, like a good hunting dog. And I am also following your scent. I am tracking you down. . . . I'm the one who shoots. I'm the one who kills" (62–63).

The hunt mentality is one of violence, domination, and survival of the fittest, all of which play a major role in the relationship between George Nelson and Antoine Tassy. Nelson's motives are in part explained in terms of his having himself been "chassé": "Turned out [chassé], your father turned you out of his house" (125); "Exiled so young [chassé si tôt] from the world of kindness, are you going to find your lost kingdom and make it your own again?" (162). In addition, the chess game that is used repeatedly to sum up the Nelson-Tassy relationship is essentially a mutual "chasse."

In all of these examples there is an uncanny identification between hunter and hunted. One is not surprised to note that George Nelson, driven from his home, becomes Antoine Tassy's tormentor, that Antoine Tassy, tormented at school, becomes Elisabeth's tormentor. Thus, while in the second chapter Elisabeth finds comfort and security in thoughts of George Nelson—"One thing I am sure of and it keeps me going despite all the nagging fears, and the horror of my days. A man. . . . Day by day love cleanses me. *It washes away* [*Il chasse*] my every misdeed, my every fear, my every shame" (8, emphasis added)—nevertheless the misdeeds, the fear, and the shame cannot be held at bay; they turn on the lover and the love and drive them both away.

Hanging On

Elisabeth is terrified of being alone. When she is sent away from the sick-room, she reflects upon the meaning of solitude:

> Have to get used to sleeping alone. To bear the horror of my dreams. All alone, *without a man to run to, without a man to protect you* [*sans le recours à l'homme, sans le secours de l'homme*]. Presence of a body under the covers. Radiating warmth. *The embrace that reassures.* Absolving every ill, brief eternity, reconcili-ation with the whole world. (25, emphasis added)

It is the man whose embrace (or stranglehold?) reassures, the man whose presence offers absolution, reconciliation. Elisabeth calls out to her dying husband: "Dear little Jerome, I can admit it to you now: if not for you I would have died of terror. . . . Take me in your arms one more time, just once more so I may find my lost salvation" (25). Elisabeth will not accept becoming, like her aunts, "husbandless, hopeless [sans homme et sans espoir]" (40).

Elisabeth's attachment to George Nelson is a struggle against solitude. When, in the beginning, George tries to avoid her, warning that he is a foreigner, that he cannot help her, that he fears nothing as much as being "discovered [découvert]," she will not allow him to barricade himself in his house "like a criminal":

> *I approach his solitude*, I venture as close as I can. . . .
>   I'm concentrating. Closing my eyes. As if I were trying to conjure up spirits and yet *it's life I'm after . . . There, at the other end of Sorel.* A man, all alone, leaning on a kitchen table. A book lying open in front of him, not a page mov-ing. Reading over his shoulder. Working my way into the innermost recesses of his daydreams. (124, emphasis added, second ellipsis in the original)

Yet combating the solitude does not guarantee salvation. Man may be "secours" and "recours" (help and recourse) but he is also somehow con-tingent to Elisabeth's damnation. This man is not only Antoine Tassy ("Good God, I'm doomed [je me damne]! Married to a man I don't love" [66]), not only George Nelson whose "last words" effectively *damn* her ("It is that damned woman . . ."), but even and especially Jérôme Rol-land, the husband whose uncritical acceptance had sheltered Elisabeth for eighteen years. The underside of Elisabeth's "if not for you, I would have died of terror" ("sans toi, je serais morte de terreur") is her accusation directed at Jérôme Rolland: "If not for you, I would have been free. I'd have made my life over" (31).[17]

Jérôme, in marrying Elisabeth, had offered her a sanctuary in which to remake her innocence. Now, about to die, he will not accept the inevitable separation. The narrative voice that resembles a chorus counsels him:

> At your bedside your wife has reclaimed her solitude.
>
> You should call that woman back. Hurry! Make her return to this slender brink of life [l'étroite margelle de ce monde], Monsieur Rolland, here where you're spinning out the last few threads of your sickly days. You cannot remain alone like this, it is intolerable, this agony, this narrow little plank [cette mince passerelle]. (19)

His need is urgent. Elisabeth must not be allowed to remain behind, untouched: "Oh, to be well enough to rape that woman. To force her back with us onto the marriage bed. Lay her out on our deathbed, here beside us. Force her to think about us, to suffer with us, to share our agony, to die with us" (19).

The tenuous line Elisabeth walks throughout the novel is in part a result of Jérôme's uttering (in implied accusation) the name of Aurélie Caron. When Jérôme utters this name, it is in order to convict Elisabeth of her unpardoned sin ("la convaincre du péché"), to catch her out in her absence ("la prendre en flagrant délit d'absence"), to bring her to him and with him by force (20). Everything occurs on this "narrow plank," this "mince passerelle," on the brink of some violent and ultimate act of separation.

Thus, the counterpart of the complicitous male abandonment that haunts Elisabeth is her own complicity in that abandonment, that is, her refusal to accompany the man beyond a certain point. Elisabeth's refusal finally to share man's transgression may be *her* greatest and final transgression. There is a striking similarity between Elisabeth's descriptions of Jérôme Rolland's impending death and of George Nelson's murder of Antoine Tassy:

> Keep watch over my husband. Follow him every step of the way, as far as I can. Over this narrow plank that leads to death. Until I can't take one more step without dying myself. Then at the very moment prescribed by law, leaving him alone to take the last step over the . . . On a thread, thinner and thinner. Watching him disappear into the distance. Remaining here, living. (90–91, ellipsis in the original)

> Again I beg you to spare me the rest of your story. All this is a man's affair. A score to settle between men. I don't mind waiting here by the side of the road (like a good little girl, lost in the snow), waiting for Antoine's execution to be over. But don't count on me to follow you all the way to . . . (231–232, ellipsis in the original)

Rather than combat the solitude, Elisabeth invokes it:

> My heart, bent on its own damnation, praying that the darkness never ends. That the light will never shine on that man, lying there in the depths of darkness. My dying heart, praying that never again will he come before me, run to me, hold out his arms to me, take me in his arms, this man who just killed another man. In the cove of Kamouraska. His unimaginable solitude. . . .
>
> . . . .
>
> Here I am walled up in my solitude. Transfixed in my own dark dread. . . . I can no longer take even a step towards you . . . (215–216, first and last ellipses in the original)

Unable or unwilling to bridge the separate solitudes, her choice is to "remain living [demeurer vivante]" and to survive *alone*.

Elisabeth does survive at the end of *Kamouraska*. Indeed, we find her and leave her at her dying husband's side. Jérôme has received the last sacrament and, absolved of his sins, is prepared to die.[18] Both he and Elisabeth appear to manifest the "admirable tact" with which the day (and the novel) began. The novel closes with the words of a servant who, upon seeing Elisabeth holding her husband's hand and weeping, comments: "Just look how Madame loves Monsieur! You see, she's crying." Elisabeth is, however, no longer "dutiful and above reproach," peacefully awaiting her husband's death. Terrified, she clings to his hand "as to a fragile thread that still holds her to life and might break at any moment." The novel thus ends, as it began, with an unstable *tableau vivant*, a precarious peace in which the woman walks the very edge of something irrevocable.

Monstrous Survival

The apparent ease of the final parting, marked (ironically) by Jérôme Rolland's words, "Don't worry, Elisabeth. I'm here," is overshadowed by the penultimate scene. While Elisabeth Rolland, the model wife, sits quietly by her husband, Elisabeth d'Aulnières is visited by a horrifying nightmare. Beneath an imperturbable and inscrutable exterior, Elisabeth succumbs to the vision: A woman had been buried alive. Disinterred, she now runs crying and pleading through the streets of a city whose fearful inhabitants have barricaded their doors against her. "Everyone thinks that that woman, buried alive, so long ago, must have a ferocious hunger to live. A ferocious and awesome hunger growing and growing underground for centuries" (249). And because of her hunger to live, this horrifying stranger is permanently exiled: "All that can remain for her to do is to die of hunger and solitude." Her hunger is monstrous, her survival is monstrous, and, monster that she is, she can only die—unsatisfied, unconsoled, alone.

As this enormous image looms over the final scene (that model of tact and propriety), words of judgment are pronounced by the "chorus" voice: "Wicked Elisabeth! Damnable/damned woman! [Malfaisante Elisabeth! Femme maudite!]." Like the woman of the nightmare, monstrously refusing to die, Elisabeth is damned and doomed. This vision of unbearable solitude drives Elisabeth to clutch at Jérôme, seeking again her connection with him, with any man, as "secours," "recours," *life* itself.

Elisabeth survives, but the price of her survival is guilt. If we try to locate the source of her guilt, the nightmare at the end certainly suggests that her survival has contributed to her sense of culpability. There seems to be something monstrous in her double widowhood. Such an interpretation is supported by the fact that, in the course of the story, both Tassy and Rolland have occasion to accuse Elisabeth of being responsible for their deaths. Yet as long as Elisabeth recognized and desired a complicitous union with George Nelson, she could balance death's law with love's law. She could refuse to allow her husbands' deaths to incriminate her. Thus, it is the outcome of the third and central drama, that of her relationship with Nelson, that fixes the final judgment upon Elisabeth. When Elisabeth, cursed by George, curses him in return, her fate is sealed:

> Damned, he called me damned. If your love shocks you so, rip it out of your heart. Which of us first betrayed the other? . . . Let him return then, anathema, to his native land. After thirty years away. Henceforth banished in/into his own country. A stranger/foreigner everywhere forever.
>
> Myself a stranger and possessed, pretending to belong to the land of the living. *Traitorous Elisabeth, here you are rejecting your deepest allegiance.* (247, emphasis added)

Refusing to cross the border of the crime with him, refusing to know him on his return, she relegates them each to a separate solitude, *étranger* and *étrangère* to one another forever: "I'm the one who pushed you from the other end of the world. (I stood back, off by the side of the road, while you . . . in the cove of Kamouraska . . .) *Crime and death to be crossed. Like a border.* When you return, your face, your look against mine, for ever and ever unknowable" (248, emphasis added, ellipses in the original). It is too late. They can no longer share "an exile, utter and complete," and "a madman's solitude" (248). But even in this separate solitude there is a threat: "Could it be that he is still living? And if he were married? No, no! I would not bear it! I'd sooner he were dead, lying at my feet, than . . . Than that any other woman might ever . . ." (248, ellipses in the original). In *Kamouraska*, ellipsis repeatedly covers the place of the crime. The murder of Antoine Tassy, which is elided, is undeniably a central and motivating force in the novel. Similarly, here at the end, when ellipsis is used to cover the possibility of George Nelson's final abandonment of Elisabeth, the possibility of his commitment to another woman, it again marks the place of transgression. And once again the transgression is both George's and Elisabeth's since, preferring him to be victim rather than betrayer, Elisabeth chooses at this moment to survive George Nelson as well. Threatened by his separate solitude that has the power to exclude her, she desires his death. In a sense, the triptych is complete and Elisabeth is *thrice* widowed (and thrice responsible). The ellipsis here establishes an analogy between Tassy's murder and the unspeakable that occurs in the space of Elisabeth's unspoken thought. In both cases, narrative suppression attempts unsuccessfully to cover transgression, but actually ends up (re)producing it and leaving a thick residue of guilt. Three men have crossed over, and Elisabeth has remained behind, "living." She does not "transgress"; she has even declared her innocence. Yet it is precisely this refusal to "cross over [franchir]" the inarticulable boundary that seems to mark her trespass and her transgression.

In the nightmare, the woman who will not die is exiled from the human community. At its climax, the nightmare gathers force to accuse Elisabeth directly, to declare her guilt and her sentence: "Malfaisante Elisabeth! Femme maudite! [Wicked Elisabeth! Damnable/damned woman!]." The sentence seems clear, but crucial questions remain. If Elisabeth is guilty of living, we need to question the voice that accuses her. We need to question the law that defines her guilt. *Who* is calling her hunger, her solitude, and her difference monstrous? According to *whose* law is her survival a crime?[19]

Four

Speaking Madness: *Mrs. Dalloway*

"Then the hour, irrevocable"

After the graphically explicit crime and gothic plotting of *Kamouraska*, Virginia Woolf's novel can only appear, at first glance, a model of propriety, supremely safe and civilized, the story of how Mrs. Dalloway, a respectable, middle-aged wife and mother, spent her day.[1] The events are decidedly mundane: Mrs. Dalloway runs errands, walks through London, mends a dress, receives the visit of an old friend, rests, muses about many things, prepares for and finally gives a party. What could there possibly be in Clarissa Dalloway's day to bring the police onto the scene?

Although the "story" of Mrs. Dalloway (with its everyday situations and its paucity of plot) might seem to be at the farthest remove from a murder mystery or detective story, it does share essential formal elements with such tales of crime. As in *Kamouraska*, there is a "charged" past that intrudes almost immediately upon the present. Indeed, in the fourth sentence, we are made privy to Clarissa Dalloway's thoughts:

> And then, thought Clarissa Dalloway, what a morning—fresh as if issued to children on a beach.
>
> What a lark! What a plunge! For so it had always seemed to her, when, with a little squeak of the hinges, *which she could hear now*, she had burst open the French windows and plunged at Bourton into the open air. (3, emphasis added)

As the novel progresses, it becomes clear that Bourton (and the social drama of friendship and courtship played out there so many years before) is a powerful and significant part of Clarissa's *present*. Freud showed how an irrepressible past may be telling the story of an uneasy conscience. Indeed, "case histories" read remarkably like detective stories.[2] The role of this past as traumatic history is suggested in the parallel development of Mrs. Dalloway's "double," Septimus Warren Smith, who is carrying around with him a past "charged" with the story of love, war, death, and betrayal.[3]

Not only does the past strain the seams of "London; this moment of June," but there is also a sense of impending future, which tends to turn the *present* moment into a *pre*moment. The anticipation of the party (the event that is to mark the culmination of Mrs. Dalloway's day and of the novel) is reflected and expanded in the novel's first few pages by Clarissa's memory of standing at the open window at Bourton and feeling "that something awful was about to happen," and by the "indescribable pause; a suspense . . . before Big Ben strikes. There! Out it boomed. First a warning, musical; then the hour, irrevocable."[4] Big Ben continues to sound the hours throughout the day—marking time between ponderous pauses and "leaden circles dissolv[ing]."

The irrevocability of time *past* is echoed by Clarissa's thoughts as she sits with her old friend Peter Walsh: "It was all over for her. The sheet was stretched and the bed narrow," and again "it was as if the five acts of a play . . . were now over and she had lived a lifetime in them and had run away, had lived with Peter, and it was now over" (70–71). *It was over*—Peter Walsh thinks these same words when he remembers the "final scene, the terrible scene" (95), the night at Bourton when Clarissa broke with him: "'Clarissa!' he cried, 'Clarissa!' But she never came back. It was over. He went away that night. He never saw her again" (97). But he *did* see her again. Indeed, with every irrevocable ending there seem to arise new expectations. Even Peter Walsh, though professing to believe that one could, with age, learn to come and go "without any very great expectations," reflects toward the novel's end that "here he was starting to go to a party, at his age, with the belief upon him that he was about to have an experience" (247).

In *Mrs. Dalloway*, the present moment into which Clarissa "plunges" is at one point described as "the moment of this June morning on which was the pressure of all the other mornings" (54). For Clarissa especially, something has happened; something is going to happen. Describing the temporal complexities of *Mrs. Dalloway*, J. Hillis Miller writes:

> In one sense the moment is all that is real. Life in the present instant is a narrow plank reaching over the abyss of death between the nothingness of past and future. . . . In another sense, the weight of all the past moments presses just beneath the surface of the present, ready in an instant to flow into consciousness, overwhelming it with the immediate presence of the past. (184)[5]

The first image unites past and future in nothingness. In the second, past and future conspire as the (narrating) consciousness draws them into circles of repetition. In the accumulated past lies the future threat: Miller describes a present both weighted and waiting.

In addition to the evocation of an insistent and telling past, the danger and suspense upon which a good crime novel depends are also present in *Mrs. Dalloway* and made particularly if oddly explicit through the agency of Septimus Warren Smith. Clarissa's memory of feeling, as a girl, that "something awful was about to happen" is repeated and magnified *in the present* by Septimus in Regent's Park, where he feels "something tremendous about to happen. He had only to open his eyes; but a weight was on them; a fear" (104). Septimus manifestly confronts and suffers what, in Clarissa, is controlled and repressed. When Clarissa looked into a mirror, "collected the whole of her at one point," and saw herself ("That was her self when some effort, some call on her to be her self, drew the parts together" [54–55]), she kept her knowledge of the internal fracturing to herself as her social role demanded: "The parts . . . she alone knew how different, how incompatible and composed so *for the world only* into one centre" (55, emphasis added). Septimus greeted a similar experience with terror, feeling himself to be a fragile and very temporary hindrance to a violent and ineluctable future: "this gradual drawing together of everything to one centre before his eyes, as if some horror had come almost to the surface and was about to burst into flames, terrified him. The world wavered and quivered and threatened to burst into flames. It is I who am blocking the way, he thought" (21). Clarissa had "always had the feeling that it was very, very dangerous to live even one day" (11). But it is through Septimus's mad lucidity that we come to see clearly the dimensions of that volatile and perilous present.

If Clarissa Dalloway's "story" were taken alone, one might perhaps overlook the troubling intrusions, the "monsters" ("hatred" on page 17; "being in love" on page 67) and the "deaths" ("the death of the soul" on page 88; Clarissa's sister "Sylvia's death—that horrible affair" on page 117), for in general the passions can be (and are) neatly packaged and put aside. When Peter Walsh, visiting Clarissa on the morning of the party, suddenly and unaccountably wept, Clarissa, kissing him, "actually had felt his face on hers *before she could down the brandishing of silver flashing*— plumes like pampas grass in a tropic gale in her breast, which, subsiding, left her holding his hand, patting his knee" (69, emphasis added). Such intensity of passion, such intimacy between two people passes quickly. So Clarissa imagines herself retiring to an attic room, a narrow bed, for "women must put off their rich apparel" (45). The "scenes" of Bourton are long past; it is unlikely that anything *momentous* will happen now: "never would she have a moment any more."[6] In Clarissa's world, reason and decorum will triumph: "She stiffened a little; so she would stand at the top of her stairs" (25). Mrs. Dalloway, the public figure, "the perfect hostess" Peter called her (93), would be always present and presentable when called upon to "be her self." For indeed "all was for the party" (56).

Were it not for Septimus's madness and suicide, Clarissa's day might have proceeded respectably, despite the turmoil of her thoughts, from early morning errands through evening party uninterrupted by crime, death, and police. It is Septimus's discourse (alternately confessional and accusational) that introduces crime into Woolf's novel, and the climax of *his* day is not a party but a fatal confrontation with authority.

On the Side of the Normal

At first glance, policemen in *Mrs. Dalloway* appear to play a very minor role. They are traffic cops, part of the daily London scene: a policeman helps Clarissa to cross a road; a policeman directs an omnibus to move aside so that the mysterious motorcar may pass; another policeman "ought to have stopped the traffic" at Piccadilly, thinks Richard Dalloway, watching a small child cross alone. Richard "had no illusions about the London police. Indeed, he was collecting evidence of their malpractices" (175). But these are not the men doing the serious policing in *Mrs. Dalloway* (nor are they those responsible for the most blatant "malpractice" described in the novel). "Bobbies" may patrol the streets, directing traffic, chasing away street vendors, harassing prostitutes, but the heavy-duty policing is done by those who force their way into homes, families, minds: the medical men. In her reading of *Mrs. Dalloway*, Maria DiBattista describes the "authoritarian figure" of the great doctor "administer[ing] and execut[ing] the law of social happiness" as he executes the will of "the prosperous England."[7]

There are two doctors at work in *Mrs. Dalloway*—Dr. Holmes and Sir William Bradshaw. Their titles confirm that they possess the necessary credentials of education or class (in addition to the necessary gender, of course) to allow them to claim positions of authority within the bourgeois society. That medical men should occupy such positions is hardly surprising. After all, do not healthy individuals secure the health of a society? This is a correlation that Virginia Woolf describes somewhat more cynically in her essay "On Being Ill": "In health the genial pretence must be kept up . . . to communicate, to civilise, to share. . . . In illness this make-believe ceases."[8] It is perhaps even less surprising that an eminent specialist in "nerve cases" should be found exercising "England's will," for as Michel Foucault has pointed out, "the prestige of patriarchy is revived around madness in the bourgeois family."[9]

Men's claim to authority within traditional bourgeois society probably needs no elucidation—the privilege of that (rather than the *other*) gender is one of the givens of patriarchy. Virginia Woolf makes clear the masculine bias of the Law. Those who mete it out, *lay it down*, are clearly defined as male:

Sir John Buckhurst, the old Judge . . . [who] had laid down the law for years and *liked a well-dressed woman*. (24, emphasis added)

Big Ben . . . all very well with his majesty laying down the law, so solemn, so just. (193)

Indeed, Woolf underlines the rather comic revelation that even Lady
Bruton, who gave "masculine lunch parties" (to which Clarissa was not
invited) (160), who "had power . . . , position, income" and who had
"known the ablest men of her day" (169), even Lady Millicent Bruton,
confidante of the Prime Minister himself "often suspended judge-
ment upon men in deference to the mysterious accord in which they, but
no woman, stood to the laws of the universe" (165). Septimus Warren
Smith, however, does not share men's privileged status in relation to the
law, for "the law is on the side of the normal."[10] Septimus may have "developed manliness" in the War, but he is clearly not *normal*. When he
makes his first appearance in the novel, his eyes have "that look of apprehension in them which makes complete strangers apprehensive too" (20).
Septimus hears voices, he hallucinates, he talks to himself, he threatens
suicide.

Most strikingly perhaps, Septimus's relation to language shows clear
signs of disturbance: language is freed from its customary restrictions.
There is a loss (and at the same time a curious surplus) of significance
in what Septimus receives and understands from the world. The smoke
letters left by the airplane do not spell out an advertisement for toffee—
instead "they are signalling to [him]. Not indeed in actual words; that
is, he could not read the language yet" (31). A sparrow chirps "Septimus, Septimus" and sings "piercingly in Greek words how there is no
crime" (36). When Rezia (Septimus's wife, Lucrezia) announces simply, "It is time," "the word 'time' split its husk; poured its riches over
him," and he sings an "immortal ode to Time" and sees walking toward him Evans, who had been his friend and had died in the War
(105).

Sir William notices the linguistic disorder immediately:

> "You served with great distinction in the War?"
> The patient repeated the word "war" interrogatively.
> He was attaching meanings to words of a symbolical kind. A serious symp-
> tom, to be noted on the card. (145)

At the same time, the "revelations" that Septimus strives to communicate to the world are also so heavily laden with significance (for him) that
they become incomprehensible. Rezia, whom he compels to write down
his messages, thinks, "Perfect nonsense it was" (101). Dr. Holmes accuses
him of "talking nonsense to frighten [his] wife" (141); and Sir William
Bradshaw refuses even to listen to his haltingly begun "confession." The
first time Septimus tries to confess, Bradshaw withdraws immediately to
an adjoining room in order to consult alone with Lucrezia; and later,
when Septimus again tries to confess, he cuts him off abruptly because the
analytic three-quarter hour is up (149).

A statement of Woolf's may shed some light on how inadequate per-
ception or conveyance of meaning may come to be considered not only
crazy but criminal:

> Incomprehensibility has an enormous power over us in illness, more legiti-
> mately perhaps than the upright will allow. In health meaning has encroached
> upon sound. Our intelligence domineers over our senses. But in illness, *with the
> police off duty*, we creep beneath some obscure poem by Mallarmé or Donne,
> some phrase in Latin or Greek, and the words give out their scent and distil their
> flavour, and then, if at last we grasp the meaning, it is all the richer for having
> come to us sensually first, by way of the palate and the nostrils, like some queer
> odour.[11]

Meaning is here clearly allied to a police function. Septimus, who does not
understand properly and does not make proper sense, is not only ill, he is,
as Woolf says in the same essay, an "outlaw."[12] Septimus himself certainly
feels that he is being viewed and treated as a criminal. Not only does he
directly and literally introduce a vocabulary of crime and confession into
the novel, the entire scenario of his madness and treatment is marked by
imagery of pursuit and the threat of incarceration.

In addition to his language disorder, Septimus shows other symptoms
of madness that may likewise be interpreted as *criminal transgressions*. He
has threatened suicide. For this reason, Sir William explains, he must be
sent away, to rest, for "it was a question of law" (146). Another symptom
of Septimus's madness seems to be the closely related fact of his refusal to
father a child and his homoerotic bond with Evans.[13] There is something
socially unacceptable, verging on criminal, in thus resisting heterosexual
convention.[14]

The extent of Septimus's departure from accepted and civilized norms
is evident in his view of heterosexuality. Claiming that Shakespeare came
to view love between man and woman as "repulsive," he declares that
"one cannot . . . increase the breed of these lustful animals, who have no
lasting emotions" (134–135). Human beings, in their heterosexual "business of copulation," come to represent "bestiality" for Septimus. Thus, for
him, humans are beasts, human nature a repulsive, bloodthirsty brute,
while nature (for instance, the trees, beauty) offers the possibility of a
transcendent experience. Significantly, it is the image of a *dog* turning into
a *man* that horrifies Septimus (102). The metaphor of two dogs playing
which he uses to describe himself and Evans places *that* relationship on the
side of nature and beauty.[15]

Septimus's idealization of his relationship with Evans and his failure to
prove a "good husband" for Rezia combine with his allegiance to nature
and against *human* nature to set him apart. His aloneness is a symptom
both of his illness (the unhealthy introspection for which Holmes pre-

scribes that he take an interest in things outside himself) and of his devi-
ance from the social order. His marriage to Lucrezia epitomizes that
order: as they sat in Regent's Park it was the "tremendous weight" of her
hand on his knee that held him down, he thought, and kept him from
going mad (32). When she removed her wedding ring, it was "with
agony, with relief" that he thought "their marriage was over" (101). In
the freedom (and madness) that resulted, he saw himself as "the lord of
men" possessing a "supreme secret" to impart to the Prime Minister and
the Cabinet. In other words, he felt himself suddenly in some way *above
the law*.

Septimus's selfish refusal to fulfill his duties as a husband precipitated
his first crisis. When his wife, confronting him with her desire for a child,
began to cry, "far away he heard her sobbing; he heard it accurately, he
noticed it distinctly; he compared it to a piston thumping. *But he felt nothing*" (136, emphasis added). He was, in every sense of the word, detached. While *not feeling* was the single symptom of his illness that
alarmed Septimus and the primary crime of which he accused himself, this
was not, however, one of the primary "transgressions" recognized by society. In the novel it is clearly *feeling too much* that transgresses acceptable
and normal behavior. Peter Walsh reflects on the inappropriateness of his
"astonishing accesses of emotion" (121) and his propensity to cry at the
wrong times (230); Septimus congratulates himself on having had the appropriate and manly reactions of a brave soldier, "feeling very little and
very reasonably" when he survived the War and the loss of his friend
(130). In *Madness and Civilization*, Michel Foucault notes that "the possibility of madness is . . . implicit in the very phenomenon of passion," and
he indirectly suggests an analogy between this mad passion and "crime":
"There comes a moment in the course of passion when *laws are suspended*
as though of their own accord.[16]

The crimes of which Septimus accused himself—that he does not feel,
that he has betrayed his wife (seduced her, married her without loving her,
lied to her)—are, indeed, quite different from those for which the *authorities* reproached him. His suicidal tendencies, his homosexual orientation,
and his excessive introspection were all treated (and treated seriously) by
the doctors; but the *lack* that lay behind his original crisis was unrecognized. It was, in fact, only when "with a melodramatic gesture which he
assumed mechanically and with complete consciousness of its insincerity,
he dropped his head on his hands" (136), that the doctor was called in.
Septimus's complete lack of feeling could be expressed only by its opposite (melodrama), one symptom masking another. And yet the order of
symptoms was understood differently by those who intervened to help
him. Tending rather to consider Septimus's lack of feeling as an attempt
to repress his far more dangerous *excesses* of feeling, the medical men were

concerned only that his nonfeeling failed to produce appropriately moderate (and civilized) behavior. "Wouldn't it be better to do something instead of lying in bed?" asks Holmes (139). "Nobody lives for himself alone," says Bradshaw (148).

The interpretive act of diagnosis depends upon tracing symptoms to causes. If true symptoms go unrecognized or if the *direction* of influences is incorrectly mapped, then the diagnostic language fails, and the failure is maddening. Septimus, caught between the contradictory demands of personal and socially prescribed conscience, could hardly fail to go mad (especially since it was by definition crazy to have such a *split* conscience in the first place).

In both diagnosis and treatment Septimus is a victim of medical malpractice. For Bradshaw's "treatment" of his "symptoms" conflates crime and punishment, prolonging the "criminal" behavior. In response to his social and matrimonial failings, Septimus is to be isolated from society and forbidden to procreate. When symptoms are twisted into treatments and punishments reproduce transgressions, is it any wonder that, having threatened suicide, Septimus should feel driven to kill himself precisely by and for those doctors who condemned the impulse?

Laying Down the Law

I have already suggested that madness is considered "criminal" inasmuch as it transgresses social norms. The law that defines the crime is that of Society and Civilization, and in *Mrs. Dalloway*, the two major instruments of that law are Holmes and Bradshaw. These two doctors share certain fundamental values. Both insist upon the importance of marriage and the family. They further agree that Septimus is too preoccupied with himself, that he must undertake to focus on things *outside* himself. They heartily condemn his selfish egotism.

Yet Holmes and Bradshaw come from very different social and educational backgrounds. Holmes is "Mrs. Filmer's Dr. Holmes" (137), a family doctor with an interest in old furniture; Bradshaw is a specialist who drives a fancy motorcar and, with Lady Bradshaw his wife, attends Dalloway parties. Holmes prescribes from personal experience, suggesting bromide, porridge, and hobbies. Bradshaw is a professional, with a "reputation . . . not merely of lightning skill, and almost infallible accuracy in diagnosis but of sympathy; tact; understanding of the human soul" (144).[17] Indeed, if Holmes is the friendly neighborhood policeman on the beat, Bradshaw spends most of his time at Headquarters. Not a mere patrolman but a *lawgiver*, it is Bradshaw, the theorist, who first defines the terms and the seriousness of Septimus's transgression.

Bradshaw's theory is concerned with restoring health, and health means law and order, for according to Bradshaw's theory the reigning principle is proportion. "Worshipping proportion, Sir William not only prospered himself, but made England prosper" (150). The manner in which the law of proportion is executed, however, is exposed by Woolf as far from benevolent. For as Sir William "secluded [England's] lunatics, forbade childbirth, penalised despair, made it impossible for the unfit to propagate their views until they, too, shared his sense of proportion," he was worshiping not only Proportion but her sister Goddess, Conversion, who "offers help, but desires power" (151).

Sir William's role as policing agent for English society comes through clearly in his description of what amounts to a comfortably complicitous arrangement between champions of proportion and law enforcement officials:

> Sir William had a friend in Surrey where they taught, what Sir William frankly admitted was a difficult art—a sense of proportion. There were, moreover, family affection; honour; courage; and a brilliant career. All of these had in Sir William a resolute champion. *If they failed him, he had to support police* and the good of society, which, he remarked very quietly, would take care . . . that these unsocial impulses . . . were held in control. (154, emphasis added)

Sharing the common goal of "controlling unsocial impulses," doctors and policemen are on the same side—the side of the law.

Despite their professional rivalry and mutual disdain, Holmes and Bradshaw also end up on the same side. Though they offer diametrically opposed diagnoses (Holmes declaring that there is "nothing whatever the matter" [139] and Sir William immediately recognizing "a case of extreme gravity" [144]), Septimus easily conflates them. When Sir William informs Septimus of his plan to send him to a rest home, Septimus's sneering response ("One of Holmes's homes?" [147]) underlines the fact that the patient hardly distinguishes between the two doctors. The identification becomes explicit when Holmes and Bradshaw *together* come to represent for Septimus that "human nature" which pursues him mercilessly: "Once you fall . . . human nature is on you. Holmes and Bradshaw are on you" (148). Holmes and Bradshaw are metamorphosed into "the brute with the red nostrils," a single monster to be feared and fled (223). Only minutes before his final plunge, Septimus expresses his sense of the Holmes/Bradshaw complicity: "Holmes and Bradshaw, men who never weighed less than eleven stone six, who sent their wives to Court . . . ; who different in their verdicts (for Holmes said one thing, Bradshaw another), yet judges they were; who mixed the vision and the sideboard; saw nothing clear, yet ruled, yet inflicted" (224–225). Though Holmes and Bradshaw may reach different verdicts (*conclusions*) about Septimus's illness, they both bring in the same verdict (*judgment*): he is guilty of socially unacceptable behavior. In this way roles blend together and lawgivers, policemen, judges combine to produce a single authoritarian force, as the opposing "verdicts" are summed up in Septimus's mind in a single "verdict": "The verdict of human nature on such a wretch was death" (138). In his analysis of *Mrs. Dalloway*, Garrett Stewart offers insightful and provocative comments on the significance of this sentence:

> Though he feels "condemned to death" for not having "cared" when Evans was killed, there is a more telling phrasing of his fate that discomfits legal terminology, offering a "verdict" determined where we would expect the resulting sentence. "The verdict of human nature on such a wretch was death" (138). In the daily disposition of Septimus's prolonged trial, as itself a vicious circle of expiation, living death sentences the soul to suspended animation.[18]

I would add that when analysis is presented as verdict, and when a verdict becomes its own sentence, there can be no practical difference between doctor and warden, judge and executioner. Bradshaw, the magistrate, and Holmes, the bloodhound, may not frequent the same circles—but they collaborate (unwittingly yet unerringly) to maintain the same precinct in good order.

As Stewart's analysis suggests, Septimus's "trial" presupposes his guilt and incessantly pronounces his death sentence. As soon as doctors must be called in, the victim is condemned; it is fundamental to the doctors' "profession" that Septimus is guilty of transgression (in Bradshaw's office his patients "learnt the extent of their transgressions" [153]). But to what extent do they respond to an existing situation, and to what extent do they define and create it?

Although one of Septimus's revelations is that "there is no crime," in the presence of Holmes and Bradshaw he grows horribly obsessed with his sin, his crimes, his vice. In Bradshaw's office the desire to confess becomes overwhelming:

> He had committed an appalling crime and been condemned to death by human nature.
>
> "I have—I have," he began, "committed a crime." (145)

Septimus, "the most exalted of mankind," but also "the criminal who faced his judges," responds to the accusation that Sir William embodies by assuming the guilt:

> But if he confessed? If he communicated? Would they let him off then, his torturers?
>
> "I—I—" he stammered.
>
> But what was his crime? He could not remember it.
>
> . . . .
>
> Love, trees, there is no crime—what was his message? (148)

This is the language of a forced confession: anything to make the punishment stop. When Septimus commits his last, irrevocable "criminal" act—throwing himself onto Mrs. Filmer's area railings—he validates the doctors' diagnoses, finally producing the crime by and for which he has been condemned. In Holmes's and Bradshaw's eyes there is no rational explanation for such a curtailment of treatment—such an act can be committed only by a deeply disturbed individual.

Whether Septimus is in fact guilty *of* anything is quite irrelevant to the fact that he is assigned and assumes the guilty role. Indeed, as a number of critics have noted, Septimus conforms to the classic definition of a scapegoat.[19] It is Maria DiBattista's analysis, however, that most eloquently describes society's interest in the scapegoating of Septimus: "it is the war that transforms Septimus, the lower class upstart . . . , into Septimus the scapegoat who assumes society's burden of guilt. The Prime Minister is a symbol of Empire without guilt, for all disgrace has been displaced onto Septimus" (43). The scapegoat answers society's need to contain its guilt. When a scapegoat is used for ritual sacrifice, it is society as a whole (and not the individual) whose crime is being expiated. Thus are judges, lawmakers, psychiatrists, police (all "instruments" of that society) unquestionably implicated in the production and perpetuation of transgression.

Lucrezia the Lawgiver

The one person whose life interacts with Septimus's, and the one person, besides the doctors, who in any sense "analyzes" his situation is his wife Lucrezia. Unlike the doctors, however, Rezia reacts complexly, her feelings often as difficult to locate as Septimus's "crimes." She is unquestionably alienated from him by her appreciation of his "bravery" in the War. When, in response to Bradshaw's questions about his military service, Septimus thinks, "Had he served with distinction? He really forgot. In the War itself he had failed," Rezia hastens to assure the doctor: "Yes he served with the greatest distinction. . . . He has done nothing wrong whatever" (145). Rezia's admiration of traditional emblems of maleness and mastery contributes to the failure of communication in the doctor's office and thus to the gross misinterpretation of Septimus's "War" that leads to Bradshaw's malpractice.

As long as war is responsible both for Septimus's manhood and for his illness ("deferred effects of shell-shock" [279]), he is indeed getting mixed messages about crime. When Rezia admires Septimus's "maleness," she aligns herself with the doctors on the side of the normative impulse toward separateness and the sexual politics of dichotomy. She rewards the soldier's stoicism, though it is precisely that lack of affective reaction which seems to Septimus to seal his fate.

Rezia at first has a comfortable relationship with Dr. Holmes. He is "a kind man. . . . [He is] so interested in Septimus. He only wanted to help them, he said. He had four little children and he had asked her to tea" (139). She is at first equally optimistic about Sir William: "She thought his name sounded nice; he would cure Septimus at once" (125). But her trust in the doctors is quickly disappointed. Having consulted the specialist when Holmes's treatment was not producing results, Rezia is soon horrified by Sir William's decision to separate husband and wife: "She had asked for help and been deserted! He had failed them! Sir William Bradshaw was not a nice man!" (149).[20]

Rezia's attitudes toward the doctors shift as she responds to parts of Septimus that they do not and cannot condone: the poet and the child. For Septimus the poet, Rezia is not just scribe. She is to some extent muse as well, a conduit to a certain natural beauty and creativity. When "the panic was on him [in Milan]—that he could not feel" (131), he was drawn to Rezia because of her gaiety and the way in which she felt the beauty of the world. For Septimus the child, Rezia offers a maternal sanctuary: "hats being made protected him; he was assured of safety; he had a refuge" (131). Sir William wants to lock Septimus away, to isolate him and to make him be a man. Rezia would like him to be a man, too, but she wants above all to *communicate* with him. She is not ready to sacrifice the poet and the child. When Rezia and Septimus play together, creating Mrs. Peters's hat, the communication established between them helps to preserve the poet and child in the man. Finding beauty in some of Septimus's writings, and comparing him to a "young hawk" (222), Rezia in a way repeats the important emotional connections in Septimus's past: for Septimus wrote poetry for Miss Isabel Pole and played like a young dog with Evans. By refusing to deny these parts of Septimus's identity, and by thus offering some continuity (in spite of the War), Rezia is able to represent a law of understanding that transcends the doctors' analyses.

Against Bradshaw's doctrine that "health is proportion" (149) and that "people we are most fond of are not good for us when we are ill" (223), Septimus puts forth that "communication is health; communication is happiness" (141). The mutual building of Mrs. Peters's hat therefore takes on an epiphanic quality. Septimus could "feel [Rezia's] mind, like a bird, falling from branch to branch . . . ; he could follow her mind" (222). And Rezia knew that "they were perfectly happy now . . . she could say anything to him now" (221).

Their communication is *not* total: Septimus is withholding (for although he can follow Rezia's mind, he is totally alone with his own nightmare visions), and Rezia, in her simple optimism, is naive. Something important is, nevertheless, communicated. Through a process of mutual recognition and naming, Septimus and Rezia redefine each other, giving their relationship a lasting *meaning*. Rezia "called [Septimus] by the name of that hawk or crow which being malicious and a great destroyer of crops was precisely like him. No one could separate them, she said" (225). In this way, she redefines his bravery. He is no longer a courageous soldier, distinguishing himself *in the ranks* of men and in the cause of England; he is a fierce and powerful bird eternally allied *with her* against the establishment that desires to separate them (as the war machine always separates men and women). Septimus in turn redefines Rezia:

> She was a flowering tree; and through her branches looked out the face of a lawgiver, who had reached a sanctuary where she feared no one; not Holmes; not Bradshaw; a miracle, a triumph, the last and greatest. Staggering he saw her mount the appalling staircase, laden with Holmes and Bradshaw, men who never weighed less than eleven stone six. . . . Over them she triumphed. (224–225)

The image of the feminine lawgiver triumphing over the weighty authority of the masculine judges recalls the "giant figure" in Peter Walsh's dream of the solitary traveler (just as that traveler, "haunter," "disturber," "devastator," in some ways reminds us of Septimus):

> The solitary traveller, haunter of lanes, disturber of ferns, and devastator of great hemlock plants, looking up, suddenly sees the giant figure at the end of the ride.
>
> . . . .
>
> Nothing exists outside us except a state of mind, he thinks. . . . But if he can conceive of her, then in some sort she exists, he thinks, and advancing down the path with his eyes upon sky and branches he rapidly endows them with womanhood; sees with amazement how grave they become; how majestically, as the breeze stirs them, they *dispense* with a dark flutter of the leaves *charity, comprehension, absolution* . . .
>
> . . . .
>
> and myriads of things merged in one thing; and this figure made of sky and branches as it is, had risen from the troubled sea . . . as a shape might be sucked up out of the waves *to shower down from her magnificent hands compassion, comprehension, absolution*. So, he thinks, . . . let me walk straight on to this great figure, who will, with a toss of her head, mount me on her streamers and let me blow to nothingness with the rest. (85–87, emphasis added)

The "reign of the feminine lawgiver" establishes charity, compassion, comprehension, and absolution in place of judgment, separation, and conversion. Whereas Bradshaw's myth secures masculine authority, the

feminine lawgiver challenges the sexual politics of dichotomy and the tyranny of normalcy upon which that authority rests. Her "law" is the law of
communication.[21]

Connecting Caves

What authority does Clarissa answer to? Unquestionably a snob, Clarissa
naturally invites prime ministers and the likes of the Bradshaws to her parties, yet she is not a thrall to their laws.[22] Unlike Mrs. Bradshaw, who is
thoroughly subjected to the Bradshaw law ("fifteen years ago she had
gone under" [152]), Mrs. Dalloway gives parties where the unexpected
may still occur. The sense of risk and possibility breathes life into Clarissa's
gatherings, for *if* the party worked, "it was possible to say things you
couldn't say anyhow else, things that needed an effort; possible to go
much deeper" (259–260). In contrast with the rising, opening, merging
movement of Clarissa's parties (and Clarissa standing there at the top of
the stairs, able to pull it all off, "to combine, to create" [185], to sum it
all up), dinners at the Bradshaws' (where the hostess "cramped, squeezed,
pared, pruned, drew back, peeped through") tended to produce a dis-
agreeable "pressure on the top of the head" (152).
    Clarissa's own view of Sir William is unequivocal:

> A man absolutely at the head of his profession, very powerful, rather worn. . . .
> One wouldn't like Sir William to see one unhappy. No; not that man. (278)

> A great doctor yet to her obscurely evil, without sex or lust, extremely polite to
> women, but capable of some indescribable outrage—forcing your soul. . . .
> (281)

Clarissa is immediately and personally concerned with the difference between conversion and communication, a difference that is summed up for
her in the contrast between her daughter's teacher, Doris Kilman, and
"the old lady opposite climbing upstairs":

> Let her climb upstairs if she wanted to; let her stop; then let her, as Clarissa had
> often seen her, gain her bedroom. . . . Somehow one respected that—that old
> woman looking out of the window, quite unconscious that she was being
> watched. There was something solemn in it—but love and religion would de-
> stroy that, whatever it was, the privacy of the soul. The odious Kilman would
> destroy it. (191–192)

Reading this old woman as "the most imposing avatar of [the] female lawgiver," DiBattista emphasizes the distinction between Bradshaw's imperative "must" and Clarissa's "authoritative yet self-absenting word, 'let.'"

As she notes, "Clarissa's party preserves the principle of voluntary, unenforced participation."[23] Clarissa's connection to Septimus as an instance of this principle is evident in the way in which she understands and interprets his suicide. For she never met Septimus Warren Smith; she knows him only *as his death*, yet "death was an attempt to communicate" (280). Like Septimus, Clarissa is aware of the many obstacles to communication. Just as there is no one to receive Septimus's "confession," so, too, Clarissa's parties are "an offering; to combine, to create; but to whom?" (185).

There seems, furthermore, to be a particular difficulty in completing communication between men and women. Though Clarissa and Peter "had always had this queer power of communicating without words" (90), "[going] in and out of each other's minds without any effort" (94), there is still some barrier: "What's your love? she might say to him. And she knew his answer; how it is the most important thing in the world and no woman possibly understood it. Very well. But could any man understand what she meant either? about life?" (184).

In addition to the impossibility of ever communicating *enough*, however, one must paradoxically reckon with the danger of communicating too much. In marriage such communication can come frighteningly close to conversion (Lady Bradshaw serves as a prime example), threatening to rob one of "one's independence, one's self-respect—something, after all, priceless" (181). Clarissa recognizes that "in marriage a little licence, a little independence there must be between people living together" (10). The alternative is too complete a marriage, such as she would have had with Peter: "But with Peter everything had to be shared; everything gone into. And it was intolerable" (10). Intersubjective intimacy is of course desirable, and to some extent even *necessary*.[24] Despite the risk to the self of annihilation, the business of combining and creating, of bringing together disparate elements, matters very deeply to Clarissa.[25] Yet for her it is not a question of choice but of continuum. Peter Walsh and Richard Dalloway do not, after all, really represent polar opposites. Excessive intimacy with Peter is tempered not only by Clarissa's restraint (marrying Dalloway, hiding her dress "like a virgin protecting chastity, respecting privacy" [59]), but as much by Peter himself (who appreciated "the triumphs of civilisation" and knew sentiment to be "fatal to art, fatal to friendship" [229]). Similarly, while, in her marriage to Dalloway, Clarissa tempers her retreat to the attic room by her sense that "quite often if Richard had not been there reading the *Times*, . . . she must have perished" (281–282), it is equally true that Richard himself, "eager . . . to travel [the] spider's thread of attachment between himself and Clarissa" (173–174), gently invades her privacy. For after Lady Bruton's luncheon Richard goes hurrying home carrying roses for Clarissa, and before he returns to his committees at the House of Commons he fetches her a pillow and quilt and settles her down for a rest—not in the narrow attic bed, but on the sofa in the drawing room.

Clarissa is described variously as lacking "something central which permeated" (46) and as composing "for the world only into one centre" (55). Decentered and centering, she assumes no fixed stance; rather she moves organically, expanding and contracting, like breathing, like waves, describing a pendular arc between communion (for she needs people and things to complete her) and the privacy of the soul. Representing this communion as "the collective mental experience of the individual human beings in the story," J. Hillis Miller notes that "deep down the general mind and the individual mind become one." Confirmation for this notion is found in Woolf's own theory of the "tunnelling process," the method that she describes using in the creation of *Mrs. Dalloway*. Woolf's imagery is striking: "[digging] out beautiful caves behind [the] characters. . . . The idea is that the caves shall connect."[26] Significantly, Woolf elsewhere offers an equally compelling description of the individual's essential separateness and of the soul's need for privacy. Instead of the "collective" landscape of connecting caves, she paints a picture of isolated and private interior worlds:

> We do not know our own souls, let alone the souls of others. Human beings do not go hand in hand the whole stretch of the way. There is a virgin forest in each; a snowfield where even the print of birds' feet is unknown. Here we go alone, and like it better so. Always to have sympathy, always to be accompanied, always to be understood would be intolerable.[27]

The "dialectic of communion and individuation"[28] suggested by these two strong images may also be said to find expression in the crowning image of *Mrs. Dalloway*: the party. "All was for the party." Clarissa's parties might seem (as Peter Walsh hints, though neither he nor Sally Seton can stay away) to represent passionless conventionality, artificiality, empty social intercourse, the worst of the English class system, yet for Clarissa they offer not only an alternative to the suffocating passions of intimacy, but just as significantly the very opposite of her retreat from passion, which she envisioned as going "slowly upstairs, with her hand on the bannisters, as if she had left a party" (45).

Criminal Circumstances

Septimus, as Clarissa's double, may be the sacrificial repository of transgressive behavior. Yet, as both are shown resisting Bradshaw's "law of conversion," one can read backward through Septimus to find Clarissa as well in potentially "criminal" circumstances.

Clarissa commits her own versions of Septimus's crimes. His suicidal tendencies have a counterpart in her retreat to the narrow, coffinlike bed. He refuses paternity; she, decidedly unmaternal, is unable to "dispel a virginity preserved through childbirth" (46). He is described as having failed Lucrezia; she as having failed Richard. His homoerotic attachment to Evans is doubled by her feelings for Sally. Finally, his lack of feeling might have a counterpart in what Peter Walsh termed in Clarissa "the death of the soul" (89).

The textual connections between Septimus and Clarissa are many and well-documented. Both are described in terms of the plunging and rising metaphors so well analyzed by J. Hillis Miller. One cannot help but feel, for instance, the resonances of Clarissa's meditation on death—

> on the ebb and flow of things, here, there, she survived . . . she being part, she was positive, of the trees at home . . . being laid out like a mist between the people she knew best, who lifted her on their branches as she had seen the trees lift the mist . . . (12)

—in Septimus's excited realization that

> leaves were alive; trees were alive. And the leaves being connected by millions of fibres with his own body, there on the seat, fanned it up and down; when the branch stretched he, too, made that statement. . . . All taken together meant the birth of a new religion. (32–33)

Septimus and Clarissa are joined by metonymic movements of the text (the most striking of which is probably the "Fear no more" verse from *Cymbeline* that passes from Clarissa's to Septimus's mind [211]) and by formal symmetries—for instance, the parallel of the old man coming down the staircase opposite when Septimus flings himself from the window and the old woman going to bed in the room opposite when Clarissa withdraws from her party to think about Septimus's suicide. They share a preoccupation with death and a belief in the ultimate inevitability of solitude. They also share a dilemma: how to reconcile the private with the public and death with life.

Béatrice Didier, reading Virginia Woolf's autobiographical writings in *Moments of Being* where the act of looking in the mirror is associated for the young Virginia with guilt, notes that "autobiographical" mirroring may prove an especially complicated undertaking for women, often involving a frightening confrontation with an identity that bears "a burden of ancestral guilt."[29] Some of the guilt associated with mirroring may derive from the fact that women are often expected to react and reflect, to be *men*'s mirrors, focusing on them, framing them, putting them in the best possible light. A woman regarding *herself* is somehow improper: "The mirror is forbidden to—and coveted by—the woman, because, if she saw herself reflected in it, she would become aware of her totality and would cease to be a body in pieces."[30] Thus, what a man reflects back to a woman of herself may be pointedly diminishing. Clarissa Dalloway experienced something of this with Peter Walsh: "He made her see herself; exaggerate. It was idiotic. But why did he come, then, merely to criticise? Why always take, never give? Why not risk one's one little point of view?" (255). What Peter Walsh reflects back to Clarissa is his judgment of her, inasmuch as she, in her own assumption of guilt, recognizes and locates truth in that mirror, and bestows on it the power to judge. Septimus Smith is therefore perhaps a truer mirror, for Clarissa sees herself *in* him without ever being seen *by* him. Clarissa acknowledges recognizing herself there ("She felt somehow very like him—the young man who had killed himself" [283]), and she to some extent assumes Septimus's guilt: "Somehow it was her disaster—her disgrace. . . . She had schemed; she had pilfered. She was never wholly admirable" (282). Note, however, that the language Clarissa uses here expresses more shame than guilt. She feels "disgrace" and that she is not "wholly admirable"; she is concerned above all with how others might view her or how her actions might reflect upon her.[31] Thus she may recognize and identify with the "disgrace" and the "disaster" without assuming "guilt" for a "crime," and indeed, in the end, there seems to be no question of guilt: "She felt glad that he had done it; thrown it away. . . . He made her feel the beauty; made her feel the fun" (283–284). Through the mirroring, Clarissa is able to arrive at a place of acceptance, exculpation, absolution.

Clarissa's absolution is not in reaction to or in contrast with Septimus's suicide; it is rather a natural extension of his act. His plunging and her soaring are intimately connected mirror images in a shifting pattern that describes the pulse, the respiration of the novel. As waves and hours gather until they are too full, then empty to begin again, as past meets future, as crests and troughs are joined in an instant, so death communicates: Clarissa is filled with the beauty of life precisely as and because Septimus throws it away. It is their *moment*.[32]

Of course, the violence and madness that contributed to force consciousness to the extreme where there could be such a moment are not unprecedented in Clarissa's experience. Clarissa may be proper and decorous, but she is not dispassionate. On the day of the party the detestable Miss Kilman excites what are probably Clarissa's strongest and most sustained excesses of emotion. Furthermore, the hatred that she feels for her daughter's teacher is monstrously satisfying: "Kilman her enemy. That was satisfying; that was real. Ah, how she hated her—hot, hypocritical, corrupt; with all that power; Elizabeth's seducer; the woman who had

crept in to steal and defile. . . . She hated her: she loved her. It was ene-
mies one wanted, not friends" (265–266). The pull of hatred can be just
as strong as that of love, but it is an attraction that opposes intimacy and
thus perpetuates the pendular movement between the individual and the
universal. Secured by age, by choice, by propriety from the excess passions
of her past, Clarissa could for a while subsist on "what other people felt";
but the "semblances," the "triumphs" begin to have a "hollowness"—she
needs to engage with the enemy. She needs passionately to hate passion—
for the struggle of passion *is* the struggle of communion with the precious
privacy of the soul. Indeed, it is what Clarissa learns from "hating" Doris
Kilman that she relearns from Septimus's death—for death also is the desired enemy and the enemy of desire. The attraction of death repeats the
pendulum swing: "Death was an attempt to communicate; people feeling
the impossibility of reaching the centre which, mystically, evaded them;
closeness drew apart, rapture faded, one was alone. *There was an embrace
in death* (280–281, emphasis added). "Closeness drew apart" and "there
was an embrace in death" describe a "natural" law of human intercourse
whereby feeling and not feeling coexist, constantly and inevitably attract-
ing and repelling. The movement is life, though at the extremes are madness and death.

The pendular nature of this "law" of course affects the nature of
"crime" as well. All of the mad and illegal acts in *Mrs. Dalloway* cut
through areas of the "law" where they are emptied of their culpability.
Suicide is both failure and triumph, the final mad act and the ultimate sane
one. Refusing to procreate, on the one hand an abdication of one's social
duty, may appear in a different light when considered alongside those
models of paternity, the patresfamilias Bradshaw and Holmes, not to mention narrow-minded old Justin Parry (in some obscure way responsible for
his daughter Sylvia's death). In similar fashion, the "perversion" of homo-
sexuality is, by a twist, idealized in the novel when compared with the
many failed or oppressive "marriages" that are portrayed.

Septimus vacillates between guilt and innocence (moving between
fields of self-accusation and self-glorification, between crime and "no
crime; love" [102]). "But if he confessed? If he communicated?" (148).
Though Septimus uses the words almost interchangeably, the difference
between confession and communication is, as Garrett Stewart points out,
capital: "Septimus cannot in his desired sense really confess, he can only
begin communicating."[33] Indeed, it is not his confession (of) which
Clarissa hears when she learns of his suicide; for her, his death rather enacts that communication. Just as Septimus, in dying, was able to reflect
back to Clarissa an image that absolved her, so Clarissa, in the way in
which she receives Septimus's death, exculpates *him*.

Mad Scenes

> Rebecca West . . . defined genius as "the abnor-
> mal justifying itself"; "those who know that
> they are for whatever reason condemned by the
> laws of life . . . make themselves one with life by
> some magnificent act of creation."[34]

Confession, communication—but Septimus produces something else as
well. His visions, his ravings, his delusions and revelations are not only the
language of madness, they are also the language of beauty and of witnessing: the language of poetry. Septimus's role as witness comes through
clearly in his image of himself as knower ("He knew the meaning of the
world" [100]) and interpreter: "He lay back in his chair, exhausted but
upheld. He lay resting, waiting, before he again interpreted, with effort,
with agony, to mankind. He lay very high, on the back of the world"
(103). Bearing witness to the connections underlying "normal" appear-
ances, for "scientifically speaking, the flesh was melted off the world"
(102), Septimus uncovered truths both terrifying (dogs will become men)
and wonderful (music is visible). Claiming the authority that only death
can bring to witnessing ("I went under the sea. I have been dead, and yet
am now alive" [104]), he would speak of that which had the power to
move people and the world: "he muttered, gasping, trembling, painfully
drawing out these profound truths which needed, so deep were they, so
difficult, an immense effort to speak out, but the world was entirely
changed by them for ever" (102). He *would* speak, but the difficulty was
immense, and most of the "poetry" (the beauty that "sprang instantly"
[104]), which as readers we are tempted to associate with Septimus, may
never in fact have passed his lips.

The "immortal Ode to Time" is described as a song of revelation: "The
word 'time' split its husk; poured its riches over him; and from his lips fell
like shells, like shavings from a plane, without his making them, hard,
white, imperishable words, and flew to attach themselves to their places in
an ode to Time; an immortal ode to Time. He sang" (105). Yet the music,
the poetry, the beauty (though, or perhaps because, they fall from the lips
of the "poet," "without his making them") are not communicated. Rezia
hears mad, insignificant nonsense ("He was talking, he was starting, this
man must notice him" [106]), and it is paradoxically only through Virginia Woolf's *own* language and voice communicating Septimus's
thoughts that the poetry (*Septimus's* poetry) is *realized*.

Virginia Woolf had great difficulty anticipating the writing of the "mad
scenes" in *Mrs. Dalloway*: "Of course the mad part tries me so much,

makes my mind squint so badly that I can hardly face spending the next weeks at it."[35] That she succeeded so brilliantly attests to the fact that she was capable of that "magnificent act of creation" by which "the abnormal" could "justify itself." For to write Septimus's madness was at least in part to assume it. Further, Virginia Woolf unquestionably drew from her own experiences with "illness" in order to "create" Septimus. Yet Virginia Woolf "ill" and Virginia Woolf "writing Septimus's illness," though adjacent entities, nevertheless occupy essentially and significantly distinct spaces.

E. M. Forster wrote of *Mrs. Dalloway* that it was "a civilised book," adding that "in her work, as in her private problems, [Woolf] was always civilised and sane on the subject of madness."[36] Of course, Woolf, who could be so lucid "*on the subject of* madness," when she was *herself the subject of* madness did not feel herself fit company for the rest of the human race. Maria DiBattista has written that madness and sanity are always adjacent but "*never identical* . . . aspects of the same reality."[37] As a writer, Virginia Woolf walked along this line of demarcation, and when she crossed the line, she no longer wrote.

Michel Foucault has also articulated the discrete proximity of madness and art: "There is no madness except as the final instant of the work of art—the work endlessly drives madness to its limits; *where there is a work of art, there is no madness*, and yet madness is contemporary with the work of art, since it inaugurates the time of its truth."[38]

Virginia Woolf, writing *Mrs. Dalloway*, is "driv[ing] madness to its limits," walking the line, forcing the borders—snatching poetry from the jaws of silence and annihilation, challenging madness with genius and thus at least temporarily rewriting what Rebecca West called the "laws of life."

Meaning and Mattering

> Transgression is an action which involves the
> limit, that narrow zone of a line where it dis-
> plays the flash of its passage, but perhaps also its
> entire trajectory, even its origin; it is likely that
> transgression has its entire space in the line it
> crosses.[39]

The limit contains its own transgression. The border defines the fugitive. As Foucault puts it, "The limit and transgression depend on each other for whatever density of being they possess: a limit could not exist if it were absolutely uncrossable and, reciprocally, transgression would be pointless if it merely crossed a limit composed of illusions and shadows."[40]

Not only do the "police" in *Mrs. Dalloway* help to set the limits that in turn establish the existence of transgression; the limits also assert themselves directly through the very form and substance of the novel. Both DiBattista and Stewart have remarked that Septimus is referred to in the novel as a "border case." Capable of inspiring widely divergent diagnoses, "limning in his demented insight the thin line between psychosis and Orphic power,"[41] Septimus is both literally and figuratively at the very limit of his own existence. He is at the margin with death: "the dead were with him" (140). And it is here, in the shadow of death, that revelation, art, and life take place. The sense of anticipation, the awareness that something momentous is about to happen, temporally situates the novel on the brink of its own achievement, just as Septimus "sat on the sill" determined to "wait till the very last moment" (226) before flinging himself onto Mrs. Filmer's railings—just as Clarissa, bidding her guests goodnight, appeared to Peter Walsh: "as if she wished the whole world well, and must now, *being on the very verge and rim of things*, take her leave" (265, emphasis added). Thus, the entire day of *Mrs. Dalloway* is a "border case" with the threatened "transgression" being both retreat and embrace, plunge into death and brush with life.

Septimus, who "did not want to die" (226), and Clarissa, who had always felt that "it was very, very dangerous to live even one day" (11), help to define a life/death border in the novel. Not only does each of them privately negotiate that line, the line itself is also traced between them, he who dies and she who survives. For even as Septimus doubles Clarissa, he opposes her; and the matter of death permeates this opposition.

Septimus, epitomizing the antisocial in his self-absorption, "knew the meaning of the world" (100), while Clarissa, who like Lucrezia could not help caring "what people think," "knew nothing; no language, no history. . . . Her only gift was knowing people" (11). Septimus, in his knowledge, communes with the dead; Clarissa, without pretending to "know the meaning," is rooted in a world of "real things": flowers, gloves, shoes, parties.

Certain women in Virginia Woolf's novels exhibit a special relationship with the seemingly accessory "things" of women's everyday existence. Clarissa recalling her Uncle William's assertion that "a lady is known by her shoes and her gloves" (15) and Lucrezia insisting that "it is the hat that matters most" (132) both allow these trappings suggestive of female vanity and shallowness to signify far beyond their ability to embellish and alter surfaces. Clarissa Dalloway's parties continue the metaphor. Clarissa is not made "thinner" by association with these apparently superficial preoccupations; rather the party is fleshed out and given weight by her. Though Peter and Richard might scoff and think her parties snobbish or foolish (183), Clarissa "did think it mattered, her party" (255). The artificiality ("every one was unreal in one way") was only part of the story (for every one was "much more real in another" [259]). In the end, the weight of the shoe or the hat or the party was the weight of *mattering*—of being matter—of being "real."

Septimus has a hard time with "real things." Dr. Holmes insists that he must be made "to notice" them. Yet it is not inattention but fear that holds him back: "He began, very cautiously, to open his eyes, to see whether a gramophone was really there. But real things—real things were too exciting. He must be cautious. He would not go mad" (215). He actually does succeed in crossing, temporarily, from his place of "miracles, revelations, agonies, loneliness, falling through the sea, down, down into the flames" (216) to the very real place and business of trimming Mrs. Peters's hat: "It was wonderful. Never had he done anything which made him feel so proud. It was so real, it was so substantial, Mrs. Peters' hat" (218). But for Septimus this "reality" inevitably entails its opposite, its loss—and the subsequent aloneness and death. He is plunged back into the abyss.

For Clarissa, too, the question of mattering extends beyond "things"— extends indeed into death. Walking toward Bond Street, she asked herself: "Did it matter that she must inevitably cease completely; all this must go on without her; did she resent it; or did it not become consoling to believe that death ended absolutely? but that . . . on the ebb and flow of things, here, there, she survived" (12).

Clarissa's reflections on Septimus's death are also concerned with the relationship of death to mattering: "A thing there was that mattered; a thing, wreathed about with chatter, defaced, obscured in her own life, let drop every day in corruption, lies, chatter. This he had preserved. Death was defiance" (280). The question of mattering extends for Clarissa beyond the real things of the world into the living of them *in the face of and through death*. Clarissa is as caught up between the real and death as Septimus is. It is on this border that she and he "communicate." Death, in some ways the ultimate expression of unreality, nevertheless makes *things* (as Mrs. Dalloway's parties made people) not only unreal but at the same time "much more real." If living and mattering coextend, it is *in the place of death*.

> There must be a reality which is not human beings at all. What about death for instance? But what is death? Strange if that were the reality—but in what sense could this be so?

ON AUGUST 2, 1923, Virginia Woolf wrote the above words in her notes for *Mrs. Dalloway*. She had already noted, nine months earlier, "Suppose the idea of the book is the contrast between life and death."[42] Describing

Woolf's treatment of life and death as "looking-glass counterparts," Miller suggests that *Mrs. Dalloway* seems to end in their "confrontation" and that "reality, authenticity, and completion are on the death side of the mirror, while life is at best the illusory, insubstantial, and fragmentary image of that dark reality." Miller notes, however, what Woolf clearly knew only too well: "Death is incompatible with language, but by talking about life, one can talk indirectly about death." The very nature of language puts death on the scene. "Words . . . designate not the material presence of the things named but their absence from the everyday world and their existence within . . . the space and time of literature," says Miller. "A novel, for Woolf, is the place of death made visible. Writing is the only action which exists simultaneously . . . within death and within life at once."[43]

It is in this sense that death communicates, both within and as the novel. Septimus's death, defiant, incomprehensible, throwing "it" away and therefore demanding no return, is able freely to communicate to Clarissa; and what it communicates, what she understands, is "a thing there was that mattered" (280).

Rezia also understands something from Septimus's act: "Rezia ran to the window, she saw; she understood" (226–227). Like Clarissa who first asked herself not why Septimus had done it but how ("He had killed himself—but how? Always her body went through it first. . . . He had thrown himself from a window. Up had flashed the ground" [280]), Rezia also needs to enter into and experience Septimus's death, as narration, in order to "understand" it. Drifting into sleep and memory, she comes to know his death in her own narrated terms:

> In London too, there they sat, and, half dreaming, came to her through the bedroom door, rain falling, whisperings, stirrings among dry corn, the caress of the sea, as it seemed to her, hollowing them in its arched shell and murmuring to her laid on shore, *strewn she felt, like flying flowers over some tomb.*
> "He is dead," she said, smiling. (228, emphasis added)

In contrast, Holmes and Bradshaw read and tell and understand nothing. Dr. Holmes, mainly concerned with judgment and justification, cries, "The coward!" as Septimus leaps from the window; but "who could have foretold it?" (227). Holmes cannot figure out "why the devil he did it": the act was inexplicable, the result of "a sudden impulse" (227). What Holmes reads as senseless and arbitrary, Bradshaw interprets as strictly motivated and easily explicable. The pat postmortem diagnosis that he utters at the Dalloway party refers to "the deferred effects of shell shock" (279). Both Holmes and Bradshaw are concerned with what Septimus's suicide *means*, and therefore, though they come up with different answers, neither of them understands.

The distinction here is between significance that is meaning and significance that is mattering. If we compare two questions, what does it mean to me? and does it matter to me? we find that while mattering is a direct relationship between me and an object, meaning requires a third term (*what* it means) and thus implies representation (as compared with the significant *presentation* that mattering enacts). Septimus is tortured by the problem of meaning, vacillating between feeling that "he knew the meaning of the world" (100) and fearing that "the world itself is without meaning" (133). Clarissa and Lucrezia place a much greater value on mattering ("it mattered, her party"; "the hat . . . matters most" [132]), knowing that mattering is significant and that one *can communicate* mattering without being able to explain "what it means."

In similar fashion, Peter Walsh is constantly running up against the impossibility of deciphering Clarissa's "meaning." He refers to her "impenetrability" (91), to the fact that he is still "after thirty years, trying to explain her" (115), to come up with a theory "to account for her" (117). And yet, in the final scene, Clarissa does not communicate anything to Peter—rather, in her very essence, she communicates *herself*, she *matters*:

> What is this terror? What is this ecstasy? he thought to himself. What is it that fills me with extraordinary excitement?
>
> It is Clarissa, he said.
>
> For there she was. (296)

Yet meaning and mattering are not wholly unrelated. For Clarissa, mattering is meaning *on the verge* of realizing itself. The "moment," which for Clarissa, as for Virginia Woolf, is a privileged instance of power and significance, is at one point described in relation to Clarissa's feelings when "yielding to the charm of a woman . . . confessing":

> It was a sudden revelation, a tinge like a blush which one tried to check and then, as it spread, one yielded to its expansion, and *rushed to the farthest verge* and there quivered and felt the world come closer, swollen with some astonishing significance, some pressure of rapture. . . . Then, for that moment, she had seen an illumination; a match burning in a crocus; *an inner meaning almost expressed*. But the close withdrew; the hard softened. It was over—the moment. (47, emphasis added)

The "match burning in a crocus," the pregnancy of *almost divulged meaning*, is what constitutes the moment, a moment that *matters* precisely because it cannot last. Woolf is here once again attesting to the powerful attraction of the border, the verge, the margin that stands in privileged relationship to the real and mattering.

There are, of course, different ways of marking these borders and different ways of mattering. The marking of the hours that Woolf uses in part to structure *Mrs. Dalloway* provides a good illustration of these differences. "Shredding and slicing, dividing and subdividing, the clocks of Harley Street nibbled at the June day, counselled submission, upheld authority, and pointed out in chorus the supreme advantages of a sense of proportion" (154).[44] These are clearly "Bradshaw" clocks, marking off each irrevocable hour in the just march of time with measure and cold precision. These are the clocks of "laying down the law" and keeping order in the city. Their "policing" role is most clearly evident when they are compared with the alternative, the "other clock . . . which always struck two minutes after Big Ben" (193):

> Volubly, troublously, the late clock sounded, coming in on the wake of Big Ben, with its lap full of trifles. Beaten up, broken up by the assault of carriages, the brutality of vans, the eager advance of myriads of angular men, of flaunting women, the domes and spires of offices and hospitals, the last relics of this lap full of odds and ends seemed to break, like the spray of an exhausted wave, upon the body of Miss Kilman standing still in the street for a moment to mutter "It is the flesh." (194)

The violence and frightening disorder of this image that contains in telegraphic form both female sexuality ("flaunting women") and illness ("hospitals"), and that describes both a city and a body out of control and abandoned to the ravages of passions, emblematizes the threat of disproportion and lawlessness to Sir William's ordered and civilized world. The border laid down by Big Ben and transgressed by the late clock describes correctness and exactitude according to the "Greenwich mean." On this border propriety demands a heartless concern with *matter* (not "mattering"). Minutes and seconds, the precise units of "slicing" and "subdividing," keep things in line. The "late clock," whose "flooding and lapping and dancing" are somehow messy and irresponsible, tends to obscure the definition of the border. Yet it is not offered as the only alternative to the police state. One need not necessarily choose between stifling order and reckless disorder: a border may be retained as a sign of *access* rather than of *limitation*. There is another clock in London that marks time's passing:

> Ah, said St. Margaret's, like a hostess who comes into her drawing-room on the very stroke of the hour and finds her guests there already. I am not late. No, it is precisely half-past eleven, she says. Yet, though she is perfectly right, her voice, being the voice of the hostess, is reluctant to inflict its individuality. Some grief for the past holds it back; some concern for the present. It is half-past eleven, she says, and the sound of St. Margaret's glides into the recesses of the heart and buries itself in ring after ring of sound, like something alive which wants to confide itself, to disperse itself, to be, with a tremor of delight, at rest—like Clarissa herself, thought Peter Walsh, coming down the stairs on the stroke of the hour in white. It is Clarissa herself, he thought, with a deep emotion. (74)

The bells of St. Margaret's do not flaunt their difference. It is not a question of opposing and breaking the Bradshaw law, for St. Margaret's is "perfectly right"—proprieties and temporal precision are respected. It is rather a question of *style*. Maria DiBattista has located a "complex pattern-ing" in Woolf's novel whereby "between the woof of time the preserver and the warp of time the destroyer is woven—the self" (32 and 33). Inas-much as, in DiBattista's formula, opposing tendencies combine to pro-duce a cohesive, complexly patterned fabric able to declare itself, might not this metaphor also suggest Woolf's vision of the artist's necessary an-drogyny? Without directly challenging the (male) law and "reluctant to inflict" her (female) individuality, St. Margaret's style nevertheless stands in marked contrast to that of Big Ben, for her sound (wanting not to im-pose but to "*confide* itself, to *disperse* itself") glides modestly but trium-phantly right to the heart of the matter. St. Margaret's "style," while man-ifestly that of the self-assured but unassuming hostess, is also, as Miller has pointed out, that of *Mrs. Dalloway*'s narrator: "the narrator possesses the irresistible and subtle energy of the bell of St. Margaret's striking half past eleven. Like that sound, the narrator 'glides into the recesses of the heart and buries itself.'"[45]

Yet as we follow Peter Walsh's thoughts, we learn that of course *death* is the *heart* of the *matter*:

> It is Clarissa herself, he thought, with a deep emotion, and an extraordinarily clear, yet puzzling, recollection of her, as if this bell had come into the room years ago, where they sat at some moment of great intimacy, and had gone from one to the other and had left, like a bee with honey, laden with the moment. . . . Then, as the sound of St. Margaret's languished, he thought, She has been ill, and the sound expressed languor and suffering. It was her heart, he remem-bered; and the sudden loudness of the final stroke tolled for death that surprised in the midst of life, Clarissa falling where she stood, in her drawing-room. (74–75)

The heart, the body's clock, gathers life's "moments" into itself until (like the waves, like the hours) it must finally empty, "committing its burden to some sea, which sighs collectively for all sorrows, and renews, begins, col-lects, lets fall" (59). In the heart resides the precious mortality of the self, and it is therefore the heart, in *Mrs. Dalloway*, that says to the body not only "That is all," but also "Fear no more" (59). Death is beyond the brain's comprehension, but not the heart's: marking a life/death border, the heart with each beat comprehends both sides. Further, the heart, priv-ileged threshold of life and death, is also and therefore the privileged place of *mattering*. As Sally Seton says of Richard Dalloway at the very end of the novel, "What does the brain matter . . . compared with the heart?" (296). On numerous occasions, the novel clearly shows that the heart *is the matter* and the heart *does matter*. It is no coincidence that Clarissa's weak heart keeps her "at death's door." Both Clarissa and Septimus must push their lives to that limit, not only because "death seems to complete rather than disrupt . . . life,"[46] offering the final "tremor of delight" and then "rest," but also because this border eventually demands the greatest and final trespass that, because it *is* the heart of the matter, must be the price of both life and art.

Post(modern)script _____

D'une langue à l'autre or
Speaking in Other Tongues:
Le désert mauve

A New Generation

In the four novels studied thus far, female characters are implicated in a number of gender-inflected "crimes," incriminated by their desire, their subjectivity, their autonomy, their presumptuousness, their endurance. Each crime has a narrative dimension. In *L'Invitée*, Françoise's criminal passions subtend her "défense légitime"; in *Lol V. Stein*, the female subject is a persistent and inarticulate challenge to Jacques Hold's narration; in *Kamouraska*, Elisabeth incessantly flees her own voice telling the tale of her monstrous survival; in *Mrs. Dalloway*, Clarissa's testament to mattering defines Septimus's trespass and her own border crossings. Furthermore, women in these stories live to tell, and each story tells of that survival. But all four novels also suggest the vicious circularity that incriminates women telling. Caught between the guilty plea and the death sentence, the woman is damned if she lives to tell, and damned if she doesn't.[1]

This is the story that women writers of the post–World War II generation inherited and set out to put into their own generation's terms. A newly articulated feminist consciousness inspired and empowered young writers like Nicole Brossard, deeply immersed in the feminist movements of the 1960s and 1970s, to try to tell the story differently, to try to break the vicious circle.

Brossard's 1987 novel *Le désert mauve* contains many pieces of the incriminating story of "women telling."[2] The text reverberates with women's voices and women's desires, and ends with Angela Parkins's murder witnessed by the young narrator Mélanie. Yet the inexorable logic incriminating "women telling" is somehow incomplete. Whereas in the earlier novels that we studied, it was possible to locate signs of policing and law enforcement, and from these proceed to identify the prohibition and its violation, here the emphasis seems to be on the summary execution. Everything comes down in the end to a man with a gun.

A Man with a Gun

6 décembre 1989
Ecole Polytechnique
Montréal

All things considered, M.L. was no young man. He was as old as all the sexist, misogynist proverbs, as old as all the Church fathers who ever doubted women had a soul. He was as old as all the legislators who ever forbade women the university, the right to vote, access to the public sphere. M.L. was as old as Man and his contempt for women.

As for the women who died, they were young, as young as the gains of feminism. They were even younger than they thought, much too young for a lone man armed with ancient mental equipment. They were as fresh as new life, which springs from the hope of each generation of women.

Nicole Brossard published these words in *La Presse* after the December 6, 1989, massacre of fourteen women students at the University of Montréal's school of engineering.[3]

(He made all the women stand apart. He shouted that they were feminists and that he hated feminists. He yelled at them: "You have no business being here!" He began shooting.)[4]

————————

In the bar, Mélanie Kerouac and Angela Parkins are dancing. Singing, laughing. Suddenly Angela Parkins sinks to the floor, a small black hole in her temple. They never saw it coming. And "at the far end of the room, there is *l'homme long*'s impassive stare."

They never saw it coming. Mélanie, narrating, never saw the man with the gun, though he was there, from the beginning, threading his way toward her through the spaces in her text. At the climax of *Le désert mauve*, in a brutal and calculated act of violence, a woman is gunned down because of who she is, who she *dares* to be.[5]

In a 1991 interview, Nicole Brossard remarked about *Le désert mauve*: "The ending seems very surprising, even gratuitous, but it's exactly what happened at the Ecole polytechnique, it's exactly the same kind of hatred. So I haven't imagined anything, I have only decoded a pattern that does not explode all the time, but is there all the time."[6]

The story within Brossard's novel is about the killing of Angela Parkins, but it is also about the "decoding" of that "pattern." *It is about noticing the man with the gun.* Noticing the man with the gun raises the possibility of shifting the blame off the victim. Noticing the man with the gun raises the possibility of a radical "translation" of the viciously circling story of "guilty women telling."

Plotting the Explosion

Begin with the ending. *La fin de l'histoire*. Apocalypse. Destruction. Angela Parkins dead on the dance floor. The end of the story. The end of history. Precisely and perfectly postmodern.

The term "postmodernism" (itself characteristically "postmodern" in its refusal authoritatively to represent any single reality) has been used in many different contexts to mean many different things.[7] "Postmodern" is frequently used somewhat loosely to refer to many of the strategies and innovations associated with what has often been called in French "la modernité": genre instability, narrative self-reflexivity, the explosion of meaning, the deconstruction of the subject. But in the context of Québec literature, as Sherry Simon quite aptly points out, there is a recent tendency to identify "the formalist *nouvelle écriture* of the early 1970s with modernism, and [to link] the production of the later 1970s and especially the feminist writers (Brossard, Théoret, Bersianik) with postmodernism."[8]

It is not possible, however, to define the postmodern simply and exclusively in terms of an intersection between a certain modernity and a feminist consciousness; it is a concept that already has currency within contemporary cultural and literary discourses, a concept that already has other political associations. In a transcribed conversation on the subject of "la post-modernité" among six Québec feminist writers in the journal *Tessera*, a number of those writers to whom the category of postmodernism as "modernity with a feminist twist" could naturally be applied quite vehemently refuse the label, evidently drawing a clear distinction between feminist versions of "modernité" and *something else* that they feel is implied by "la post-modernité." From their discussion, it emerges that this "something else" has at least in part to do with the relationship between the writing project and history.[9] The postmodern under discussion among these six women may share many of the strategies and qualities that characterized modernity, but in its grounding in a consciousness and inscription of History radically contested, it is one step removed from that project. The question, as Gail Scott puts it, is then whether that crucial step is a "faux pas" or a "step beyond [un pas au-delà]."[10] Does "la fin de l'histoire" (the apocalyptic postmodern catchphrase around which much of the discussion seems to circulate) inscribe cataclysm, closure, and despair, or might it paradoxically suggest a different kind of overture?

One's answer to these questions will of course depend largely upon one's angle of interpretation. While some might define "la post-moder-nité" in terms of the limitations imposed by its regressive perspective, there are other theorists of postmodernism who insist upon the expansive potential of the radical break that it figures. Janet Paterson, for instance, has written that the rupture which characterizes the postmodern "estab-lishes the order of plurality, fragmentation, overture," and that "what ani-mates the postmodern spirit is not lassitude and certainly not a death drive but rather a liberating force."[11] Such an interpretation of the postmodern might help to explain why, as Catharine Stimpson put it, "many of the most spacious, provocative, interesting contemporary critics would no more isolate feminism from postmodernism than they would isolate figure from ground, figure of speech from conversation."[12] Indeed, Louise Dupré suggests that "it is in fact to the end of history/the end of the story that feminism invites us, [for feminism is] a thought outside of the patri-archy situating itself in a posthistoric consciousness." She argues that in bringing a feminist perspective to "the end of History," and "without closing its eyes to the nuclear threat, feminism allows us to envisage 'la fin de l'histoire' beyond the catastrophe, to associate *postmodernism with possibility.*"[13]

It is in the light of a feminist/postmodern "coalition" (to borrow Stimpson's term) that I propose to look at what is happening on the level of narrative in *Le désert mauve*.[14] With references to an explosion and to the death of Angela Parkins, Brossard does inscribe a devastating "fin de l'histoire" in *Le désert mauve*—but is this the end of it? The novel is com-posed of three parts: "Mauve Desert," Laure Angstelle's text of which Mélanie is narrator; "A Book to Translate," in which translator Maude Laures reads and prepares to translate Angstelle's book; and "Mauve, the Horizon," Maude Laures's translation of Laure Angstelle's "Mauve De-sert." In other words, even as *Le désert mauve* comes to its inevitable and apocalyptic climax with the killing of Angela Parkins, it at the same time contains and encircles that climax within a story of women narrating, writ-ing, reading, translating. Women's voices rising to meet the explosion.[15]

Patricia Smart has shown that within the master plot of a patriarchal literary and cultural tradition, the woman is frequently inscribed as "an object-woman constructed to serve as reflection and medium through which to express masculine subjectivity."[16] The eruption into writing of that *other* voice and subjectivity—or even the perceived risk of such erup-tion—has frequently been met by a swift and merciless narrative response, a violent plotting against the woman who, as victim in and of *his story*, can tell hers only (and I am here using the terms of Smart's paradigm) as or from the buried place of the cadaver under the edifice of the father's house of writing. There are certainly elements of this plot evident in *Le désert mauve* in the methodically plotted trajectory of *l'homme long* traced to its culmination, the death of Angela Parkins. This old story is, however, not the whole story or even, I would venture to say, the main story here. It is told otherwise, not foregrounded or highlighted, but imbedded and contained within the multidimensional narrative structure of the novel. Smart makes this point in her book's conclusion where she analyzes *Le désert mauve* in terms of the still unresolved struggle between the old story of destruction and what she calls "the transformation toward which women's sensibility strives."[17] What is perhaps most significant about this struggle is its narrative inscription—for it is, in fact, the narrative structure of Laure Angstelle's story that triggers our recognition of the old familiar plot and our anticipation of its inevitable and violent climax. And it is likewise in narrative, through new plottings and scriptings, that the transformation Smart refers to is occurring.

The Gun Is Always Loaded

Even on the most fundamental and seemingly straightforward narrative level there is both assertion and subversion of the old story of destruction. Looking at the first part only—that is, Laure Angstelle's "Mauve Desert"—we can relatively easily identify and follow the plotting of two distinct narrative threads. The details and events of fifteen-year-old Mélanie's first-person narrative are recounted in nine sections (plus one short italicized section of which I will speak later). These nine sections, resembling short untitled chapters, set off by white space and page breaks, alternate with the eight titled chapters of the third-person narrative of *l'homme long*. The juxtaposition and formal interweaving of the two narrative strands emphasize their contrast and their interimplication. The parallel development of the two stories anticipates their intersection, each thread tracing a chronological and spatial approach toward the other. The isolation of each narrative and the contrasts between them (first- and third-person narration, untitled and titled, many female characters and relationships and a lone and solitary male, the open desert and the enclosed motel room) increase the reader's awareness that the moment of impact must, calamitously, arrive. Even before *l'homme long* steps out of his own story and appears at the margin of Mélanie's we know, as readers of narratives, that this is inevitable.

Furthermore, if one's first impression, triggered by the obvious formal and technical differences between the two narrative strands, is that they are indeed distinct and ostensibly not directly engaged with one another, still an awareness of lexical and episodic echoings and parallels both heightens the sense of contrast and suggests that the formal divisions between the two sections are penetrable. There is *already* a confrontation working here, prefiguring the clash of two realities that is the climax in the final section.

By lexical echoings I am referring to the recurrence of key words and phrases within markedly different contexts. For instance, in the opening section Mélanie refers to the "magical power [pouvoir magique]" of her mother's comb. When, in *l'homme long*'s first chapter, we read that he knows the "magic value [valeur magique] of formulas," there is, especially in the French, an intratextual resonance. Similarly, vocabulary from the crucial last sentence of Mélanie's first section infiltrates *l'homme long*'s first chapter. The sentence reads, "I was fifteen and with every ounce of my strength I was leaning into my thoughts [j'*appuyais* sur mes *pensées*] to make them slant reality toward the light [pour qu'elles *penchent* la réalité du côté de la lumière]." In *l'homme long*'s chapter, "he thinks about the explosion [il *pense* à l'explosion]," "he does not bend down [il ne se *penche* pas]," "[he] rests his head on the equation [(il) *appuie* sa tête sur l'équation]." Such free circulation of vocabulary establishes textual echoes that show the formal divisions between the two stories to be permeable.

Just as lexical border crossings are significant to our reading, so episodic parallels also compel the reader to become aware that the juxtaposition itself is telling a story about different narrative economies. The scene in chapter 2 in which *l'homme long* masturbates while looking at photographs in a porno magazine is framed by two sections in which Mélanie's physical pleasure (her *jouissance*) is evoked. In the first section Mélanie comes to embody the violence and splendor of the natural world: "On dry storm nights I would become tremors, detonations, total discharge. Then surrender to all the illuminations, those fissures which like so many wounds lined my virtual body. . . . And so the body melts like a glimmer of light [comme une lueur] in the abstract of words" (20). In the second section her self-pleasuring is associated with play and invention in language: "Crazy gleam of light in my room and my fingers there, that's it, there, yet sways, amuses me, *aways* me" (24). ("Folle lueur dans ma chambre et mes doigts là, c'est ça, là, *yet* vacille, m'amuse, m'*envas*" [26].) The "lueurs" of these two passages are very different from the shadows and exploding white circles associated with the sexual climax of *l'homme long*. His masturbation and orgasm are starkly portrayed as man-made, business as usual, directly connected to the degradation and destruction of women, and by extension, in references to the explosion, to the destruction of the planet:

> The explosion will occur. In the silence of the room the man eyes the genitals, their coloration. He does not see the faces. The faces, shadow of shadows, make white circles around the genitals. Then the circles make a noise like an explo-

sion. He shuts his eyes. Dust falls slowly. . . . *L'homme long* hears the noise of the explosion. Heart leaps, body leaps. [Haut-le-coeur, haut-le-corps.] A final shiver. He strokes his felt hat. He lights a cigarette. (21)

The differences thus figured between *l'homme long*'s climax and Mélanie's *jouissance* lend themselves to a reading of the difference between two kinds of story: a certain traditional narrative and the narration of heretofore untold stories such as are frequently associated with the unfigurable that is women's desire and pleasure. One cannot help being struck by the expansion, abandon, connection, and open-endedness of Mélanie's pleasure (epitomized by the neologism "*m'envas*") as compared with the concentration, self-possession, dispassion, and finality of *l'homme long*'s climax. It is his narrative that inscribes and privileges climax and denouement, necessary closure, "a final shiver" and then the return, diminished, re-composed. If *Le désert mauve* has a climax, it is because of (the presence of) *l'homme long*.

The episodic counterpointing continues: Mélanie writes words in her little notebook and *l'homme long* traces figures (*chiffres*) on the walls full of his shadow. The connection, comprehension, and intimacy (verbal, sensual, sexual) associated with Mélanie's visit with her friend Grazie contrast sharply with *l'homme long*'s "bitter solitude." As the parallels continue, we become more and more aware that what is for Mélanie multiplication and expansion, is always for *l'homme long* reduction and division and fracturing. Indeed, though each is associated with solitude, their solitudes are radically different: Mélanie's is the spacious solitude of the desert ("I was driving, perfect on the edge of solitude" [33]); *l'homme long*'s is the claustrophobic solitude of an anonymous motel room with the curtains drawn.

The climax that comes in the final section is inevitable from the moment we read in the last sentence of *l'homme long*'s last chapter that "he put on his jacket and headed for the Bar." For at the end of the preceding section the narrator Mélanie had announced her intention to finish swimming, take a shower, and go to the bar. These parallel moments of anticipation place *l'homme long* and Mélanie clearly on a collision course. In the last section, echoes and parallels give way to the violent reality of that moment of impact, marked not only episodically, by the appearance of *l'homme long* in Mélanie's story, but also lexically, by the attachment of what can only be considered *his* word, "allongée," to the dying body of Angela Parkins: "At the far end of the room there is *l'homme long*'s impassive stare. The desert is big. Angela Parkins is stretched out, there [allongée, là]."[18]

New Geometries: Angela Parkins

L'homme long's masturbation scene makes obvious the association between the destruction of women and the destruction of the planet. Indeed, the explosion encompasses both. A number of readers have analyzed
the ways in which the explosion described in the text is referentially linked
to the development and testing of the atomic bomb.[19] That there *is* this
reality beyond the walls of *l'homme long*'s room and beyond the textual
boundaries of his chapters is also made very clear.[20] Thus when *l'homme
long* is suddenly there—in the space of Mélanie's narration, at the scene
and on the margin of "the disaster"—his very presence establishes the relationship between Angela Parkins's murder and the explosion of the
bomb. And it is through *this* association that one might say that the old
plot is to the first degree *postmodernized*. The end of the story, the inevitable climax, through this identification can indeed be read to figure the
apocalyptic triumph of the senseless, "la fin de l'histoire."

But this "postmodern" plot is already and continually *decentered* by a
series of what I have chosen to call feminist plots. There is, of course, the
fact, already discussed, that the inevitable linear progression of *l'homme
long*'s story is surrounded by Mélanie's differently figured and transfig-
ured narrative space (his the plotting of a line on a graph; hers the plots
that are spaces, areas of land in three dimensions, like burial plots or garden plots). If *l'homme long*'s plotting is both singular and universal,
Mélanie's is both individual and collective. The universality of *l'homme
long* is implied by his lack of a proper (personal) name and by references
to "the civilization of men who came to the desert to watch their equations explode," but also to "some guys who 'came from far away'" and set
fire to a nearby shack, according to Mélanie's mother. "Only one of them
was armed, she had sworn to me. Only one among them. All the others
were blond" (11).

The third part of the novel extends and makes explicit the anonymous
universality of *l'homme long*, for in Maude Laures's translation he becomes "*l'hom'oblong*." Karen Gould has commented on the echoes of
"l'homme-au-blanc" in this new name—a reference to the photo of his
face figured/transfigured as/by a white explosion.[21] I would add to this
that the echoes of "au blond" recall as well the early reference to the one
man who was armed: "All the others were blond [Tous les autres étaient
blonds]." While Maude Laures's translation has rendered this distinction differently ("all the others had blue eyes"), the "blond" that separated him from them in the original passage has crossed over and very
discreetly attached itself to him, making the one man and all the others

fundamentally indistinguishable. His new name epitomizes this as the word "homme" ("man") disappears into the word "homo" ("hom'o")— meaning same.

By contrast, Mélanie's narrative space is anything but homogenized. It is full of women, different women in complex relationships to one another and in different and complex relationships to language, voice, and story. It is a plural, multidimensional space of lesbian experience and sensibility, a space of many angles and many points of view.

Mélanie's encounters and relationships with her mother, with Lorna, with Grazie, and with Angela Parkins bring into circulation different perspectives on language, intimacy, and solitude. But it is Angela Parkins who becomes the focal point, the target of the assassin's bullet, and who therefore may be read as a key to the novel's feminist plotting.

While *l'homme long* is closed in a room with his calculations, Angela Parkins is (like Mélanie) all over the desert. *L'homme long* is associated with the cold perfection of mathematics: *figures, calculations, formulas, equations*. Angela Parkins is a *géomètre*, a geometer or surveyor. Hers is the mathematics of measuring spaces, measuring the earth. *L'homme long*'s abstractions wreak real destruction on the planet: "The slightest error could have disastrous consequences. . . . the ground beneath his feet turns to jade" (17). Angela Parkins's mathematics is not concerned with equations (reduction, proof, and balance) but with angles and points and lines of view. Note that the essential linearity of *l'homme long* comes through in his name that names one dimension: length.[22] Angela Parkins's name, on the other hand, associates her with angles, with distances (*là*), and with spaces (parks). Further, she is a figure of multiplicities, she is ex-centric and excessive, at the intersections of science and language and desire, at once charting and transgressing the knowable and the speakable.

If Angela brings in all the angles and pushes all the limits, she also achieves and embodies a vision that Mélanie profoundly desires to share: "What did she see, Angela Parkins, when she looked through her theodolite?" (36). As Angela tells Mélanie in the scripted scene in "A Book to Translate," she spends her life watching the horizon in detail. The horizon that is the geometer's point of reference is in a sense the figure that Mélanie is trying to approach.

The very first sentence of the novel made room for this figure in a declaration that has implications for both writing and geometry: "The desert is indescribable." If the desert is indescribable, then no language can contain and confine it. Nor can a geometer trace its outline as one would describe a circle on a sheet of paper, because it has no fixed outline. And yet there *is* the horizon which figures precisely that unfixable boundary in relation to one's vision. For the horizon is a line that is in fact a space between earth and sky—always in the distance but never out of sight. It is "a mirage that orients the thirsting body" (28), the endless end, in space, and in time.

As a horizon is a limit that is forever beyond, it suggests a plotting that continues to outdistance itself. One key element of this plotting is what I call the feminist postscript or post(modern)script. This postscript is not an inconsequentially appended afterthought, but rather the considered appropriation of formerly unused space to write beyond an ending. It is the perspective from which the text is always in the process of crossing its own boundaries, the transgression *in* narrative *of* narrative.[23]

One example of this in *Le désert mauve* is the short italicized passage to which I earlier referred. This passage appears on a separate page between Mélanie's first section and *l'homme long*'s first chapter (15). Not only does this passage break with the formal symmetry of Laure Angstelle's "Mauve Desert," it also breaks with the temporal logic of the narratives in which it is embedded. Beginning "And now [Et maintenant]," it situates the narrator, in the present, already at a moment that is, in fact, to come later, right before the final scene. It is in Mélanie's seventh and eighth sections that this moment is being approached: in the seventh section when a conditional tense is used to inscribe an intentional future in relation to the past tense of the narration ("I had been driving all night. . . . I would stop at that motel" [38]); and in the eighth section, in which Mélanie anticipates the final scene in a move from present tense narration ("Everything is so real around the pool. I have entered the life of my fifteen years like a character. . . . I am up to my neck in reality") to the future tense ("I will go take my shower when the tourists leave for a brief outing into the desert, at that hour of the day when everything is so beautiful. When they return I will be at the bar . . ." [40]). Placed as it is, however, out of order, almost at the beginning of the text, the italicized postscript baffles any reading of the final scene. What is this "maintenant," this "now"? Inasmuch as the conditional and future passages that anticipate it come later, it might seem to leave that anticipation intact, to suggest that the climax—the killing of Angela Parkins—is not necessarily the end, the *point final*. Furthermore, this italicized passage also represents the tantalizing *elision* of an important space suggested only in the conditional of the seventh section: "I would take out my composition book and the pen. All morning, I would write." The importance of this elided space/time of writing is even more clearly articulated in Maude Laures's translated version of the scene: "Then I would take possession of *my* room [*ma* chambre]. I would write all morning." The addition of and stress upon "*my* room" clearly establishes the importance of this episode in juxtaposing Mélanie's story and that of *l'homme long*.

The early italicized postscript points to the later sections that anticipate it, and the three sections together describe, but indirectly (since only in the conditional and through obvious elision), a crucial possibility, another plot, but one that remains virtual: Melanie in her motel room writing all morning.

Trespassers Will Be

In "The Utopia of Language," Roland Barthes suggests that all writing is inevitably both transgression of and exercise of (and within) existing power structures. Noting that "in every present mode of writing [there is] a double postulation: there is the impetus of a break and the impetus of a coming to power [un avènement]," he goes on to declare that "revolution must of necessity borrow, from what it wants to destroy, the very image of what it wants to possess."[24] Maurice Blanchot comes to basically the same conclusion:

> To write then becomes a terrible responsibility. Invisibly, writing is called upon to undo the discourse in which—however unhappy there we might believe ourselves to be—we who make use of it remain, comfortably installed. Seen in this way, writing is the greatest act of violence, for it transgresses the Law, every law, and its own law.[25]

Recognizing and describing the unavoidable and transgressive violence of their literary undertaking, Barthes and Blanchot know that writing is "a terrible responsibility." Yet they seem capable of assuming the role of revolutionary or lawbreaker without reading "responsibility" as "guilt." If writing is transcending borders, transgressing its own law, always endeavoring to speak beyond itself, these writers are apparently not loath to venture forth as explorers or outlaws. The images that they use to describe the realm entered by the outlaw writer (Blanchot's "never-ending discussion [l'entretien infini]" and Barthes's "utopia of language") furthermore seem to stress *boundlessness* rather than lawlessness, to take pleasure in the artist's transcendence rather than to derive anxiety from the criminal's transgression—although Blanchot does seem willing to acknowledge the underlying anxiety: "Transcendence, transgression: names too close to one another not to make us suspicious [pour ne pas nous rendre méfiants]."[26]

The difference for the woman writing is that she is an outlaw even among these outlaws. Her trespass is compounded by her gender for, unlike her male colleague, she has no comfortable claim on the laws she is breaking. When Blanchot refers to "the discourse in which we . . . remain, comfortably installed," he is speaking for an "us" that has traditionally excluded women writers. Women have written a great deal through the years, but they could hardly have described themselves or been described as "comfortably installed." In Elizabeth A. Meese's words, "from the beginning, women have been trespassers in the world's literary communities."[27] With the advent of a feminist consciousness, women writing have begun more and more to see and to describe themselves in such terms, as trespassers and thieves.[28]

Twentieth-century women writers are in general less afraid to appear presumptuous than were their forebears. Many of them are, moreover, supremely aware of the dilemma they face in attempting the activity of breaking and entering when they have themselves long been defined as that which is only meant to be broken and entered. The encouragement that women have begun to give one another then often clearly takes the form of incitement to riot/incitement to write.[29] Virginia Woolf, perhaps the most eloquent rabble-rouser of all, uttered the following supremely civilized call to arms:

> But let us bear in mind a piece of advice that an eminent Victorian who was also an eminent pedestrian once gave to walkers: "Whenever you see a board up with 'Trespassers will be prosecuted,' trespass at once."
>
> Let us trespass at once. Literature is no one's private ground; literature is common ground. It is not cut up into nations; there are no wars there. Let us trespass freely and fearlessly and find our way for ourselves.[30]

Woolf's "us" is clearly not "comfortably installed," yet Woolf does not regard this as an insurmountable obstacle to progress or production. On the contrary, she would have us meet the anxiety of boards and fences with fearless determination, for in this call to trespass, transgression *is* transcendence. The trespasser who proceeds "freely and fearlessly" apparently need feel neither anxiety nor guilt, but may rather experience the pleasures that those who posted "No trespassing" signs had previously claimed as their own exclusive privilege.

There is a certain utopian innocence to Virginia Woolf's belief that one may trespass "freely and fearlessly," ignoring posted laws that one does not accept. Her story recalls to mind the sign on Piglet's house in *Winnie the Pooh* that read:

Trespassers W

In the innocent fantasy world of the children's book, grown-up society's proscription had been reduced (probably by the forces of nature) to a harmless relic. Its original signifying power eroded, it could then be given a new and benign significance with a newly reconstructed *history*: "it was [Piglet's] grandfather's name, and had been in the family for a long time. . . . it was short for Trespassers Will, which was short for Trespassers William."

Adult readers of *Winnie the Pooh*, however, automatically reconstruct and *understand* a different original message: Trespassers Will Be Prosecuted. In fact, as adults, our particular pleasure in reading children's books may derive in large part from just such contrasts between the worlds therein imagined and our own, contrasts frequently inscribed in references meaningful only to the adult reader. Children's literature offers a glimpse of the lost pleasures and freedoms of naive readings. But naïveté once lost can never be completely regained. In fantasy, the law may be disarmed and pieces of it used to rename an innocent world, but when we are no longer children we can no longer *not know* that the full sentence will be pronounced (has already been pronounced in our heads), and that trespassers *will be prosecuted.*

Sentencing

In the stories of "guilty women," one hears many different voices, many different pleas.[31] Nevertheless it does seem, as I suggested in my Prologue, that no matter how the woman pleads, she has already been incriminated: by pleading at all she pleads guilty. What makes this double bind even more binding, however, is the fact that her guilty plea determines and produces her final sentence. One might even go so far as to maintain (as Garrett Stewart by way of Nabokov seems here to be implying) that the (final) sentence is invariably a death sentence:

> What Nabokov sets about to suggest later in his career is that the very discovery of pattern within the process of life's story or text is the uncovering not of life's truth in the act of death but of death's finality in the work of a summarized life. Every "coherent sentence" thus seems gathered from flux into an orderly death sentence of a sort.[32]

In Stewart's discussion of *Mrs. Dalloway,* he had already complicated the idea of the death sentence by showing how Woolf's "phrasing of [Septimus's] fate . . . discomfit[ed] legal terminology," making the sentence the *verdict.*[33] The leap from (guilty) plea to (death) sentence leaves no room for variations in judgment. But to call the sentence "verdict" is at the same time to carry the guilt over into that death. How can the "guilty woman," answering to the *letter of the law,* expect any other sentence?

"Are you ready to be sentenced?" [asked the policeman.]

"Only a judge can sentence you," said Milo, who remembered reading that in one of his schoolbooks.

"Good point," replied the policeman, taking off his cap and putting on a long black robe. "I am also the judge. Now would you like a long or a short sentence?"

"A short one, if you please," said Milo.

> "Good," said the judge. . . . "I always have
> trouble remembering the long ones. How
> about 'I am'? That's the shortest sentence I
> know."
> —Norton Juster, *The Phantom Tollbooth*

> "Let the jury consider their verdict," the King
> said, for about the twentieth time that day.
> "No, no!" said the Queen. "Sentence first—
> verdict afterward."
> —Lewis Carroll, *Alice in Wonderland*

The judge's sentence in *The Phantom Tollbooth* does exactly what "Trespassers W" did: it radically subverts the entire "legal system" by offering a conclusion that is neither guilty verdict nor death sentence, one that in fact precedes and precludes them both. The short sentence "I am" may contain traces of and references to longer sentences ("I am *guilty*" is one longer version that comes to mind), but it is also completely readable on its own. Unlike the sentence "I am guilty," which is a sentence containing a verdict, the short sentence "I am" *precedes* any possible verdict. The pronouncing of this sentence thus speaks *being* but never reaches the conclusion of that being; in other words, it never arrives at the conclusion of either guilt or death. In fact, it makes being its own interminable conclusion.

Such alternative readings of the "guilty woman" on trial may be possible only in Wonderland, through playful manipulations of the language of the law. It might nevertheless be argued that "I am" is the implicit final sentence of every one of the five novels considered in this study. It certainly seems that this short sentence is seeking to affirm itself through the female protagonists' solitary survival at the novels' ends:

Françoise: "She had at last made a choice. *She had chosen herself.*"
Lol: "*Lol had arrived ahead of us.* She was sleeping in the field of rye, worn out, worn out by our trip."
Elisabeth: "Léontine Mélançon (unless it was Agathe or Florida?) murmurs softly. '*Just see how Madame loves Monsieur! See how she is weeping.*'"
Clarissa: "It is Clarissa, he said. *For there she was!*"
Mélanie: "There are memories for digging into words without defiling graves. *I cannot get close to any you.*"

But what is the declarative force of an *implicit* "I am"? Or, to put the question somewhat differently, what is an affirmation of existence without the voice that in affirming it confirms it?

In my first chapter, I argued that Françoise's final self-affirmation was seriously compromised by the author-narrator's policing of the protago-

nist's voice. At the same time, I suggested that the female protagonists in
the other novels, insofar as they exceeded narrators' attempts to speak of
and for them, could be seen as somehow scandalous, and that even without declaring themselves explicitly, they seemed to be challenging the
processes that would incriminate them. Thus Lol sleeping evades Jacques
Hold, Elisabeth weeping is rendered unrecognizable through the irony of
that final *tableau vivant*, and Clarissa, recognized and appreciated by
Peter Walsh, still stands above and beyond him, inarticulable. Yet if one
looks closely at the literal endings of the novels by Beauvoir, Duras,
Hébert, and Woolf, one cannot help noticing the way in which each sur-
viving woman is seen through another person's eyes, described and objectified by another person's voice. The female protagonists' evasions may be
interpreted as subversively undermining textual closure, but the fact remains that at the end of each of these novels the reader is to some extent
left in the (often awkward) company of a narrator who seems determined
to have the last word. Only in *Le désert mauve* is the woman still speaking—on her own behalf, in her own "first person"—at the end.

It is true that Mélanie, having witnessed the cataclysmic end of the
story, can only speak her solitude. "I" without "thou," she speaks of the
impossibility of reaching, touching anyone through language: "je ne peux
tutoyer personne [I cannot use the familiar form of address with any-
one]." Yet it is precisely this inability to communicate that she *is communicating*.

In Translation: Rewriting the Sentence

> D'une langue à l'autre, il y aurait du sens, juste
> distribution, contour et rencontre du moi, cette
> substance mouvante qui, dit-on, entre dans la
> composition des langues et qui les rend sa-
> voureuses ou détestables.

> From one tongue to the other there would be
> meaning, fair distribution, contour and self-en-
> counter, that moving substance which, it is said,
> enters into the composition of languages and
> makes them tasteful or hateful.[34]

Translation—the writing *after* that is also a writing *with*—is a powerful
postscript in *Le désert mauve*. Engaged in the feminist plot of reading,
Maude Laures enters the margin that is the reader's/translator's narrow
space for maneuvering. She then inscribes that margin *as* "A Book to

Translate," the long central section of Brossard's novel, and *in* "Mauve, the Horizon," the third, translated section. "A Book to Translate," the scripted space of Maude Laures's reading, both postscripts Laure Angstelle's *récit* and pretexts Maude Laures's own translation. In this way it opens up a little space in each one, a perspective from which the text is always in the process of crossing its own boundaries. Thus when Angela Parkins is called back to life and given voice by her translator in that middle section, she speaks directly both to Laure Angstelle, her *auther* [*sic*],[35] and to Mélanie, the survivor and witness who will continue to speak beyond her ending.

"A Book to Translate" begins with a series of short passages in which Maude Laures, reader and would-be translator of Laure Angstelle's book, is herself narrated. In the first sentence she is inscribed as if emerging from (her reading of) Angstelle's "Mauve Desert" through future, past, and present time into a virtual existence analogous to those of both narrator and auther of "Mauve Desert": "She will never know why her whole being plunged into a book, why for two years she spent herself, stretched herself through the pages of this book written by a woman she knows nothing about except the presumed evidence of an existence cloistered in the time and space of a single book" (51). This is not the voice of a detached, omniscient narrator. But neither is it a typical *style indirect libre*, for it has no hidden agenda aimed at securing narrative authority by subsuming one voice into another. The intimate third-person voice that narrates the opening passages of "A Book to Translate" glides lovingly in and out of Maude Laures's thought, reading her reading as if hearing into another's listening. As she is narrated, Maude Laures infiltrates the language and the voice that narrate her. The narration is *of* her in every sense: "She was thinking slowness while with her gaze she abstracted the book's equilibrium"; "She was a minimal presence, a misted space in front of the window"; "Through an incalculable returning-effect of words, she knew herself to be no longer in a position of absconding from that which, deep under tongue, wanted." The time of this wanting is the passage from abstraction into being, until finally, "one heavily snowing morning, [Maude Laures] decided upon existence among the scenes and the sure symptoms which, in Laure Angstelle's language, had seduced her."

The pages that follow resemble a translator's journal in which Maude Laures engages with and processes Angstelle's book, reading it into existence. The entries fall into four categories: Places and Things, Characters, Scenes, and Dimensions. There follows a final section called simply "A Book to Translate (continued)," in which Maude Laures is once again intimately narrated as she gradually approaches the moment when there will come substitution and she will enter her own text, the translated book "Mauve, the Horizon."

One of the most striking examples of feminist postscripting occurs in the section "Scenes" where Maude Laures scripts four dialogues (Kathy Kerouac with Mélanie; Kathy Kerouac with Lorna; Mélanie with Angela Parkins; and Maude Laures herself with Laure Angstelle). In these four scenes of "speaking together," Maude Laures seems to be teasing voices out of Angstelle's text by evoking both speakers and listeners. In the shared intimacy of conversation, the voices in these four scenes essentially break open "Mauve Desert" and create a space (both internal and external to the original text) into which Maude Laures will carry over—translate— Angstelle's words. It is no accident that all four scenes center on questions of aloneness and closeness, fear and hope.

The last of the scenes might almost be considered a rite of passage as "the distance [between auther and translator] is abolished." Both women are "looking to understand how death transits between fiction and reality," for it is death that they have in common, death that separates them. In addition, Maude Laures wants to hear from Laure Angstelle "what [she] can make her own." Thus, when Laure asks, "What would you like to talk about?" Maude replies, "One thing only: Angela Parkins' death." But what Maude Laures really wants is not to speak of Angela Parkins across the writer/translator barrier, as if Angela Parkins were no more than a shared fiction. She wants to draw Laure Angstelle into the space of her reading where she, Maude Laures the reader, can lend her voice to Angstelle's protagonist and give her a chance to speak directly to her auther about her death. Speaking for and as Angela Parkins, Maude Laures asks Laure Angstelle, "—*Why did you kill me?* [*Pourquoi m'as-tu mise à mort?*]*.*"

In response, Laure Angstelle reminds Angela Parkins about reality: "*you forgot to look around you. . . . You forgot about reality. . . . That man exists. . . . I'm not responsible for reality*" (132 and 133). But Maude Laures reinhabits her own voice to remind Laure Angstelle that "reality is what we invent." In the ebb and flow of voices imagined and invented, the two women, translator and auther, come fiercely and gently to an understanding that they are not in competition for authority but are rather sharing a space to which both of them have a right: "there are true landscapes that pry us from the edge and force us onto the scene" (133).

The scene ends with an exchange in which Maude Laures affirms the paradoxical coexistence of solitude and communion (an affirmation that is to become the organizing principle of her translation): "—I mostly wanted to hear you talk about death. But no matter what happens, *we're alone, aren't we?*" (134, emphasis added). And as if in answer to what Maude Laures's question is *really* asking, Laure Angstelle answers by giving the translator her blessing: "—Keep to beauty, have no fear. Muffle civilization's noises in you. Learn to bear the unbearable: the raw of all things" (134).

The importance of this scene in giving Maude Laures a way to "slip anonymous and *whole* between the pages" (161, emphasis added) is evident in the changes worked upon Laure Angstelle's "innocent book" (162) by Maude Laures's translation. For instance, Angstelle's Mélanie had said:

> Some day I would know the perfect moment of exaltation and *indifference* in synchrony. Some day I would know the silence and *the secret that lives on inside beings so that other civilizations may be born*. Beauty was before reality and reality was in writing, *open work* [*un jour*]. (36, emphasis added)

In Maude Laures's rendering of this passage there are small but significant variations:

> Some day I would experience everything in synchrony, ecstacy, *the secrets which from within undermine dear civilization*. Beauty was before reality and reality was in writing, *a gaping* [*béance*]. (192, emphasis added)

In Maude Laures's translation, Mélanie has lost her "indifference"; she no longer believes naively in futures. Her lucidity is poignant: the secret that "lives on" so that "other civilizations may be born" has, in translation, become "secrets [that] undermine dear civilization." To Angstelle's Mélanie, writing suggested openness and promise (*un jour*, literally "one day"); but Maude Laures's Mélanie sees the space of writing also as a space of loss (*béance*).[36] Conceived in the *passage* from one text to another, the translation must always be marked by loss. Thus, as "Mauve, the Horizon" depends upon the memory of "Mauve Desert," so Mélanie, in the translator's mind and in the translated book, can never be entirely what she was before Angela Parkins's death. An awareness of the inevitable connection between intimacy and loss pervades the translated text. For instance, in Angstelle's version we read:

> It was cold in the desert night and everywhere heat brought beings to life, I trembled about turning reality into an episode by getting close to beings. (33)

But in Maude Laures's version the danger is far more explicit:

> But it was cold in the desert night and everywhere that heat gave life, I trembled *that it would shift everything over onto the side of death*. I was trembling with the fear of turning reality into an episode by getting close to beings. (189, emphasis added)

There is no going back to a time before death. Marked by what she witnessed in her reading, Maude Laures is motivated by the end that she

senses herself approaching and by the need to know whether at that ultimate textual boundary, there is any way to get beyond the—indisputable—facts of Angela Parkins's murder and Mélanie's solitude.

Maude Laures's translation of Angela's final discourse includes the sentence "In reality a few concise words are enough to change the course of
death [En réalité il suffit de quelques mots concis pour changer le cours de
la mort]" (201). This does not correspond closely to anything in the original passage of which it is a translation, *but* it does now resonate with a
sentence in Maude Laures's translation of *l'homme long*'s first chapter: "A
single mathematical error could alter the course of history [le cours de
l'histoire]" (173). That sentence also departed significantly from its corresponding original: "The slightest error could have disastrous consequences" (17). This new articulation of two decidedly (and differently)
postmodern conclusions in dialogue with one another might be understood to be a product of translating *through* the scripted space of "A Book
to Translate." At the end of Laure Angstelle's story, Angela had only been
able to talk to Mélanie of "our attachment to certain words, that they are
like small slow deaths in concise reality" (45). (Note that there is no mention here of "*changing* the course of death.") But translation will make
crucial if virtually imperceptible changes in "le cours de l'histoire" (the
course of history . . . the course of the story).

The importance of what appear to be slight changes in wording is suggested in "A Book to Translate" when Maude Laures works on the word
"ricochet"—"a word that could save many a situation" (159). At this
point she begins to tick off—the verb in French is *cocher*—in the margins
"other words that could in her language get meaning restarted [relancer
le sens] and spare her from facing Angela Parkins's brutal end" (159).
Furthermore, "ricochet" is already a product of the shared space of translation. The word was first uttered by Angela Parkins in the scripted scene
where Maude Laures had (and heard) Angela say to Laure Angstelle: "—
But imagining the scene, you could have changed its course. *You could
have made the bullet ricochet* or wound me slightly" (132, emphasis
added). Even though Laure had answered that no, it was you or him and
"I didn't kill you. That man killed you," still Maude Laures has carried
away from that encounter the idea of a ricochet. In a sense, because Laure
Angstelle's story and words have ricocheted through Maude Laures's "A
Book to Translate," *Angela herself* comes to suggest in the end of
"Mauve, the Horizon" that "a few concise words may be enough to
change the course of death."

There *are* a few concise words in the ending of "Mauve, the Horizon"
that seem to be trying to make a different sense out of what is happening.
For one thing, Maude Laures's inscription of the horizon throughout her
translation but especially in the conclusion is tied to an expansion of an

important element at the end of Laure Angstelle's text. The words completing Mélanie's description of Angela's discourse in Maude Laures's
conclusion, "she is talking and awakening in me the horizon" (201),
forcefully inscribe a connection between voice and vision. The possibility
was already there in Angstelle's "Mauve Desert," when Angela said, "but
the eyes, Mélanie [mais les yeux, Mélanie]" (45). Since the scene of
Mélanie's original naming by her mother had played on her name in
French as "*mais la nuit [but the night]*, Mélanie," Angela's words were
effectively *renaming* Mélanie in terms of vision. In Maude Laures's translation, then, this phrase is repeated and its significance enhanced. The passage from vision to horizon is strikingly clear: "she is saying that one must
hope, that memory can still accomplish works of beauty, but the eyes,
Mélanie, she is saying that in reality a few concise words are enough to
change the course of death, to frighten away little pains, she is talking and
awakening in me the horizon" (201).

Again, it is in the scripted middle sections that Maude Laures was able
to open the space within which Mélanie can realize this vision. When
Laure Angstelle insisted to Angela Parkins, "*Swear to me that you didn't
see anything coming [Jure-moi que tu n'as rien vu venir]*," she provided an
opening that could be taken up in Maude Laures's conclusion. Whereas in
Angstelle's version, after Angela Parkins's killing, Mélanie said, "I didn't
see a thing [Je n'ai rien vu]," in the translation her "I didn't see anything
coming [Je n'ai rien vu venir]" leaves Mélanie capable of witnessing and
telling. Even if she did not see the end coming soon enough to change the
course of the story, she sees enough to change, with a few words, not
death but the course of death.

Angela Parkins's body stretched out on the dance floor is described
now as "forever inflexible, displayed, point of viewing [à tout jamais inflexible, exhibé, point de mire]." The French is difficult to translate. A
"mire" is a surveyor's rod for sighting, and a "point de mire" may be a
(literal) target or a (figurative) focal point. Angela, no longer the surveyor
("point de mire"—that is, she has "no surveyor's rod"), is now the "point
of viewing," her own point of view forever inflexible but somehow now
the whole point of *Mélanie's* viewing. So we may recall Maude Laures's
description of Angela in "A Book to Translate": "Like a witness-mound
that has escaped erosion [comme une butte-témoin échappée à l'éro-
sion]" (94). Indeed, she does seem now to be that witness-mound—the
reference point, the focal point for Mélanie's vision, but also perhaps the
voice that survives her own death and tries to witness: "Mélanie, daughter
of the night, what happened? [Mélanie, fille de la nuit, que s'est-il donc
passé?]" (202). In the translation we no longer read that "Angela is dissolving in the black and white of reality" (46). Neither is Mélanie any
longer described by the play on words in English in Angstelle's text: "*Of*

course Mélanie is night teen."[37] In the translation, "night teen" has become "night's *daughter* [fille de la nuit]." Once again the changes are traceable to and through "A Book to Translate" where the translator spoke of "the narrator, whose name, Mélanie, let her [Maude Laures] glimpse a profile outlined against the night" (52). Thus Mélanie's name is associated with Maude Laures's vision that later, in a kind of ricochet, becomes Mélanie's vision again. So Mélanie's eyes at the end, not bound to the chalk outline around the body, nor to the "mauve dawn, the desert and the road like a bloody profile," are vigilant, able to see "the threatening profile of every thing. Then dawn, the desert and mauve, the horizon." The danger is incontestable, but as Angela Parkins's eyes fade away, Mélanie is there, perhaps to see beyond "la fin de l'histoire." And the fact of her witnessing may keep alive some small hope for the possibility of rewriting the final (death) sentence.[38]

Where I now find myself, it is possible to hone hope
among the dense lightrays.

Notes

Prologue

1. *Random House Dictionary of the English Language*, 2d ed., unabridged, s.v. "incriminate."

2. The desirability and the difficulty of considering an accused person as "innocent until proven guilty" is widely recognized. Incriminating evidence *may not prove* anything, but it arouses suspicions—and one tends to assume that where there is suspicion there is probably reason for suspicion.

3. Just as "incrimination" refers both to proofs and to accusations, "guilt" too has different meanings that enforce and reinforce one another. One may be guilty of a crime, but inasmuch as guilt is essentially the assumption or assignment of responsibility, it always involves some subjective process. Whatever the "crime," one may or may not feel guilty, one may or may not plead guilty, one may or may not be found guilty. Although we want to believe that one is guilty (and is found guilty) by virtue of the *facts*, we must remember that guilt is finally determined or proven on the basis of an interpretation or *judgment*. A jury *decides* the guilt or innocence of the accused. The apparently well-defined and methodical functioning of our legal apparatus tends to give the reassuring impression of objectivity and thus effectively to obscure guilt's incessant semantic slippage. Guilt's many meanings contaminate one another. The most supposedly judicious guilty verdict still contains bias just as the most subjective sense of guilt carries an incriminating force of its own.

4. I am here proposing not a historical but a symbolic reading of the practice of witchducking. In actual practice, men as well as women were tried as witches (although fewer) and a person who sank during the water test was not *supposed* to be allowed to drown (although some did). Such historical facts do not, however, diminish the symbolic force of the fiction of drowning witches as "guilty women telling." For an account of the history of the centuries-old practice of witchducking, see George Lyman Kittredge, *Witchcraft in Old and New England* (Cambridge: Harvard University Press, 1929), 232–238.

5. Women may of course also be read as nonreflexive subjects. The polysemy of "incriminations" allows for the possibility of women incriminating (that is, implicating) *others*, but the placement of the word "guilty" acts to de-emphasize this reading in favor of those that blame women.

6. Garrett Stewart, *Reading Voices: Literature and the Phonotext* (Berkeley and Los Angeles: University of California Press, 1990), 37.

7. Henry Louis Gates, Jr., *Figures in Black: Words, Signs and the "Racial" Self* (New York: Oxford University Press, 1987), xxx.

8. An obvious allusion to Stanley Fish's inquiry into the relationship of readers to texts (*Is There a Text in This Class? The Authority of Interpretive Communities* [Cambridge: Harvard University Press, 1980]), my opening question also, and perhaps more pertinently, echoes that posed, of and after Fish, by Mary Jacobus

("Is There a Woman in This Text?" in *Reading Woman: Essays in Feminist Criticism* [New York: Columbia University Press, 1986]).

9. See Jacques Derrida, *La Voix et le phénomène* (Paris: Presses universitaires de France, 1967), translated in *Speech and Phenomena and Other Essays on Husserl's Theory of Signs* by David B. Allison (Evanston, Ill.: Northwestern University Press, 1973). See also Derrida, *Of Grammatology*, trans. Gayatri Spivak (Paris: Seuil, 1967; Baltimore: Johns Hopkins University Press, 1976), and *Writing and Difference*, trans. Alan Bass (Paris: Seuil, 1967; Chicago: University of Chicago Press, 1978). For a useful analysis and discussion of Derrida's position on the relationship between speech and writing, see Jonathan Culler's chapter "Writing and Logocentrism," in *On Deconstruction* (Ithaca: Cornell University Press, 1982). Culler notes that Derrida essentially makes speech "already a form of writing" since, like writing, it "works by the differential play of signifiers, though it is precisely this work of difference that the privileging of speech seeks to suppress" (95 and 108–9). All of this suggests that the eradication of voice is decidedly not the point or intention of Derrida's critique of phonocentrism. Nevertheless, it is undeniable that, as part of the fallout of this critique, "voice" became something of a dirty word.

10. It was Roland Barthes who wrote in 1971: "There now arises a need for a new object, one obtained by the displacement or overturning of previous categories. This object is the *Text*." Barthes, "From Work to Text," in *Textual Strategies*, ed. Josué Harari (Ithaca: Cornell University Press, 1979), 74.

11. Stewart, *Reading Voices*, 27.

12. In the first chapter of *Fictions of Authority: Women Writers and Narrative Voice* (Ithaca: Cornell University Press, 1992), Susan Sniader Lanser makes this same point and includes a long list of titles with the word "voice" in them.

13. Stewart, *Reading Voices*, 6.

14. In his subtle and ingenious study of "textual effects," Stewart sets out to save the *phonotext* (ibid., 15, 28). Yet the metaphor of voice *is* seductive and tenacious, as we see in his claim that "literature . . . perhaps *speaks through* us," and that "we *speak* to [a text], silently, in the loose sense of moving to a beat" (37, emphasis on "speaks" added). Stewart's contention is that such statements in no way contradict the fact that literature has no voice. He notes rather that "[texts are] produced in reception. Such is the auditory leeway opened precisely by the lack of literature's *inherent* voice" (38). Voice and voicing are on the *reader's* side only of the process, "a somatic *effect* at the site of reception" (9).

15. Geoffrey Hartman, *Saving the Text: Literature/Derrida/Philosophy* (Baltimore: Johns Hopkins University Press, 1981), 121.

16. Ibid., xxii, emphasis added.

17. Lanser's *Fictions of Authority* offers perhaps the best discussion of the status and function of "narrative voice." Recognizing that narrative voice is a powerful convention that in fact does more than just name a "textual practice," she notes: "Although many critics acknowledge the bald inaccuracy of 'voice' and 'teller' to signify something written, these terms persist even among structuralists. . . . The narrative voice and the narrated world are mutually constitutive. . . . the narrator has no existence 'outside' the text yet brings the text into existence" (4–5). In an important codicil, Lanser defines the connection between stories and tellers as

"not essential but conventional: narratives have narrators because Western literature has continued to construct reading and listening in speakerly terms" (4n.3).

18. Ibid., 4.

19. Ibid., 6.

20. Alice A. Jardine, *Gynesis: Configurations of Woman and Modernity* (Ithaca:
Cornell University Press, 1985), 117, emphasis added.

21. Joanne S. Frye, *Living Stories, Telling Lives: Women and the Novel in Contemporary Experience* (Ann Arbor: University of Michigan Press, 1986), 76 and
58.

22. Is this experience any less problematic? For an important discussion of "the
problem of experience," see Elizabeth Weed, "A Man's Place," in *Men in Feminism*, ed. Alice Jardine and Paul Smith (London: Methuen, 1987; New York:
Routledge, 1989), 71–77. On page 76, Weed credits Teresa de Lauretis with having described the need to "theorize experience on our way to theorizing and tex-
tualizing the female subject" (de Lauretis, "Semiotics and Experience," in *Alice
Doesn't: Feminism, Semiotics, Cinema* [Bloomington: Indiana University Press,
1984]). Weed and de Lauretis both recognize experience as problematic but in
some complex way vital to feminist theory, their formulations recalling Stephen
Heath's oft-cited remark that "the risk of essence may have to be taken." See
Heath, "Difference," *Screen* 19, no. 3 (1978): 99. See also Diana Fuss, "The
'Risk' of Essence," in *Essentially Speaking: Feminism, Nature and Difference* (New
York: Routledge, 1989), 1–21; Alice Jardine, "The Demise of Experience: Fiction
as Stranger Than Truth?" in *Gynesis*, 145–155; and Teresa de Lauretis, "Upping
the Anti (sic) in Feminist Theory," in *Conflicts in Feminism*, ed. Marianne Hirsch
and Evelyn Fox Keller (New York: Routledge, 1990), 255–270.

23. My question intentionally recalls Alice Jardine's definition in *Gynesis* of the
business of "[putting] the signifier woman into circulation" (the process she
names "gynesis") as a *risk* "feminists *must* take" (155). Jardine's formulation is
itself of course an amplification of Stephen Heath's remark that "the risk of essence
may have to be taken."

24. Lanser, *Fictions of Authority*, 3.

25. The "voices coming from the margins" echo the title of Arnold Krupat's
book *The Voice in the Margin: Native American Literature and the Canon* (Berkeley and Los Angeles: University of California Press, 1989). In his introduction,
Krupat writes, "It is no accident that those of us who work with hitherto marginal-
ized materials show a certain reluctance to give up voice in favor of text as recently
defined" (20).

26. The French have a word to denote specifically *women's* gossip: *commérages*.
This word derives from the French word for godmother, *commère*. It might also be
argued that the English word *gossip* (derived from the Old English *godsibb*, meaning godparent) is, in usage if not in strict etymological terms, equally gender-specific.

27. Other variations on the Siren figure include the nymph Lorelei luring sail-
ors to shipwreck on her rock in the Rhine and Delilah wheedling out of Samson
the secret source of his strength and invulnerability.

28. Also known as *The Arabian Nights*, this collection of Arab tales dating
from tenth-century sources was first translated into French and published by An-

toine Galland between 1704 and 1712 (with two volumes published in 1717 after Galland's death). The framing narrative can be read in a number of different ways. The sultan, having acquired a hatred for all women upon discovering his first wife's unfaithfulness, vows to marry and kill a new wife every day. What Scheherezade accomplishes with her stories is both to keep the sultan's desire (and herself) alive and also ultimately to work a change in him. She is an adept tease but also an able teacher. When the sultan, having been converted by her stories, finally abandons his murderous project, Scheherezade has clearly saved not only herself but all of the women in her country.

29. For a particularly astute and subtle reading of Ovid's Philomela, see Elissa Marder, "Disarticulated Voices: Feminism and Philomela," *Hypatia* 7, no. 2 (1992): 148–166. Marder insists that the severed tongue "does not merely function as a narrative consequence of the rape, but rather becomes a figurative representation of it" (158).

30. For three different readings of the Philomela myth, see Geoffrey Hartman, "The Voice of the Shuttle: Language from the Point of View of Literature," in *Beyond Formalism, Literary Essays 1958–1970* (New Haven: Yale University Press, 1970), 337–355; Jane Marcus, "Liberty, Sorority, Misogyny," in *The Representation of Women in Fiction*, ed. Carolyn Heilbrun and Margaret Higonnet (Baltimore: Johns Hopkins University Press, 1982), 60–97; and Patricia Klindienst Joplin, "The Voice of the Shuttle Is Ours," *Stanford Literature Review* 1, no. 1 (1984): 25–53. Exposing the fact that a woman's voice may become the story and *still* be silenced by male readings, both Marcus and Joplin challenge Hartman's universalizing reading of "the voice of the shuttle" as an "archetypal" metaphor for the poet's art, "a symbol for oracular utterance" (337 and 351). Marcus bases her critique on Virginia Woolf's incisive reading of Philomela and Procne in *Between the Acts*, a reading that "tells us that 'what we must remember' is the rape; 'what we must forget' is the male rewriting of women's history" (62). Joplin brilliantly critiques Hartman's appropriation of Philomela in an eloquent reading (more prereading than rereading) of the "the voice of the shuttle": "Philomela and her loom speak to us because together they represent an assertion of the will to survive despite everything that threatens to silence us, including the male literary tradition and its critics who have preserved Philomela's 'voice' without knowing what it says" (52).

31. To say that silence is a gendered question in no way imposes a univocal answer. I am reading silence and voice here in terms of a model of suppression and resistance that owes an obvious debt to the theoretical writings of Virginia Woolf and Tillie Olsen—but this is not the only possible model. One exciting foray into new territory is Patricia Yaeger's *Honey-Mad Women: Emancipatory Strategies in Women's Writing* (New York: Columbia University Press, 1988). Tipping the suppression/resistance model on its head without (I would submit) invalidating it, Yaeger's "alternate mythology of feminine speech" (3), in its own playfully provocative way, sets out to "multiply the paradigms available to the feminist critic" (239) and in so doing *performs* the emancipatory strategies that it describes.

32. "Nous pouvons même aller jusqu'à la proposition absurde: «l'interdit est là pour être violé.»" Bataille, "La Transgression," chapter 5 of *L'Erotisme* (Paris:

Minuit, 1957), 71–72. All translations of Bataille are my own. The "absurdity" of the proposition, attributed by Bataille to the "irrational nature of interdictions," in no way invalidates it.

33. Ibid., 72–73.

34. Michel Foucault, "A Preface to Transgression," in *Language, Counter-Memory, Practice: Selected Essays and Interviews*, ed. Donald F. Bouchard, trans. Donald F. Bouchard and Sherry Simon (Ithaca: Cornell University Press, 1977), 33–34. Foucault's essay first appeared as "Préface à la transgression," in "Hommage à Georges Bataille," *Critique*, nos. 195–196 (1963): 751–769.

35. Bataille, "La Transgression," 144.

36. Susan Rubin Suleiman, "Pornography, Transgression, and the Avant-Garde: Bataille's *Story of the Eye*," in *The Poetics of Gender*, ed. Nancy K. Miller (New York: Columbia University Press, 1986), 128.

37. Ibid., 131 and 132.

38. Luce Irigaray, *Speculum of the Other Woman*, trans. Gillian C. Gill (Ithaca: Cornell University Press, 1985), 135. See also Christa Wolf, *Cassandra: A Novel and Four Essays* (1983; New York: Farrar, Straus and Giroux, 1984). Wolf's questions echo Irigaray's: "Do people suspect, do *we* suspect, how difficult and in fact dangerous it can be when life is restored to an 'object'? When the idol begins to feel again? When 'it' finds speech again? When it has to say 'I,' as a woman?" (298).

39. When we feminize "l'interdit qui est là pour être violé," the word "interdite"—with its feminine marker—can no longer be read as the (neuter) interdict; it now indicates "the woman under interdiction" and simultaneously suggests that she is, in this position, dumbstruck.

40. Jardine, *Gynesis*, 69–71.

41. Ibid., 72, 88.

42. Tillie Olsen, *Silences* (1965; reprint, New York: Dell Publishing Co., 1983), 46.

43. To the list of those already mentioned in connection with such a script (Scheherezade, Lorelei, Philomela and Procne, the Sirens), we might add the temptress Eve, the demanding Salome (and her vengeful mother Herodias), Pandora who cannot refrain from opening her box, Cassandra who sees and says too much, Lady Macbeth whose taunts incite to murder, not to mention the Harpies and Furies, the beguiling femmes fatales, the harridans and shrews, and a colorful fairy-tale assortment of duplicitous stepmothers and spell-casting witches. Obviously the "narration" part of the script—transgression enacted through *language*—is more literal and more explicit in some of these stories than it is in others.

44. I do not in any way mean to suggest that there were no important feminist articulations and mobilizations before the nineteenth century. I agree, however, with Adrienne Rich that the feminist movement has historically had difficulty in conceiving of itself: "The entire history of women's struggle for self-determination has been muffled in silence over and over. One serious cultural obstacle encountered by any feminist writer is that each feminist work has tended to be received as if it emerged from nowhere; as if each of us had lived, thought, and worked with-

out any historical past or contextual present." Rich, *On Lies, Secrets, and Silence: Selected Prose 1966-1978* (New York: W. W. Norton, 1979), 11. It was, of course, Kate Millett who introduced the term "sexual politics" in her ground-breaking study, *Sexual Politics* (Garden City, N.Y.: Doubleday and Co., 1969). Millett also focused her analysis on the nineteenth and twentieth centuries, although she noted that "if the sexual revolution was born in the thirties and forties of the nineteenth century, it enjoyed, nevertheless, a very generous period of gestation in the womb of time" (65).

45. For a particularly illuminating reading of the historical and literary contexts for "the battle of the sexes," see Sandra M. Gilbert and Susan Gubar, *No Man's Land: The Place of the Woman Writer in the Twentieth Century*, vol. 1, *The War of the Words* (New Haven: Yale University Press, 1988). References to "the woman question" (sometimes referred to as "the woman problem"!) may be found on pages 12 and 21. Gilbert and Gubar identify a crucial moment in the articulation of sexual politics within the literary tradition, noting that "in the mid-nineteenth century when female resistance becomes feminist rebellion . . . the battle of the sexes emerges as a trope for struggle over political as well as personal power" (6).

46. Ibid., 4.

47. A perceptive analysis of the relationship of historical and political developments to women's literary traditions in nineteenth-century France, Britain, and the United States may be found in Ellen Moers, "The Epic Age: Part of the History of Literary Women," in *Literary Women: The Great Writers* (New York: Doubleday, 1963; New York: Anchor Books Edition, 1977), 19-62.

48. Jane Flax, *Thinking Fragments: Psychoanalysis, Feminism, and Postmodernism in the Contemporary West* (Berkeley and Los Angeles: University of California Press, 1990), 136. As Elizabeth V. Spelman has noted, "although not all feminists subsequent to de Beauvoir referred to her work, or even necessarily knew about it, there is hardly any issue that feminists have come to deal with that she did not address." Elizabeth V. Spelman, *Inessential Woman: Problems of Exclusion in Feminist Thought* (Boston: Beacon Press, 1988), 58. Spelman's critique of Beauvoir targets "the serious discrepancy between the potential broad scope of her views and the actual narrow focus of her position" (58).

49. Elaine Marks and Isabelle de Courtivron, eds., *New French Feminisms: An Anthology* (New York: Schocken Books, 1981), 7. Marks and de Courtivron stress the fact that by not participating in the "dialectic pro and con" of the debates surrounding "the woman question in France," Beauvoir's work opened the way for a radical reorientation in the discourse of feminism. See also Jane Flax's *Thinking Fragments* for a brilliant analysis of the ways in which psychoanalysis, feminist theory, and postmodernist philosophy are uniquely interarticulated in the twentieth century. The concept of "previously unaskable feminist questions" was suggested to me by the title of Flax's account of Beauvoir's crucial role in the generation of modern feminisms: "The Emergence of a Distinctively Feminist Question: The 'Other' Says No" (136).

50. Where Woolf stressed the androgynous ideal ("one must be woman-manly or man-womanly"), Beauvoir favored an existentialist humanist concept of the universal. One of the most celebrated of Woolf's statements is probably her caveat

in *A Room of One's Own* that "it is fatal for a woman to lay the least stress on any grievance; to plead even with justice any cause; in any way to speak consciously as a woman." *A Room of One's Own* (1929; reprint, New York: Harcourt, Brace, and World, 1957), 108. Beauvoir expresses a similar conviction about the challenge facing women writers: "By aspiring to clear-sightedness women writers are doing the cause of women a great service; but—usually without realizing it—they are still too concerned with serving this cause to assume the disinterested attitude toward the universe that opens the widest horizons." *The Second Sex*, trans. and ed. H. M. Parshley (1949; New York: Knopf, 1952, 1980; New York: Vintage Books, 1989), 709–710.

51. Jardine, *Gynesis*, 24.

52. The work of French feminist theorists like Hélène Cixous, Luce Irigaray, and Julia Kristeva comes immediately to mind, of course. See also, for instance, the anthology edited by Sally McConnell-Ginet, Ruth Borker, and Nelly Furman, *Women and Language in Literature and Society* (New York: Praeger Pubs., 1980); and Jean Bethke Elshtain's article, "Feminist Discourse and Its Discontents: Language, Power, and Meaning," in *Feminist Theory: A Critique of Ideology*, ed. Nannerl O. Keohane, Michelle Z. Rosaldo, and Barbara C. Gelpi (Chicago: University of Chicago Press, 1981), 127–145.

53. Nicole Brossard, *L'Amèr ou le chapitre effrité* (Montreal: Quinze, 1977), translated by Barbara Godard as *These Our Mothers or: The Disintegrating Chapter* (Toronto: Coach House Quebec Translations, 1983), 45.

54. I am thinking here not only of the fact that the story recounted in *Kamouraska* was based on an actual historical event, but also of one of the more obvious literary intertexts, François Mauriac's *Thérèse Desqueyroux*.

55. Queen Victoria died in 1901, seven years before Simone de Beauvoir was born. Obviously, generations of women writers cannot be clearly delineated by years alone—and in some ways Woolf and Beauvoir seem of the same generation. But it is worth recalling that Woolf was born more than a quarter of a century before Beauvoir, and that in 1941, the year of Woolf's death, Beauvoir was just completing her first novel, *L'Invitée*. When Beauvoir herself turned forty and was writing *The Second Sex*, Woolf had already been dead seven years, and *A Room of One's Own* was already a classic.

56. This passage from *A Writer's Diary* ([New York: Harcourt Brace Jovanovich, 1954], 46) is cited by Maria DiBattista at the beginning of her chapter on *Mrs. Dalloway*, in *Virginia Woolf's Major Novels: The Fables of Anon* (New Haven: Yale University Press, 1980), 22. DiBattista comments that "the emergence of Woolf's distinctive literary identity can be dated, as she herself dated it, to her fortieth year."

57. We tend to regard both "afterthoughts" and "postscripts" as generally insignificant inasmuch as they are supplements and therefore contingent. Our tendency to minimize their importance and our failure to recognize their provocation is, however, very likely an indication that we sense their potential to undermine what we think we know.

58. I am grateful to my student Vivienne York for this reflection on postscripts.

59. The expression is of course taken from the title of a well-known book about

women writers and subversive narrative strategies. See Rachel Blau DuPlessis, *Writing beyond the Ending: Narrative Strategies of Twentieth-Century Women Writers* (Bloomington: Indiana University Press, 1985).

60. Brossard, *Mauve Desert*, trans. Susanne de Lotbinière-Harwood (Toronto: Coach House Press, 1990), 11. Originally published as *Le désert mauve* (Montreal: Editions de l'Hexagone, 1987).

Chapter One
The Voice of Reason: *L'Invitée*

1. I have preferred to continue to use the French title of Simone de Beauvoir's novel in my text for reasons that my reading of that title later in this chapter should make clear. Beauvoir's *L'Invitée* (Paris: Gallimard, 1943) was published in English as *She Came to Stay*, trans. Yvonne Moyse and Roger Senhouse (London: Martin Secker & Warburg, 1949; New York: W. W. Norton and Co., 1954). The Norton paperback edition credits no translator but appears to be an updated version of the Moyse and Senhouse translation. The World Publishing Company holds the copyright. All references to the French text of the novel are to the 1989 Gallimard Folio paperback edition. When citing the English translation, I have tended to use the 1949 edition, which I have frequently modified, drawing on occasion from the 1954 edition as well. Page references are given to the passages in the Norton edition.

2. I provide deliberately literal translations here in order to make my point. In the published English translation of the novel, these words and lines are more freely translated. For the passages cited as well as for some of the numerous other occurrences of the kind of vocabulary referred to here, see, for example, in the French original, 138, 166, 185, 187, 205, 206, 213, 216, 246, 251, 355, 368, 401, and 434. "Complicité" and "coupable" are particularly prevalent.

3. During the years when Beauvoir was writing *L'Invitée* (1939–1941), Jean-Paul Sartre was working on *Being and Nothingness* (trans. Hazel E. Barnes [New York: Philosophical Library, 1956]). I use some of Sartre's formulations in this and other of his works to elucidate the philosophical background of Beauvoir's novel. This use of Sartre does not seem unwarranted since Beauvoir herself admitted in an interview with Alice Schwarzer that "I have adopted [Sartre's] philosophical ideas." Schwarzer, trans. Marianne Howarth, *After the Second Sex: Conversations with Simone de Beauvoir* (New York: Pantheon, 1984), 57.

4. Jean-Paul Sartre, *Existentialism and Humanism*, trans. Philip Mairet (1948; London: Methuen, 1982), 29.

5. Ibid., 30.

6. These terms, widely used by contemporary French theorists and critics, designate the words uttered (*énoncé*) and the act of uttering them (*énonciation*).

7. One might say that the "unpoliced" world of the existentialist hero is here expressed through the "well-policed" medium of the realist novel. As D. A. Miller put it in "The Novel and the Police," in *The Poetics of Murder*, ed. Glenn W. Most and William W. Stowe (San Diego: Harcourt, 1983), 299–326, "whenever the novel censures policing power, it has already discreetly reinvented it, in *the very practice of novelistic representation*" (315).

8. *The Prime of Life* (in French *La Force de l'âge*), trans. Peter Green (1960; Cleveland: World Publishing Co., 1962), 274. In quoting from *The Prime of Life* (hereafter referred to as *Prime*), I have frequently modified Green's translations.

9. One might protest that direct discourse and *style indirect libre* also "belong to" the narrator. I would argue that this is not so, that both exceed the narrator's control and function outside of the narrator's domain. Direct discourse, separated by quotation marks from the narrator's voice and judgment, evokes the speaker's authority in place of the storyteller's. *Style indirect libre*, grammatically and referentially escaping strict attribution, in both its "freedom" and "indirectness" constantly questions and challenges the narrator's place in, and authority over, the text.

10. The pretensions of *style indirect libre* are, of course, never that clear, but when it is combined with a limited point of view, as is the case in Beauvoir's novel, it can appear to be a more direct and transparent vehicle than it really is. After all, even when the attribution of point of view is *not* ambiguous, *style indirect libre* is still essentially a third-person discourse (grammatically) claiming first-person privilege while disclaiming first-person responsibility.

11. Martha Noel Evans, *Masks of Tradition: Women and the Politics of Writing in Twentieth-Century France* (Ithaca: Cornell University Press, 1987), 83 and 84.

12. Ibid., 88. While I take exception to Evans's contention that the "I" is authorial (I see it rather as stylistically smudging the boundary between protagonist and *narrator*), I would agree with her that switching away from the first person makes us at once more conscious of the fragility of first-person claims to authority and more suspicious of all other claims.

13. In the published English translation these two sentences are italicized and ellipsis points are inserted before them: "*. . . And I am here, my heart is beating. To-night the theatre has a heart and it is beating.*" The italics are undoubtedly intended to clarify this discourse as Françoise's *thought*. I have modified the translation to conform to the original French, however, since when no external marker prepares the reader for that "I," the effect is far more unsettling and in keeping with the spirit of Françoise's meditations.

14. In his analysis of Flaubert's use of *style indirect libre*, Jonathan Culler sees the abandonment of the first person plural after the opening pages of *Madame Bovary* as a kind of *piège à cons* whose purpose is precisely to "undermine narrative convention": "the text stops us short by telling us that the narrator we have identified knows nothing about the events in question." Culler, *Flaubert: The Uses of Uncertainty* (Ithaca: Cornell University Press, 1974), 112. Beauvoir is not in any way as intentionally "demoralizing," but I would contend that her occasional use of the first person combined with her refusal to surrender her narrative to that first person is Beauvoir's way of putting a check on her readers' knowledge and thus demonstrating that there is no privileged perspective from which to "comprehend" the narrative.

15. The most common use of the unmediated first person in the novel is in statements along the lines of "I am here." The fact that the ability to declare one's existence is a crucial thematic concern is supported and clearly illustrated by the interplay and struggle of pronouns in the juxtapositions of "I am here" and "she was there."

16. Peter Brooks, *Reading for the Plot* (New York: Knopf, 1984), 174.

17. Michal Peled Ginsburg, "Free Indirect Discourse: Theme and Narrative Voice in Flaubert, George Eliot, and Verga" (Ph.D. diss., Yale University, 1970), 3. Ginsburg distinguishes several kinds of free indirect discourse, and the kind we find in *L'Invitée* seems to be close to what she describes in her chapter on George Eliot. She asserts that Eliot "repeats on the level of a single utterance the problem of the relation between author and text," and she elaborates by declaring that the free indirect discourse is a "second rhetorical level which deconstructs and subverts the first level of the text" (dissertation abstract and 136). This would seem to be precisely what is going on in Beauvoir.

18. Brooks, *Reading for the Plot*, 177 and 196.

19. Culler, *Flaubert*, 109–110.

20. Miller, "The Novel and the Police," 319, emphasis added; *style indirect libre* italicized in the original.

21. The way in which Beauvoir explains the role of gender in her personal history is revealing:

> I did not deny my femininity, any more than I took it for granted: I simply ignored it. I had the same freedoms and responsibilities as men did. I was spared the curse that weighs upon most women, that of dependence. . . . [N]either Sartre nor any of my other male friends ever showed a superiority complex where I was concerned; so it never occurred to me that I was in a disadvantageous position. Today I know that the first thing I have to say if I want to describe myself is that I am a woman; but my feminine status has been for me neither an embarrassment nor an alibi. In any case, it is a given condition of my life, not an explanation of it. (*Prime*, 291–292)

Her "feminine status" may be neither alibi nor explanation, but it is rather striking that she interrupts her memoir and, addressing herself to "certain critics [who] are going to point out triumphantly that [this autobiography] flatly contradicts my thesis in *The Second Sex*" (*Prime*, 291), takes two pages to elaborate and insist upon the relative irrelevance of her "own particular brand of femininity" to her writing.

22. Beauvoir, *The Second Sex*, trans. and ed. H. M. Parshley (1949; New York: Knopf, 1952, 1980; New York: Vintage Books, 1989), xxxiv. Further references (designated *SS*) will appear in the text. The translations may be modified.

23. Beauvoir, adamantly opposed to the "roman à thèse," would undoubtedly hasten to argue here that, while such an investigation is appropriate in the essay, it has no role in the novel. See "Mon expérience d'écrivain," in *Les écrits de Simone de Beauvoir*, ed. Claude Francis and Fernande Gontier (Paris: Gallimard, 1979), 447. The question here, however, is not why *L'Invitée* is not *The Second Sex*, but rather why it seems to refuse to embrace the consciousness which that theoretical work displays, why the important role of gender is not *acknowledged*. For indeed, while resisting the limitations of "romans à thèse," Beauvoir's first novel still unabashedly acknowledges its debt to existentialism.

24. Beauvoir, "Mon expérience d'écrivain," 445, my translation.

25. Ibid., 441, my translations.

26. "A moitié victimes, à moitié complices, comme tout le monde." *Le*

deuxième sexe, vol. 2 (Paris: Gallimard, 1949), 7. The epigraphs that precede book 2 in the original French are omitted in Parshley's translation.

27. Evans, *Masks of Tradition*, 86.

28. Ibid., 94.

29. Martha Noel Evans, "Murdering *L'Invitée*: Gender and Fictional Narrative," *Yale French Studies* 72 (1986): 80. In the revision of this article as chapter 2 in *Masks of Tradition*, Evans makes the same point but does not keep this sentence.

30. In *She Came to Stay*, "a bitch" is given as the English translation for "une femelle." This retains (but somewhat more obscurely) Françoise's use of "femaleness" as an insult, emphasized in the French by the litany of feminine nouns culminating in the naming of what they have in common: "La perle noire, la précieuse, l'ensorceleuse, la généreuse. Une femelle . . ." (*L'Invitée*, 491).

31. Dominique Desanti, "Truth in Memoirs and Truth in Fiction: *Les Mandarins* and *La Force des choses* [*Force of Circumstance*]" (Paper delivered at Columbia University, April 1985).

32. Conversation with Deirdre Bair, translated and quoted by Bair in " 'My Life . . . This Curious Object': Simone de Beauvoir on Autobiography," in *The Female Autograph*, ed. Domna Stanton and Jeanine Plottel (New York: Literary Forum, 1984), 241. Not reprinted in Stanton, ed., *The Female Autograph* (Chicago: University of Chicago Press, 1987). Deirdre Bair also includes this citation in her biography *Simone de Beauvoir: A Biography* (New York: Summit Books, 1990), 468.

33. Simone de Beauvoir, *Force of Circumstance* (in French *La Force des choses*), trans. Richard Howard (1963; New York: Putnam, 1964), v, emphasis added. Hereafter referred to as *FCir*.

34. Hélène V. Wenzel, "Interview with Simone de Beauvoir," *Yale French Studies* 72 (1986): 9. "I realized that the theatre wasn't my best mode of expression, that there was a kind of lie—that there are lies in literature, and that those of the theatre didn't suit me. That the lie in the novel suited me better; and finally, that the truth of autobiography suited me better yet."

35. "Although I related this affair—very inaccurately [très inexactement]—in *The Mandarins* . . ." (*FCir*, 124).

36. Bair, " 'My Life,' " 242.

37. Yolanda Astarita Patterson, "Entretien avec Simone de Beauvoir, 20 juin 1978," *French Review* 52, no. 5 (1979): 751, my translation.

38. Ibid., my translation.

39. In his chapter "Autobiographie et roman," in *L'autobiographie* (Paris: Presses universitaires de France, 1979), Georges May, focusing on a distinction similar to that suggested here between "true" and "real," challenges "the common misconception . . . that novels are more 'true' than autobiographies." Dismissing claims of Anatole France and André Gide that the "truth" is found in novels, he writes: "The truth and the lie of which they speak do not belong to the same order of reality. The truth . . . is that of their personality, whereas the lie that they recognize only affects their text. The commonly held idea that the novel is truer than autobiography is thus partly based on a sophism" (183, my translation).

40. It is interesting that Beauvoir closes one volume of her memoirs with the passage from which I quoted above (*Prime*, 479) and that in her preface to the next volume, *Force of Circumstance*, she is quick to warn her readers that the truth of this book can be found only in an overview: "I suggest that its truth is not expressed in any one of its pages but only in their totality" (*FCir*, vii). In autobiography, as in the novel, discrepancies, inaccuracies, even lies may not be avoided. Therefore, though constantly policing for "accuracy," the memorialist also asks her readers to read *less literally*, and to remember that lies may become part of the fabric of truth.

41. Nancy K. Miller, "Women's Autobiography in France: For a Dialectics of Identification," in McConnell-Ginet, Borker, and Furman, *Women and Language*, 267 and 269.

42. Ibid., 271. Those autobiographical pacts described by Philippe Lejeune are probably the best known. See Lejeune, "The Autobiographical Pact," trans. Katherine Leary, in *On Autobiography*, ed. Paul John Eakin (1975; Minneapolis: University of Minnesota Press, 1989), 3–30. I would point out as well that the very concept of such a binding pact is resonant of (male) legislative systems.

43. Miller, "Women's Autobiography," 270.

44. In an intriguing and insightful article about some of Beauvoir's later writing, Elaine Marks notes that Beauvoir "transgresses what has become a ruling protocol for important writing in the 1970s and early 1980s: she revels in the referential fallacy and her writing remains readable." Marks, "Transgressing the (In)cont(in)ent Boundaries: The Body in Decline," *Yale French Studies* 72 (1986): 200.

45. Beauvoir as cited in Bair, " 'My Life,' " 241, emphasis added.

46. Ibid., emphasis added.

47. See, for example, Domna Stanton, "Autogynography: Is the Subject Different?" in *The Female Autograph*, ed. Stanton (University of Chicago Press), and Miller, "Women's Autobiography."

48. Miller, "Women's Autobiography," 263, emphasis in original.

49. Ibid., 263.

50. "There has certainly been an autobiographical explosion, but very often women think that all they need do is to tell their story. . . . And so they tell it, and it has no literary value whatsoever, neither in its style, nor in the universality which it ought to contain." Beauvoir in Wenzel, "Interview," 9.

51. This is very different from her approach to her fiction where she on several occasions evokes George Eliot and Virginia Woolf, implicitly placing herself among women novelists. See, for example, *Prime*, 291 and *FCir*, 46.

52. Beauvoir as cited in Bair, " 'My Life,' " 242.

53. Ibid.

54. See n. 21.

55. "Mon expérience d'écrivain," 456: "I am thinking of Proust, because he is the one who said that the work of literature, the world of literature, is the privileged locus of intersubjectivity" (my translation). Beauvoir is actually referring here to both the novel and autobiography.

56. These "equations" are derived from the sequence of sentences: *Xavière*

vivait. La trahison de Françoise vivait. Elle revit le visage de Xavière décomposé par la souffrance. Mon crime. Il existait pour toujours. Xavière existait, la trahison existait. Elle existe en chair et en os, ma criminelle figure. To read this way is admittedly to assume or impose equivalencies that the text does not directly or explicitly authorize. It is a reading that privileges formal over semantic cues, the repetitions and parallel structures in contiguous statements inviting substitutions. Furthermore, the pivotal pronoun "elle" in the above passage, because it could conceivably stand for any of the three noun subjects, further encourages and supports such a reading (as does the earlier pronoun "il," which, in a similar though less striking fashion, could claim both "Mon crime" and "le visage de Xavière" as antecedents).

57. The crime of the letters may appear to be the crime of writing, but it is important to remember here that the letters Françoise burns are *not* her own writing. They were written and addressed to her by Gerbert and Pierre. It is not Françoise the writer, but Françoise *addressed* who is thus incriminated. Nevertheless, letters evidence correspondence, and Françoise's side of the exchange is implicit. Of course, the effect of excluding Françoise's writing is to exclude it from the final purge as well. In the end, Françoise's writing then either continues to exist in a completely unpoliced state beyond the text, or it has been so thoroughly policed from the start that it never existed and never will. Françoise is either defiantly guilty of writing or disturbingly innocent.

58. It is undoubtedly significant that Xavière, originally Françoise's *protégée*, apprentices herself to Pierre in order to learn acting. What is perhaps most interesting, however, is not that Françoise is the writer and Xavière the actress, but that both women are in a sense apprenticed or appended to Pierre who is writer, director, and actor. The implications of this will be discussed at greater length in the final section of this chapter.

59. Walter Benjamin wrote that "death is the sanction of everything that the storyteller can tell. He has borrowed his authority from death." Benjamin, *Illuminations,* trans. Harry Zohn (New York: Schocken, 1968), 94.

60. I would note that a connection might be drawn between Xavière's implied indecipherability and the fact that Françoise *solves* her at the end *for the crime,* indeed for a whole series of terms, these equivalences being the necessary first step to canceling her out.

61. I am also reminded of another English verb from the same Latin root: *to convict.* Françoise may want to convince Xavière of the innocence of her intentions (although this is questionable since she never articulates any such object of her convincing), but the word "convaincre" also contains traces of her desire to shift the guilt, to accuse and even convict the other woman.

62. Albert Camus, *The Rebel,* trans. Anthony Bower (New York: Knopf, 1954), 11.

63. See *Prime,* 411, French preserved in translation.

64. In his comparison of crimes of passion and logic, Camus goes on to say that "the Penal Code distinguishes between them by the useful concept of premeditation" (*The Rebel,* 11). Françoise's murder of Xavière, appearing not in its consequences but in its preparation, is clearly represented by and as its *premeditation.*

65. Martha Noel Evans offers a good analysis of the fact that the murder is never actually committed within the novel. See Evans, *Masks of Tradition*, 97. I have already shown, furthermore, that the dedication to Olga radically subverts the criminal gesture of turning on the gas, by framing it and thereby transforming it into an eternal death threat.

66. Evans writes that "Françoise becomes in effect Pierre's writing" (ibid., 85). While Pierre's role as Françoise's "narrator" is clear, the progression from narration to writing is perhaps less obvious. I believe we may justify it on the basis of the imagery used: the operation that Pierre performs on the raw material "recounted" to him by Françoise suggests the writer's craft. *Writing* is the final achievement, the fixing of the story as text, as truth. Nor must we overlook the criminal implications of witnessing (and the consequences of locating "truth" with the witness). One can be a witness for the defense or for the prosecution. Pierre's power as a witness relates to his ability to offer a definitive version that may either exculpate or incriminate.

67. *Prime*, 270–273. Acknowledging that the ending is the weakest part of the novel, Beauvoir explains that Françoise would have been incapable of killing Xavière, that, in fact, "[to] pierce Françoise's inner defenses and turn her into a monster[,] there was only one character who possessed the necessary strength, and that was Pierre" (*Prime*, 270).

68. Ibid., 272–273. Beauvoir takes the necessity of this "autocensure" for granted. In some ways what is censored in Beauvoir's fictional and autobiographical writing (like the unexamined unconscious) is the most provocative and one might even say essential material.

69. Similarly, Beauvoir shows but refuses to condemn Sartre's complicity in the murder of Olga in *L'Invitée* (*Prime*, 252–253). Beauvoir had been intending to use Simone Weil as the model for Xavière until Sartre suggested that Olga "would suit [her] purpose far better." If it was, in fact, *Sartre* who offered Olga up as the perfect victim, Beauvoir relates this not in order to blame Sartre but only conveniently to exculpate herself. Are we to believe that it never occurred to her on her own to kill off Olga "on paper"?

70. Beauvoir, *L'Invitée* (original French edition), 157, emphasis added. ("It would have been necessary to question/reexamine everything.")

71. For this reader, there are in Françoise's litany resonances of a line from the "petite madeleine" episode in Proust's *A la recherche du temps perdu*, vol. 1 (Paris: Gallimard [Pléiade], 1954): "J'avais cessé de me sentir *médiocre, contingent, mortel*" (45, emphasis added). ("I had ceased now to feel mediocre, accidental, mortal." Translation from *Remembrance of Things Past*, vol. 1, trans. C. K. Scott Moncrieff [New York: Random House, 1934], 34.) Describing the human condition and the transcendent experience afforded by memory and art, the Proustian model seems to me to be a universal backdrop for Beauvoir's refrain. Beauvoir's version imposes two limitations on the universal model: it focuses upon criminal transgression and upon gender. Reading Proust and Beauvoir together, one may then tend to see the "universal" anguish and transcendence expressed in Proust as in fact a *male* counterpart to the limited, personal, and guilt-tainted experience in Beauvoir, which is marked by the language as female.

72. *L'Invitée, Le ravissement de Lol V. Stein, Kamouraska,* and *Mrs. Dalloway* all also *begin* with the protagonist alone. The naming of a woman in the first or second sentence and the return to her in the last creates a certain emphatic unity of form. As we shall see in the Post(modern)script, Nicole Brossard's *Le désert mauve* also conforms—in its own way—to this model.

Chapter Two
Cries and Lies: *Le ravissement de Lol V. Stein*

1. All references to the French are to the 1964 Gallimard Folio edition. Both of the published English translations of the novel (*The Ravishing of Lol Stein*, trans. Richard Seaver [New York: Grove Press, 1966], and *The Rapture of Lol V. Stein*, trans. Eileen Ellenbogen [London: Hamish Hamilton, 1967]) include some effective *literary* renderings, but also numerous errors and imprecisions and an unfortunate tendency to resolve ambiguities. My close readings requiring greater lexical fidelity (and more literal translation), I therefore chose to use the Seaver translation as a base text only, and to modify it freely and sometimes extensively, frequently consulting and occasionally borrowing from Ellenbogen (page references are to Seaver). Where I have abandoned Seaver's translation altogether (and started from scratch) I give page references to the original French, indicated thus: "fr" followed by page number.

2. I am talking only about first impressions here. The narrator's "shifty" identity is considered later in this chapter.

3. Viviane Forrester, "Voir. Etre vue," *Magazine littéraire* 158 (March 1980): 12. Translation mine.

4. ". . . il manquait déjà quelque chose à Lol pour être—elle dit: là" (12).

5. Jacques Lacan, "Hommage fait à Marguerite Duras du Ravissement de Lol V. Stein," *Cahiers Renaud-Barrault* 52 (1965): 7–15.

6. Ibid., 9. Translation mine.

7. To speak of a psychoanalytic "primal moment of truth" is, however, a gross oversimplification, for it is not a matter of returning to a fixed point, but of an endless repetition, reworking, untangling that resembles the narrative process. The moment of truth is a fallacious "emblem." Shoshana Felman makes a similar point when she asks whether interpretation might not be "a gift of language—that is, a reply to the analysand's address—rather than a gift of truth." See Felman, *Jacques Lacan and the Adventure of Insight: Psychoanalysis in Contemporary Culture* (Cambridge: Harvard University Press, 1987), 120. Such distinctions have implications for the naive and simplistic assumptions that make crime the reason behind the law.

8. In *Lol V. Stein,* we find not only the triangle of Lol, Anne-Marie Stretter, and Michael Richardson, but also that of Lol, Tatiana Karl, and Jacques Hold. I am interpreting "Oedipal triangle" as the scene in which the child is excluded from but witness to the parents' sexuality. When we say the triangles in *Lol V. Stein* "recall," we do not mean a direct reference to Freud's Oedipus in all of its complexity, but rather certain resonances of that scene's dynamics.

9. For a critique of the privileged position accorded thematic and psychoana-

lytic interpretations of Duras, see Pascal Durand, "Le lieu de Marguerite Duras," in *Ecrire dit-elle: imaginaires de Marguerite Duras*, ed. Danielle Bajomée and Ralph Heyndels (Brussels: Université de Bruxelles, 1985), 245–246.

10. The inflected French word makes clear, as the English equivalent cannot easily do, that these are women.

11. But does he *actually* follow her? Jacques Hold's story is full of contradictions and not necessarily to be believed. Does his testimony have the weight of his having *witnessed* Lol? Such questions inform the discussion of invention and authority later in this chapter.

12. On page 24 of Seaver's translation of the novel (on page 33 in the French), Lol's husband, Jean Bedford, uses the word "virtuality" to describe her gentleness.

13. What moves is still "virtual": *un corps infirme*, not a person. We always seem to end up with Lol, as Béatrice Didier suggests, able neither to possess nor to be possessed. See Didier, "Thèmes et structures de l'absence dans *Le ravissement de Lol V. Stein*," in Bajomée and Heyndels, *Ecrire dit-elle*, 72.

14. Ibid., 80. Translations mine.

15. Pages 52–57 in the French and pages 42–48 in Seaver's translation.

16. This idea seems to be related to Lacan's conception that "the unconscious of the subject is the discourse of the Other." See "Function and Field of Speech and Language in Psychoanalysis," in *Ecrits: A Selection*, trans. Alan Sheridan (New York: Norton, 1977), 3–113. An essential element in Lacan's formulation, however, is its emphasis upon intersubjectivity and reflexivity. The Other is not a locus of answers, but of responses. Jacqueline Rose ("Introduction II," in *Feminine Sexuality: Jacques Lacan and the école freudienne*, ed. Juliet Mitchell, ed. and trans. J. Rose [New York: Norton, 1982]) offers a lucid elaboration of why the question of one's identity as thus posed is unanswerable. Shoshana Felman, in *Jacques Lacan*, also usefully explores the implications of the "new mode of reflexivity" inaugurated by Freud and illuminated by Lacan:

> [It] necessarily incorporates a passage through the Other, not as a reflection of the self but as a radical difference . . . to which, paradoxically, the very movement of reflexivity is addressed . . . reflexivity, therefore, which, passing through the Other, returns to itself without quite being able to rejoin itself; a reflexivity which is thus untotalizable, that is, irreducibly dialogic, and in which what is returned to the self from the Other is, paradoxically, the ignorance or the forgetfulness of its own message. (60)

17. Michel Foucault, *The Archaeology of Knowledge*, trans. A. M. Sheridan Smith (New York: Pantheon, 1972), 7 and 138–140. Credit must go to David Krause, in his article "Reading Bon's Letter and Faulkner's *Absalom, Absalom!*" (*PMLA* 99 [1984]), for my use of "reading" here, since (Krause points out) Foucault does not speak explicitly of reading but of "archaeological analysis and the history of ideas" (229–230).

18. The interrupted sentence "You are so close to" appears here as it appears in the French text (169) without ellipsis points or other diacritical marking of the break.

19. See the discussion of this sentence earlier in this chapter.

20. "[Michael Richardson] n'a plus qu'une tâche à accomplir, toujours la même dans l'univers de Lol: . . . [il] commence à dévêtir une autre femme que Lol

et . . . il en reste là; ébloui, un Dieu lassé par cette mise à nu, sa tâche unique, et Lol attend vainement qu'il la reprenne, *de son corps infirme de l'autre elle crie*, elle attend en vain, elle crie en vain" (50–51, emphasis added). Neither of the published English translations adequately conveys the complexities and ambiguities of this passage. Lol does not cry out "with her body rendered infirm by the other" (Seaver); nor does "the frail body of her other self [cry] out" (Ellenbogen). Lol cries out "from/with her infirm body *of the other.*" Hers is now "the body of the other." This difficult phrase must be read in relation to the description, earlier in the same sentence, of Michael Richardson's task: "to undress a woman *other* than Lol." Who is the other woman? Watching that other body *mise à nue*, Lol becomes herself "the other woman" (as the other is now the one) and it is *her* body, infirm, on the way to being replaced, effaced, annihilated, that cries out.

21. Denis Donoghue, *Ferocious Alphabets* (New York: Columbia University Press, 1984). In Donoghue's terms an epireading reads *back* toward a more authentic "source" (such as speech), reconstituting an "absence," whereas a graphireading "acknowledges writing as a primary act" (160) and "disowns the dream of presence" (165).

22. Lol's silence is an essential counterpart to Jacques Hold's narration. Note, for example, that despite the fact that Jacques Hold says of Lol, "at the end she talks nearly all the time" (fr 174), by thus appropriating and muting her discourse his narration effectively silences her.

23. Even as Lol "inscribes this transgression," however, it is contained *within* the story. Jacqueline Rose reading Lacan has cautioned against assuming a radical otherness for women outside of language: "Woman is excluded *by* the nature of words, meaning that the definition poses her as exclusion. Note that this is not the same thing as saying that woman is excluded *from* the nature of words" ("Introduction II," 49).

24. This is the nature of the subject regardless of gender. It is when Lol becomes the subject/object of a masterminding analytic discourse (whether that of Jacques Lacan or of Jacques Hold) that her role as a woman seems to contribute to a certain mystification and to accentuate the problematic.

25. The title of Lacan's piece on Duras, "Hommage fait à Marguerite Duras du Ravissement de Lol V. Stein," brilliantly illustrates this endless shifting. Since none of the words is underscored or fixed as "title" and since there is no limiting and defining *punctuation*, multiple meanings circulate freely with the capitalized nouns around the prepositions, and it is impossible to tell which part of the phrase is subject of/to which other.

26. The normalization of the place names and the dropping of Lol's middle initial, V., in the English title—and generally throughout the novel—are probably Richard Seaver's most glaring and unfortunate mistranslations. Eileen Ellenbogen's title does not repeat this omission although something else is (perhaps unavoidably) lost in the rendering of "ravissement" as "rapture." Béatrice Didier refers to S. Tahla as "the name [that] does not name" ("Thèmes et structures," 79); and Didier Coste ("S. Thala: capitale du possible," in Bajomée and Heyndels, *Ecrire dit-elle*, 165–178) notes that "S. Thala is formed like a person's name: Lol V. Stein was born here in no-place-person [non-lieu-personne]" (169). The spelling of the name "Tahla" as "Thala" is not Coste's mistake: while we find

"Tahla" in the novel, the alternative spelling occurs in several other contexts, including in Duras's interviews with Xavière Gauthier, which were read and corrected by Duras prior to publication (*Les Parleuses* [Paris: Minuit, 1974], published in English as *Woman to Woman*, trans. and with an afterword by Katharine A. Jensen [Lincoln: University of Nebraska Press, 1987]). This "non-lieu," S. Tahla/Thala is clearly as unstable, *unfixable* as Lol herself.

27. Geoffrey Hartman, "Literature High and Low: The Case of the Mystery Story," in Most and Stowe, *The Poetics of Murder*, 212.

28. While this section sets out to establish *textual* connections between Lol's *crises* and the possibility of *crime*, it should also be noted that there exist in this novel pronounced sound metonymies (chains of association based on near or partial homonyms) that link *cry*, *crisis*, and *crime* (*cri*, *crise*, and *crime*). Furthermore, an analogy between writing and crime is illustrated and reinforced by a chain of word associations possible in French: crime . . . crise . . . je crie (I cry out) . . . j'écris (I write).

29. In his reading of Proust's *A la recherche du temps perdu*, in *Figures III* (Paris: Seuil, 1972), Gérard Genette uses the phrase "homonymie sur métonymie" to describe a metonymic chain of associations based upon homonyms (59). The example he gives is of Swann who, because of his passion for Odette who lives on rue La Pérouse, frequents a restaurant of the same name. Such, says Genette, is the "rhetoric" of desire. The homophonic echo in Lol's "on bat" likewise seems to indicate not an *explicit* association (one that might have been expressed as "La police est en bas. Elle bat . . ."), but rather a mechanism of subconscious association. The sounds suggest a connection between the two sentences that the signs themselves do not clearly signify. Might not such homophonically triggered metonymy be considered part of a "rhetoric" of guilt and/or fear?

30. Monique Schneider, "Au seuil de l'immolation," in Bajomée and Heyndels, *Ecrire dit-elle*, 129, translation mine.

31. There is no break, no gap, no end. Death is elided, forgotten. Yet, and this is one of the paradoxes of *Lol V. Stein*, this moment of forgetting death *is* the moment of death. The section "Traces" later in this chapter considers death and *forgetting* in their relationship to the telling of Lol's story.

32. In my chapter on *L'Invitée* the Pierre-Xavière-Françoise triangle is similarly analyzed in terms of the threats of "indifference" and "displacement." In Duras's reworking of the same kind of gendered triangulation, however, there is no longer a woman and an "other" woman. Lol and Tatiana are *each* "the other woman," and the triangle seems stable—but only through the absence of the female subject.

33. To attribute all of these statements unequivocally to Lol is to overlook the ambiguities and convolutions of this dialogue. In the complete passage from which the quoted statements are extracted, the alternating voices do not fully succeed in producing a coherent interchange, and since speakers are never named, there are moments of uncertain attribution—notably in the statement "It's a substitute." Here, through the polysemy of the text, boundaries between the past and the present, Anne-Marie Stretter and Tatiana Karl, Lol's voice and Jacques Hold's, lose their ability to delineate—voices flow together and are confused.

34. In Duras, the binary relation of love (to love is to "regard") is always com-

plicated by the triangular relation of desire (to regard the "regard"). This idea is developed later in this chapter.

35. Borgomano, "Le corps et le texte," in Bajomée and Heyndels, *Ecrire dit-elle*, 59, translation mine.

36. Lol wants to be "flesh to flesh" with the *gesture*. Yet the gesture itself is ultimately also one of flesh to flesh, and this vocabulary of bodies cannot help but refer beyond itself to the body upon which the gesture is to be enacted: the body that is then named in the following paragraph, that of the other woman. Thus "son cadavre" is both the corpse of the gesture (the impossible act) and the "corpse" of the other woman who receives the gesture. The word "cadavre" emphasizes both body and mortality.

37. Whose fantasy *is* this? We must not be blinded to the fact that what we are reading is in fact *Jacques Hold's fantasy* of Lol's desire. It is Jacques Hold who dreams of the totally naked woman on the one hand and of the other woman totally *eclipsed* in/by her on the other. This is the man attempting to know or to say "what a woman wants" (*pace* Freud). Jacques Hold can think of no other way of explaining why or how the other woman's body is so important to Lol. Hold's own investment in the woman's nudity is revealed on page 161 where he imagines her nakedness "complete, for the first time oddly enough."

38. The corresponding passages in Seaver's translation are on pages 146 and 147.

39. It is important to keep in mind that Lol's evasion is not complete. At the critical moment of indistinguishability (when there would theoretically no longer be an *other woman* and desire and crime would vanish along with the triangle) Lol still differs from Tatiana Karl in two small but significant ways: unlike Tatiana she names herself (using both their names) and her eyes are "free of remorse." These differences maintain at least vestiges of the triangle (with all of its attendant criminal baggage), but because the terms of Lol's difference are precisely her freedom from guilt and the indifference of her name (that is, her ability to designate herself by different names), she escapes the criminal implications. She never puts herself in the position of assuming criminal responsibility.

40. Hold's denial of that separation is also forcefully and poignantly inscribed in his use of the first person plural pronoun in the last scene. It is significant that the final words of his narration are "our trip," conscripting Lol into his project, his script.

41. Gérard Genette's description of "figures" illustrates this idea: "Every figure is translatable, and bears its translation, transparently visible, like a watermark, or a palimpsest, beneath its apparent text." "Figures," in *Figures of Literary Discourse*, trans. Alan Sheridan (New York, Columbia University Press, 1982), 50.

42. Duras and Gauthier, *Woman to Woman*, 169.

43. Jacques Derrida, *Positions*, trans. and annotated by Alan Bass (Chicago: University of Chicago Press, 1981), 26. Indeed, is not the unarticulated image of Lol in the rye at the end a "trace of a trace"?

44. I have chosen to use "rumor" here because it expresses the surreptitious nature of the fragment overheard. I use the word in the broad sense to include the traces of its more obsolete meanings as well: a sound, a word, a message. What is

particularly appropriate about the rumor is that it is unsubstantiated. A substantiated rumor ceases to be a rumor and becomes something else: evidence? Rumor is thus the perfect emblem for stories, those fictions whose referents cannot coexist with them on the same plane.

45. My reference to the scene of writing is an acknowledgment of the importance to this discussion of Derrida's work on memory, writing, and traces in his reading of Freud's "Wunderblock": "Freud and the Scene of Writing," in *Writing and Difference*, 196–231.

46. Lol's remark ("Des gens le font") appears on the surface to say less than this. A benign interpretation of this passage has Lol merely saying that some people destroy their own houses when they move away. Because this is a startling idea, however, one tends to question it. Do people really do that? And the same remark (in its ambiguity) seems to offer an answer to the very question it poses. People destroy their own houses precisely because *other people* will and do destroy them.

Chapter Three
Bearing Witness: *Kamouraska*

1. Anne Hébert, *Kamouraska*, trans. Norman Shapiro (New York: Crown, 1973; reprint, Toronto: General Publishing Company, 1982). All references to the French are to the 1970 Seuil edition. The 1982 General Publishing Company English edition appears to be a revision of Shapiro's translation although no translator is named. It is close but not identical in translation and pagination to the 1973 Crown edition. In general, I have used one or the other of these texts but with frequent modifications as necessary for my close textual analysis. Page references included in my text are to the 1982 English edition. When I have abandoned Shapiro's translation and that of the 1982 edition altogether and substituted my own translation, I have given references to the original French edition, indicated as "fr" followed by page number.

2. In the French original, the contrast between the formal "you" in George's letter ("Vous viendrez?") and the familiar "you" of Elisabeth's despairing cry ("Ton silence à jamais") is particularly striking.

3. The deceptive power of letters had of course been most strikingly demonstrated in the letter that Elisabeth sent to Antoine announcing her pregnancy. The language of this letter cunningly obscured the fact that it was George Nelson and not Antoine Tassy who was the baby's father: "My darling husband—your loving wife is writing—to announce a blessed event—" (149).

4. Nelson is often described as "étranger," that is, "foreigner" or "stranger." Through her desire, Elisabeth shares this exile with him: "I'm the one who calls to George Nelson in the night. The voice of desire reaches us, rules us, ravages us. One thing only is necessary. To be forever lost, both of us. Each with the other. Myself, foreigner/stranger and wicked [étrangère et malfaisante]" (125).

5. These are women of the lower classes, innkeepers' wives and servants, for the "good women" of bourgeois Catholic society, including Antoine Tassy's mother, are quite willing to perjure themselves in order to preserve the honor of one of their own. Of course, any assessment of the situation is complicated by the fact that Elisabeth was never wholly "one of their own." Despite her careful and proper

upbringing, she was drawn to the wild, pipe-smoking, fifteen-year-old Aurélie, and had also drawn Aurélie into her own world.

6. Analyzing several key "diglossic" passages in *Kamouraska*, Ben-Zion Shek shows to what extent they reveal historical and ideological tensions and "the depth of cultural alienation as seen in the symbolic clash of English and French." "Diglossia and Ideology: Socio-Cultural Aspects of Translation in Québec," *Etudes sur le texte et ses transformations: Traductions et cultures* 1, no. 1 (1988): 86. See also Janet M. Paterson, *Anne Hébert: Architexture romanesque* (Ottawa: Editions de l'Université d'Ottawa, 1985). Paterson suggests that the "direct reporting in English of the *acte d'accusation*" is part of "the code of the real" in the novel, but that as the French narration proceeds, "it is the dream that engenders the multiplicity of voices by inducing a fragmentation of narrative authority and thus creating in the discourse an ambiguity between reality and dream" (142–143, translation mine).

7. Mary Jean Green notes that in this passage Elisabeth is denying guilt by "affirm[ing] her own identity as a princess who has gone on to become a queen." "The Witch and the Princess: The Feminine Fantastic in the Fiction of Anne Hébert," *American Review of Canadian Studies* 15, no. 2 (1985): 143. Green argues subtly and persuasively that Elisabeth chooses to assume the role of the princess (rather than that of the witch) so that she may see herself "as a passive victim, powerless to control her fate, and thus innocent" (144).

8. Janet Paterson points out that the "jeu d'échecs" in *Kamouraska* is, in fact, a *mise en abyme*: the chess games that George and Antoine played in school reflect not only the fiction (George will take Antoine's "queen"); "as a *game/play* [à titre de *jeu*]," they reflect the dramatic element in the novel as well (*Anne Hébert*, 146, translation mine). I will further analyze the chess game later in this chapter.

9. In the French text, this colonizing gesture is illustrated in the language itself: "The Queen! Toujours the Queen! C'est à mourir de rire" (44).

10. Note that this closed world was also defined by a *language* of its own: Latin.

11. It is interesting to note that the society against which Elisabeth rebels is referred to by Murray Sachs as "the rigid, *matriarchal*, and Catholic society of French-speaking Canada," and by Elaine Hopkins Garrett as "a *patriarchal* and Jansenist society" (emphases mine). See Sachs, "Love on the Rocks: Anne Hébert's *Kamouraska*," in *Traditionalism, Nationalism, and Feminism: Women Writers of Quebec*, ed. Paula Gilbert Lewis (Westport, Conn.: Greenwood Press, 1985), 121; and Garrett, "Intentionality and Representation in Anne Hébert's *Kamouraska*," *Québec Studies* 6 (1988): 102.

12. "Elle a *le diable* dans le corps. Vous ne réussirez jamais à la mater!" (52, emphasis added). English translation mine. (The corresponding passage in the 1982 English edition is on page 47.) One of the important resonances in the original is lost in translation. In French, the verb "mater" again introduces the language of the "jeu d'échecs." Elisabeth would, on every level, resist being checked, being mated, being checkmated.

13. Murray Sachs quotes Anne Hébert as having said that "one of the themes of *Kamouraska* is 'la déculpabilisation de la femme'" ("Love on the Rocks," 115).

14. Given that words in George Nelson's "mother tongue" appear so rarely in

the novel, we may perhaps be excused for seeing in the following description of the trade name on Nelson's stove a metonymic connection between that inscription and the "orphaned" doctor himself: "I amuse myself by trying to decipher the slanting, rounded letters [les lettres *bâtardes*] of 'Warm Morning,' registered trademark [marque *déposée*]" (120 in French edition, translation and emphasis mine). This passage may be found (translated more freely) on page 117 in the English-language edition. Obviously, the metonymic connection to which I refer is lost in translation.

15. The translations are mine. The published English text does not distinguish between the two sentences, rendering both as "Protestants can't get into Heaven" (122 and 153).

16. Using the "subtext" of the Québécois legend of *La Corriveau* to elucidate her reading of *Kamouraska*, Mary Jean Green clearly articulates the way in which the language that condemns and imprisons is necessarily and fundamentally defined by gender: "*La Corriveau*'s cage was built for her by an English-speaking governor, whose legal language formed bars between this woman and her freedom. Elisabeth's cage, too, is built from the words of a language not her own, *a patriarchal language with its own mythology of femininity*" ("The Witch and the Princess," 145, emphasis mine).

17. The French is even more insistent, using the imperfect of the verbs where we might normally expect a past conditional. "Sans toi, j'étais libre et je refaisais ma vie." This is the "imparfait de conséquence infaillible," emphasizing the potential certainty of that unrealized result by bringing to bear on the conditional the literal sense of the imperfect: "Without you, *I was free* and was remaking my life."

18. I cannot agree with Sachs's interpretation of the novel's ending (that the "final nightmare image of Elisabeth as pariah expresses her despairing inner reaction as she takes in the truth that her husband has apparently survived the crisis and will not die" ["Love on the Rocks," 118]). Although in the novel, "Anne-Marie says her father is completely cured, now that the priest has given him the last rites" (246), I am inclined to read this "cure" as spiritual and symbolic rather than physical and to see no incompatibility between it and Jérôme's impending death. Everything still hangs in the balance, and the image that defines the novel's ending is that of "a fragile thread that . . . might break at any moment" (250).

19. For a resolutely positive answer to these questions, see Gabrielle Pascal-Smith, "La Condition féminine dans *Kamouraska* d'Anne Hébert," *French Review* 54, no. 1 (1980): 85–92. Pascal-Smith comes to a similar conclusion about the incrimination of Elisabeth at the end of *Kamouraska*, but she interprets Elisabeth's crime as an indication of her strength and power: "In a complete reversal of roles, Elisabeth is now the one who embodies strength [la force] and that is why she is judged" (91, translation mine).

Chapter Four
Speaking Madness: *Mrs. Dalloway*

1. The quotation used as a heading is from Virginia Woolf, *Mrs. Dalloway* (New York: Harcourt, 1925), 5 and 177. All future references are to this edition.

2. That the psychoanalytic paradigm might in some ways serve as a model for narrative is suggested by Peter Brooks in his analysis of Freud's "Masterplot." In

addition, Brooks notes that Tzvetan Todorov "makes the detective story the narrative of narratives, its classical structure a laying-bare of the structure of all narrative" (*Reading for the Plot*, 90–112 and 25).

3. In her introduction to the Modern Library edition of the novel, Woolf herself refers to Septimus as Clarissa's "double" (vi). The pairing of these two protagonists has been widely analyzed. See, for example, the following articles: Lee R. Edwards, "War and Roses: The Politics of *Mrs. Dalloway*," in *The Authority of Experience: Essays in Feminist Criticism*, ed. Arlyn Diamond and Lee R. Edwards (Amherst: University of Massachusetts Press, 1977), 160–177; Isabel Gambel, "Clarissa Dalloway's 'Double,'" in *Critics on Virginia Woolf*, ed. Jacqueline E. M. Latham (London: George Allen and Unwin, 1970), 52–56; Suzette A. Henke, "*Mrs. Dalloway*: The Communion of the Saints," in *New Feminist Essays on Virginia Woolf*, ed. Jane Marcus (Lincoln: University of Nebraska Press, 1981), 125–147; John Hawley Roberts, "'Vision and Design' in Virginia Woolf," in Latham, *Critics*, 61–69; and Lucio P. Ruotolo, "Clarissa Dalloway," in *Virginia Woolf: A Collection of Criticism*, ed. Thomas S. W. Lewis (New York: McGraw, 1975).

4. The anticipation of the party permeates the novel and comes to figure a much more general anticipation. This is especially evident in one image attributed to Clarissa: "[she] felt often as she stood hesitating one moment on the threshold of her drawing-room, an exquisite suspense, such as might stay a diver before plunging while the sea darkens and brightens beneath him" (44). The "plunging" imagery in the novel has been discussed in some detail by J. Hillis Miller in "*Mrs. Dalloway*: Repetition as the Raising of the Dead," chapter 7 of his book *Fiction and Repetition* (Cambridge: Harvard University Press, 1982), 176–202.

5. Miller suggests that "if there is no past in the cinema, there is no present in a novel, or only a specious, ghostly present which is generated by the narrator's ability to resurrect the past not as reality but as verbal image" (*Fiction and Repetition*, 188). This verbal image is the *present* of testimony that, reaching over the abyss of death, derives its power from the past.

6. "If ever I have a moment, thought Clarissa (but never would she have a moment any more), I shall go and see her at Ealing" (58). The empty social phrase "to have a moment" here suggests to Clarissa the special "moments" of illumination (an important concept for Virginia Woolf—see, for example, the collection of her autobiographical writings entitled *Moments of Being*) like Sally Seton's kiss ("the most exquisite moment of her whole life" [52]) that she had only a short while before been recalling. Time she may have (though "she feared time itself" [44]), but, she thinks, no more such *moments*. "Narrower and narrower would her bed be" (45–46).

7. "DiBattista, *Mrs. Dalloway*: Virginia Woolf's Memento Mori," chapter 2 of her book *Virginia Woolf's Major Novels*, 47 and 48. See also Emily Jensen's description of the medical profession as one of the "bastions of masculine power and authority." Jensen, "Clarissa Dalloway's Respectable Suicide," in *Virginia Woolf: A Feminist Slant*, ed. Jane Marcus (Lincoln: University of Nebraska Press, 1983), 165.

8. "On Being Ill" (1930), reprinted in *The Moment and Other Essays* (New York: Harcourt, 1948), 14.

9. *Madness and Civilization: A History of Insanity in the Age of Reason*, trans. Richard Howard (1961; New York: Random House, 1965), 253.

10. "On Being Ill," 20.

11. Ibid., 19, emphasis added. Maria DiBattista, in *Virginia Woolf's Major Novels*, also quotes this passage, focusing, however, not on the policing of meaning but on the association between madness and unmediated and inexpressible sensual experience. She uses this passage to conclude that "in the intemperate madness of Septimus . . . the world reveals its beauty, a beauty that words can't express nor reason explain" (51). Of course, the question of "meaning" is implicit in this observation since, as is suggested in the novel, "beauty" even as it resists meaning in one sense is clearly meaningful in another. The relationship between "beauty" and this other kind of "meaning" is clear in Septimus's incoherent writings, so when he told Rezia to write, "she wrote it down just as he spoke it. Some things were very beautiful; others sheer nonsense" (212). In *Mrs. Dalloway*, Septimus returns to the world a "meaningless" message that over time comes "to mean something" to Rezia, for when Septimus asks her to burn his writings, she does not—she ties them with a piece of silk and will put them carefully away since "some were very beautiful, she thought" (224).

12. "Rashness is one of the properties of illness—outlaws that we are" ("On Being Ill," 19).

13. Jane Marcus described Septimus's refusal to procreate as his "principal social sin." "Middlebrow Marxism," *Virginia Woolf Miscellany*, Spring–Summer 1976, 5.

14. Evidence of repressed homosexual tendencies in both Septimus and Clarissa has been noted and analyzed by a number of readers, among them Suzette Henke ("Mrs. Dalloway," 141), Emily Jensen ("Clarissa Dalloway's Respectable Suicide," 169), and Beverly Ann Schlack (*Continuing Presences: Virginia Woolf's Use of Literary Allusion* [University Park: Pennsylvania State University Press, 1979], 63).

15. Peter Walsh remembers Clarissa as having had a special and, he thinks, unnaturally demonstrative affection for her dog, an attachment that he seems to associate with her "coldness," and with something "unyielding" in her in relation to *him*—and by extension to *men* (91 and 97). In fact, Peter gives us perhaps an important insight into Clarissa's marriage when he describes Richard Dalloway as good "with horses and dogs" and recalls "how good he was, for instance, when that great shaggy dog of Clarissa's got caught in a trap . . . and Dalloway did the whole thing; bandaged, made splints. . . . That was what she liked him for perhaps—that was what she needed" (113).

16. Foucault, *Madness and Civilization*, 88 and 89, emphasis added.

17. Through the ironic juxtaposition of this sentence with Bradshaw's behavior with Septimus and Rezia, Woolf renders Sir William's "reputation" as laughable as Holmes's bromide.

18. Stewart, *Death Sentences: Styles of Dying in British Fiction* (Cambridge: Harvard University Press, 1984), 271.

19. See Suzette Henke ("Mrs. Dalloway," 126) and Avrom Fleishman (*Virginia Woolf: A Critical Reading* [Baltimore: Johns Hopkins University Press, 1975], 77) for discussion of the "scapegoat" aspect of Septimus's story.

20. Rezia had trusted Sir William because of his name. She supposed (as the law would have one suppose) that a nice-sounding name guaranteed the niceness

of its bearer. Her realization of the error of this assumption marked the beginning of her mistrust of the doctors' control and of their self-serving manipulations of "meaning."

21. Elizabeth Abel sees *Mrs. Dalloway* as built around two myths ("rhetorical [and] ideological antithes[es]"): one centers on the Goddesses Proportion and Conversion, the other on the Solitary Traveller. Abel, "Narrative Structure(s) and Female Development: The Case of *Mrs. Dalloway*," in *The Voyage In*, ed. Abel, Marianne Hirsch, and Elizabeth Langland (Hanover: University Press of New England, 1983), 182. Maria DiBattista writes that the feminine lawgiver is a "metacharacter whose function is to embody the dignity of our solitude and to suggest the infinite mystery about ourselves as 'alone, alone, alone.' She is indisputably the antitype of Clarissa and Septimus, both 'lost in the process of living'" (*Virginia Woolf's Major Novels*, 59). While I would agree with DiBattista that the lawgiver defines and occupies a sanctuary where one does not suffer "the death of the soul," I would slightly amend her claim that the lawgiver is Clarissa's antitype. Indeed, DiBattista herself describes the lawgiver "[dispensing] the law of natural, mutual and voluntary association" (60). She no longer embodies merely solitude, but a communion of solitudes. Might one not call this a law of communication?

22. Elizabeth Abel gives a strong argument for comparing Clarissa and Rezia. She shows that even as Septimus's story doubles Clarissa's, Rezia's does as well. The two women implicitly share a "pastoral, female-centered" past, and as Septimus's death releases his wife "to return imaginatively" to that world, it also "enables Clarissa to resolve the developmental impasse that appears to be one cause of her constricted vitality" ("Narrative Structure(s)," 176).

23. DiBattista, *Virginia Woolf's Major Novels*, 59 and 61.

24. The dynamics of marriage (as a prototypical instance of gender relations) fascinated Virginia Woolf, particularly in relation to her concern with an "androgynous vision" of internal harmony between the artist's male and female natures (a concern dealt with most explicitly in *A Room of One's Own*). In her article "Virginia Woolf and Androgyny," Marilyn Farwell explores the "ambivalences and ambiguities" in Woolf's use of the concept, contending that Woolf "hedges between balance and fusion, only to resort to fusion at the end." (*Contemporary Literature* 16, no. 4 [1979]: 442–443). Farwell argues that such fusion is necessarily at the expense of the female principle, privileging the "traditional male quality of objectivity" through an exorcism of the personal (450). Maria DiBattista takes issue with Farwell's use of the word "fusion," arguing that for Woolf "borders aren't that easily abolished." She notes that the "communication/identification/participation" that together define "an inter-subjective ideal" do not in any way correspond to "a fusion of minds or identities" (personal correspondence). I agree that Woolf would have wholeheartedly rejected the idea of fusion: she was interested in the permeability—and not the abolition—of boundaries. But I also feel that Farwell's point about the hedging in Woolf's use of the concept of androgyny is well taken. When borders are permeable, nothing can be as clear-cut as before. Total separateness and total fusion are the extremes that haunt Woolf's text, more often in tension with one another than in balance.

25. Miller points out that many of the characters in *Mrs. Dalloway* desire that focus, that continuity, that completion. He cites several examples of "a kind of

telepathic insight" between people whom he describes as "endowed with a desire to take possession of [the] continuities" that are there not only "between the present and the past within [a single] mind" but also "from one mind to another." This is, however, a "modified translucency," for the power of communication is in all cases either incomplete or intermittent (*Fiction and Repetition*, 191–192).

26. Ibid., 180; Woolf quoted by Miller, 180–182. Quotation from Woolf taken from *A Writer's Diary*, 60.

27. "On Being Ill," 14.

28. Fleishman, *Virginia Woolf*, 81. Miller puts this in similar terms: "The novel seems to be based on an irreconcilable opposition between individuality and universality" (*Fiction and Repetition*, 183).

29. Béatrice Didier, *L'écriture-femme* (Paris: Presses universitaires de France, 1981), 228, translation mine.

30. Ibid., translation mine.

31. Robert Karen usefully distinguishes guilt and shame, writing that "if guilt is about behavior that has harmed others, shame is about not being good enough. Shame is often, of course, triggered by something you have done, but in shame, the way that behavior reflects on you is what counts. Shameful behavior is thus often a victimless crime; and shame itself is less clearly about morality than about conformity, acceptability, or character." "Shame," *Atlantic Monthly*, February 1992, 47.

32. See also Miller's analysis of this climactic moment (*Fiction and Repetition*, 196–197). Miller stresses the fact that "death is the place of true communion."

33. Stewart, *Death Sentences*, 277.

34. Victoria Glendinning, *Vita: The Life of V. Sackville-West* (New York: Alfred A. Knopf, 1983), 301.

35. *The Diary of Virginia Woolf 1920–1924*, vol. 2, ed. Anne Olivier Bell (London: Harcourt, Brace, Jovanovitch, 1977), entry for June 19, 1923, 248.

36. E. M. Forster, *Virginia Woolf: The Rede Lecture* (1941) (Cambridge: Cambridge University Press, 1942), 12.

37. DiBattista, *Virginia Woolf's Major Novels*, 28, emphasis in original.

38. Foucault, *Madness and Civilization*, 288–289, emphasis in original.

39. Foucault, "A Preface to Transgression," 33–34.

40. Ibid., 34.

41. Stewart, *Death Sentences*, 268.

42. Woolf's notes for *Mrs. Dalloway*, holograph notebook, Berg Collection, New York Public Library.

43. *Fiction and Repetition*, 198, 201. For Miller, the communication arising from the "embrace" of death "holds [the polarities] poised in their irreconciliation" (198). "Irreconciliation" seems consistent with the interrogatory form in which Woolf asks (what probably cannot be *affirmed* through language) whether death might be the reality.

44. It is interesting to compare this description to that of Mrs. Bradshaw, who "cramped, squeezed, pared, pruned" (152).

45. *Fiction and Repetition*, 178.

46. DiBattista, *Virginia Woolf's Major Novels*, 35.

Post(modern)script
D'une langue à l'autre or Speaking in Other Tongues: *Le désert mauve*

1. I owe my use here of this particular formulation to the anonymous Princeton University Press reader who described the incriminations in my book as a situation of "damned if you do, damned if you don't."

2. Nicole Brossard, *Mauve Desert*, trans. Susanne de Lotbinière-Harwood, (Toronto: Coach House Press, 1990). Originally published as *Le désert mauve* (Montreal: Editions de l'Hexagone, 1987). Page references accompanying English citations are to Lotbinière-Harwood's translation, which I have used throughout with occasional modifications. Page references accompanying French citations are to the Hexagone edition.

3. Brossard's article is included in the anthology *Montreal Massacre*, ed. Louise Malette and Marie Chalouh, trans. Marlene Wildeman (Charlottetown, P.E.I.: gynergy books, 1991), 31–33. This collection was originally published as *Polytechnique, 6 décembre* (Montreal: Remue-ménage, 1990). As the publisher of the English edition explains, Brossard and a number of the other contributors chose to represent the killer by his initials instead of his full name in order to underline the fact that the killing of fourteen women was "not the isolated act of a madman but a horrifying reflection of misogyny in our society" (9–10).

4. *Montreal Massacre*, 34 and 43.

5. Throughout this chapter I have chosen *not* to translate "l'homme long," which the English translation renders as "longman," because the French seems to me to convey more clearly the fact that this is not a proper name.

6. Nicole Brossard, "Order and Imagination," an interview by Beverley Daurio, *Books in Canada*, March 1991, 21.

7. See Barbara Godard, Sherry Simon, and Patricia Smart, "Symposium on Feminism and Postmodernism in Quebec: The Politics of Alliance," *Québec Studies* 9 (Fall 1989–Winter 1990): 131–150. In her remarks, Barbara Godard presented an exhaustive, cogent survey and analysis of the history and varied applications and implications of postmodernism, demonstrating how "the very elasticity of the term has assured that it . . . is located in a network of contradictory meanings" (132). Linda Hutcheon makes much the same point when she sets out to "theorize" postmodernism as "a contradictory phenomenon, one that uses and abuses, installs and then subverts, the very concepts it challenges." See Hutcheon, *A Poetics of Postmodernism: History, Theory, Fiction* (New York: Routledge, 1988), 3.

8. Simon in Godard, Simon, and Smart, "Symposium," 143. Simon in fact says that there "seems to be a consensus now" on this distinction, but there are, as will be seen in my discussion of the conversation among six Québec feminists, those who are unwilling to accept the term "postmodern" as referring to a feminist practice.

9. See in particular Louise Cotnoir, "La Post-modernité? un leurre," and France Théoret, "Les femmes ont une autre version de l'histoire," both included in the transcribed conversation, "Ce qu'on se dit le dimanche," *Tessera* 5 (September 1988): 31 and 34.

10. Gail Scott, "Pas au-delà? Ou faux pas?" in "Ce qu'on se dit le dimanche," 37.

11. Janet M. Paterson, *Moments postmodernes dans le roman québécois* (Ottawa: Les Presses de l'Université d'Ottawa, 1990), 20 and 23, translations mine. Paterson offers an extremely cogent survey and analysis of the history of the use of the term "postmodern" by different theorists in different countries and in different disciplines. She herself essentially adopts Lyotard's concept of the postmodern, for reasons that she very convincingly explains. See Jean-François Lyotard, *La Condition postmoderne* (Paris: Minuit, 1979). Paterson's own translation of her book is forthcoming, with an added chapter on *Le désert mauve*.

12. Catharine R. Stimpson, "Are the Differences Spreading?: Feminist Criticism and Postmodernism," *English Studies in Canada* 15, no. 4 (1989): 366.

13. Louise Dupré, "Une conscience posthistorique," in "Ce qu'on se dit le dimanche," 36, translation mine. Also extremely useful on this subject is Karen Gould's analysis in "Feminisme/Postmodernité/Esthétique de Lecture: *Le désert mauve* de Nicole Brossard," in *Le roman québécois depuis 1960: méthodes et analyses*, ed. Louise Milot and Jaap Lintvelt (Quebec: Université Laval, 1992), 195–213. Gould clearly articulates and explores the "common ground" between poststructuralist feminisms and so-called postmodern philosophy. Without reducing either the feminist or the postmodern to the terms of the other, her reading suggests that the postmodern "delegitimation of the metanarrative of science" and the postmodern "discourse on history" are in *Le désert mauve* transformed, reoriented, re-visioned by feminist structures and perspectives (175).

14. Any reference to "la fin de l'histoire" engages in contestation not only the metanarrative of History but also every narrative, every story. That postmodernism is frequently associated with a return to narrative forms (and a turn away from the more innovative forms that characterized the feminist writing of "la modernité" in Québec) is further evidence of the extent to which *narrative* is a postmodern problem.

15. In the development of my reading and analysis of *Le désert mauve*, I was particularly challenged and inspired by the questions, ideas, and readings (in discussion and in writing) of my students Catherine Perry, Miléna Andrews, and Christine Thomas. Many of my ideas took shape in relation to and in dialogue with theirs.

16. Patricia Smart, *Ecrire dans la maison du père: L'émergence du féminin dans la tradition littéraire du Québec* (1988; rev. ed Montreal: Québec/Amérique, 1990), 22, translation mine. Smart has also translated her own book into English as *Writing in the Father's House: The Emergence of the Feminine in the Quebec Literary Tradition* (Toronto: University of Toronto Press, 1991).

17. Smart, *Ecrire*, 335, translation mine.

18. The use of the word "allongée" to describe Angela Parkins's dying body can be no accident. Not only might one consider this word a *verbal participial* equivalent of *l'homme long*, it was also explicitly and reflexively associated with him in his first chapter: "l'homme long s'allonge [*l'homme long* stretches out]. . . ." The intermediate step is the appearance of the verb used to describe the man who passes in front of Mélanie by the pool in her next-to-last chapter. This man "who is not from the area" "stretches his body out [allonge son corps] on the towel."

When the past participle "allongée" is used to describe Angela Parkins right after *l'homme long* makes his appearance, we have little trouble in seeing that *the man* has left this mark on her.

19. Karen Gould in particular has carefully elaborated a pattern of intertextual references that establishes J. Robert Oppenheimer as a "figure of inspiration" for *l'homme long*, thereby constructing within the novel "an overdetermined thematics of the violence of the Atomic Age." See Gould, "Feminisme/Postmodernité/Esthétique," 205, my translation.

20. Mélanie recognizes it. In her very first section, before *l'homme long*'s story has begun, she says: "Some day I would be fast so fast, sharp so sharp, some day, faced with the necessity of dawn, I would have forgotten the civilization of men who came to the desert to watch their equations explode like a humanity" (13).

21. Gould, "Feminisme/Postmodernité/Esthétique," 206, my translation.

22. The "long" may of course also be read as a temporal marker—signaling his duration—which in effect makes him even more of an abstraction.

23. In Anne Hébert's *Les fous de Bassan* (her 1982 novel whose plotting circulates around the rape and murder of two young girls), this "feminist postscript" might be the lingering atemporal voice of Olivia that in some ways undermines the authority of a more linear and chronological narration, refusing to allow the traditionally placed extratextual postscript of Stevens Brown to have the last word.

24. Roland Barthes, *Le degré zéro de l'écriture* (Paris: Seuil, 1953), trans. Annette Lavers and Colin Smith as *Writing Degree Zero* (London: Jonathan Cape, 1967; Boston: Beacon Press, 1970), 87.

25. Maurice Blanchot, *L'entretien infini* (Paris: Gallimard, 1969), viii, translation mine.

26. Blanchot, *Le pas au-delà* (Paris: Gallimard, 1973), 41, translation mine.

27. Elizabeth A. Meese, *Crossing the Double-Cross: The Practice of Feminist Criticism* (Chapel Hill: University of North Carolina Press, 1986), 5.

28. See, for example, Claudine Herrmann, *Les voleuses de langue* (Paris: des femmes, 1976), trans. Nancy Kline as *The Tongue Snatchers* (Lincoln: University of Nebraska Press, 1991). Also, Meese, in the "In/Conclusion" of *Crossing the Double-Cross*, describes in these terms the revolutionary stance taken by the feminist critic: "she borrows [the present order's] tools in order to subvert it" (147); and she goes on to refer in this context to Roland Barthes's comment that those "outside Power" must "steal a language," and to Hélène Cixous's use of the word "voler" to describe the woman as both thief and "in flight."

29. See Tillie Olsen, "1971—One Out of Twelve: Writers Who Are Women in Our Century," in *Silences*, 41–65. See also the last section of Virginia Woolf's *A Room of One's Own*.

30. Virginia Woolf, "The Leaning Tower" (1940), in *Collected Essays* vol. 2 (London: Hogarth, 1966), 181. I must credit Meese in *Crossing the Double-Cross* with sending me back to this important essay.

31. In the four novels considered in the earlier chapters of this study, for instance, one could identify insanity pleas (language disguising or losing the guilty subject), confessions (always less transparent than they seem), and refusals of speech (silence as self-defense), as well as the articulation of various scapegoating strategies.

32. Stewart, *Death Sentences*, 335.

33. Ibid., 271. See my discussion in chapter 4.

34. Nicole Brossard, *Le désert mauve* (Hexagone), 177. Brossard, *Mauve Desert*, trans. Lotbinière-Harwood (Coach House), 161.

35. Susanne de Lotbinière-Harwood spells "author" as "aut*her*" as a way to convey the gender-marking of the French "auteure" (a form that has entered into common usage in Québec). I have adopted her translation for the purposes of my discussion.

36. The expression "un jour" has already been shown to be common and polysemous in Brossard's novel. Note also that "béance" looks like a French-English bilingual form of "being."

37. In the French original of *Le désert mauve* this sentence is inscribed in English, with partial italics, exactly as it appears here.

38. The epigraph that follows is from the middle section of "A Book to Translate" where it appears at the end of the entry under the final category "Civilization" (150). The original French reads: "Là où je suis rendue, on peut affiner l'espoir parmi les rayons drus de la lumière" (166).

Index